*Learner strategy use and performance on language tests:
A structural equation modeling approach*

STUDIES IN LANGUAGE TESTING...8
Series editor: Michael Milanovic

Also in this series:

An investigation into the comparability of two tests of English as a Foreign Language: The Cambridge–TOEFL comparability study
Lyle F. Bachman, F. Davidson, K. Ryan, I.-C. Choi

Test taker characteristics and performance: A structural modeling approach
Antony John Kunnan

Performance testing, cognition and assessment: Selected papers from the 15th Language Testing Research Colloquium, Cambridge and Arnhem
Michael Milanovic, Nick Saville

The development of IELTS: A study of the effect of background knowledge on reading comprehension
Caroline Margaret Clapham

Verbal protocol analysis in language testing research: A handbook
Alison Green

A multilingual glossary of language testing terms
prepared by ALTE members

Dictionary of language testing
Alan Davies, Annie Brown, Cathie Elder, Kathryn Hill, Tom Lumley, Tim McNamara

Learner strategy use and performance on language tests: A structural equation modeling approach

James E. Purpura

Teachers College, Columbia University

CAMBRIDGE
UNIVERSITY PRESS

Published by the Press Syndicate of the University of Cambridge
The Pitt Building, Trumpington Street, Cambridge CB2 1RP, UK
40 West 20th Street, New York, NY 10011–4211, USA
10 Stamford Road, Oakleigh, Melbourne 3166, Australia

© University of Cambridge Local Examinations Syndicate, 1999

First published 1999

Printed in Great Britain at the University Press, Cambridge, UK

British Library cataloguing in publication data

University of Cambridge, Local Examinations Syndicate

Learner strategy use and performance on language tests: A structural equation modeling approach

James Enos Purpura

1. Education. Assessment 2. Education. Tests. Setting

ISBN   0 521–651026   hard cover
           0 521–658756   paperback

DEDICATION
In memory of my mother
Josephine L. Mercurio Purpura

Contents

Series Editor's note	**VIII**
Preface	**XII**

Chapter One
Introduction 1
    Context of the problem 1
    Structural equation modeling 3
    Purpose of the study 3
    Research questions 4
    Definition of key terms 5
    Significance of the study 9
    Limitations of the study 11

Chapter Two
Strategy use and second language performance:
Theories and empirical research 14
    Introduction 14
    Factors that influence second language test performance 15
    Cognitive factors in models of second language proficiency 17
    Learning strategies and second language development 22
    Second language strategy research and cognitive theory 31
    Methods for investigating strategy use and SLTP 37
    Summary 39

Chapter Three
The structural equation modeling approach:
Single and multi-group procedures 41
    Introduction 41
    Study participants 41
    Measurement instruments 43
    Study variables 50
    Data collection and scoring 55
    Statistical procedures 58
    Summary 65

Chapter Four
Item-level analysis 67
    Introduction 67
    The cognitive strategies questionnaire 68
    The metacognitive strategies questionnaire 73
    The *FCE Anchor Test* 78
    Summary 87

Chapter Five
Modeling strategy use and test performance:
Findings and discussion 88
    Introduction 88
    The cognitive processes 88
    The metacognitive processes 99
    The *FCE Anchor Test* 105
    Testing the validity of of the Full Latent Variable Model:
    The relationships between test-takers' reported strategy use and SLTP 110
    Summary 133

Chapter Six
Multiple-group Analyses 135
    Introduction 135
    The high and low ability groups 136
    Multi-group procedures and analyses 136
    Results and discussion of the multi-group analyses 138
    Summary 168

Chapter Seven
Conclusions 170
    Introduction 170
    The research questions: The entire-group analyses 170
    The research questions: The multi-group analyses 174
    Theoretical implications 177
    Methodological implications 183
    Implications for practice 183
    Suggestions for further research 196
    Conclusions 198

References 200
Appendices 213
Subject Index 252
Author Index 256

Series Editor's note

This volume is the result of many years of work dating back to 1991 when UCLES EFL together with a team led by Lyle Bachman within the Language Assessment Working Group at UCLA began the development of a bank of questionnaires. The bank was designed to investigate the background characteristics of Cambridge EFL Examination candidates and examine how these characteristics might relate to performance on Cambridge EFL examinations. The project was part of a wider UCLES initiative in the area of consequential validity.

In the early stages of this research Lyle Bachman, Jim Purpura and Sarah Weigle identified two sets of background factors that were hypothesized to affect second language acquisition - and by extension, second language test performance. These two factors were grouped as strategic and socio-psychological and were further subdivided as follows:

a. Strategic factors

   Cognitive strategies
   Metacognitive strategies
   Communication strategies

b. Socio-psychological factors

   Attitudes
   Anxiety
   Motivation
   Effort

Data was collected using questionnaires in all the areas listed above. However, questions were raised about the traits in the communication strategies questionnaire, and it was decided to suspend data collection until more attention could be given to the construct.

Personality factors (e.g. self-esteem, extroversion) and cognitive style factors (e.g. field dependence/independence, visual/aural, analytic/gestalt) were not included in the design for reasons of feasibility. However, these factors have drawn a considerable amount of research attention in the past few years and might be a possible direction for further questionnaire development.

Demographic factors were also excluded from the questionnaires since UCLES had already implemented a questionnaire designed to collect these data on a routine basis (i.e. the Candidate Information Sheet - CIS).

In consultation with UCLES, the UCLA team:

- proposed taxonomies for each of the seven questionnaire item banks;
- developed pilot versions of the questionnaires;
- administered the pilot questionnaires to students;
- analysed the initial questionnaire data by means of reliability analyses and
- produced a revised pilot version of the questionnaires.

UCLES then revised the questionnaires, (especially in relation to British English usage) and administered them to a number of candidate groups in order to collect more data from the target population. All of this early work was completed by 1994.

Since then Jim Purpura has continued the work on validating the questionnaires, initially in the context of research for his PhD dissertation and more recently in collaboration with UCLES EFL since he joined Columbia University Teachers College.

The project is now at a stage where the bank of questionnaires have been validated and will soon be available to be used for a number of purposes. The following uses are anticipated for a range of user groups:

- to provide test takers with information on their language learning behaviours;
- to provide teachers with a profile of their students' language learning behaviours;
- to provide curriculum planners and administrators with a profile of the language learning behaviours in their schools;
- to provide UCLES with data to continue examining the relationships between test taker background characteristics and performance on language tests.

The next phase of the development work for the questionnaires will be to produce a user-interface on computer. This is being undertaken as part of the UCLES developments in the field of Computer-based Testing (CBT). It is anticipated that users will be able to assess their language of ability using computer-adaptive tests (e.g. CommuniCAT) and also to evaluate their approach to learning using the language learning questionnaires. In this way learners and their teachers will be able to target the learners' strengths and weaknesses more effectively and thus be able to tailor the learning process to the individual's specific requirements.

Preface

This study is a revised version and an extension of my Ph.D. dissertation submitted to UCLA in February 1996. Chapter six was added as a result of a paper I presented at the 1997 Language Testing Research Colloquium in Orlando. Chapter seven is an attempt to show my students in the TESOL and Applied Linguistics Programs at Teachers College, Columbia University that quantitative research can provide insights for classroom practice.

In writing this book, I wish to express my sincere gratitude to Professor Lyle F. Bachman, who patiently taught me to begin thinking like a researcher. He gave freely of his time with guidance, support and encouragement. I am indebted to him for his insightful comments throughout the manuscript, but especially for the time and care he took with chapter six. A more discerning and sympathetic friend and mentor I would be hard put to find.

I also wish to express my appreciation to: Professor Peter Bentler for demystifying SEM in his lectures and for ongoing technical advice; Professor Victoria Fromkin for her advice in the planning and implementation of this study; and especially to Professor Marianne Celce Murcia for agreeing to teach a seminar on learning strategies at UCLA and for supporting my work in countless other ways over the years.

I wish to acknowledge Dr. Mike Milanovic from UCLES for his support and encouragement throughout the project, and for his comments and suggestions on this manuscript. Also, thanks to Mike and Lyle Bachman for including me in the Cambridge–UCLA Language Testing Project whose aim it was to pursue research on test taker characteristics.

A sincere note of thanks goes to Nick Saville from UCLES for his support and encouragement throughout the project, to Paulo Pinto da Cunha for his desktop publishing skills and his patience with my many revisions, and to the staff at UCLES for their assistance.

A special word of gratitude goes to Dr. Sara Cushing Weigle for her collaboration and good cheer in the design and development of the UCLES language learning questionnaire item bank during the initial stages of this study.

My greatest debt is owed to the 1,660 participants who graciously spent an hour reflecting on their learning strategies and two hours taking a challenging language test.

Thanks to Scott Foresman Publishing and to Denise Marmelstein at HarperCollins–Spain for financial support in carrying out this project.

I wish to express my gratitude to those who helped with data collection:

• in Barcelona, Denise Marmelstein and Eva Sabaté at HarperCollins, and Professor Ramón Ribé, Elsa Tragant and Teresa Navés at the University of Barcelona;

• in the Czech Republic at Dvorákovo Gymnázium in Kralupy, Jarmila Znojilová and colleagues; and at the Pedagogická Fakulta in Liberac, Ivana Pekarova, Vera Buresova and Donna Sarvay;

• in Istanbul, I am deeply grateful to my friend and colleague, Berin Erciyes Ertürk of Dünya Süper Dagitim, for her assistance in locating centers and helping collect data, for accompanying me to five cities all over Turkey, and especially for giving me a deep appreciation of Turkey and her people. For data collection assistance in Turkey, thanks to the principles and teachers: (1) in Istanbul at Sehremini High School, Kabatas Erkek High School, Pendik High School, ITO Anadolu Ticarest Meslek High School, Hasan Polatkan High School, and the Orhan Cemal Fersoy High School; (2) in Tekirdag at Tuglacilar High School; (3) in Buca (Izmir) at Dokuz Eylül University; (4) in Kayseri at Erciyes University; and (5) in Ankara at the Turkish–American Association and Hacettepe University.

My gratitude goes to the following for serving as informants, taking tests, proofreading and so much more: Lubie G. Alatrist, Steve Albanese, Pamela Deuel, Roger Frantz, Linda Jensen, Andrea Kahn, Sean Kilroy, JeeWha Kim, Lisa Purpura Kilroy and Howard Williams.

Finally, my heartfelt thanks to my friend, Andrea Kahn, who never failed to be there, and to Steve Albanese for his unwavering support and understanding as this project has gone from idea to ISBN.

J.E.P.

1 Introduction

Context of the problem

Since the 1970s, research and theory in second or foreign language (SL) education have shifted from examining the methods of teaching to investigating the processes of learning. This refocusing on the learner and on learning has created an explosion of research aimed at investigating learner characteristics and second language acquisition (SLA). More importantly, this shift has stirred considerable interest in the cognitive factors that underlie learning, and much research has been conducted on the relationships between learner strategy use and SL processes and products. Also, as strategic behaviors are generally believed to exert a causal effect on SLA or SL performance (SLP), numerous studies to date have focused on examining the strategies underlying the differential behaviors of successful and unsuccessful learners (e.g., O'Malley, Chamot, Stewner-Manzanares, Küpper & Russo, 1985; Oxford, 1986; Politzer & McGroarty, 1985). These studies have analyzed the type, variety and frequency of the learners' strategy use and produced a number of taxonomies. In a few studies, learner strategies have also been found to correlate with SLP. However, for the most part, these studies have been heuristic in nature and although the majority have not been rooted in any theory of cognition or submitted to powerful statistical tests, they have been useful in identifying different types of strategies, in generating taxonomies, and in setting the ground work for further empirical research on the cognitive characteristics of SL learners.

A similar trend has occurred in language testing as researchers have expressed increasing interest in investigating the cognitive background characteristics of test-takers that may influence performance on language tests, an interest which stems from a concern that a test-taker's use of strategies may well be a significant factor in test score variation. Unsurprisingly, this theoretical interest in the mental processes of language learning, testing and use is not new, as assessment researchers have long held an interest in the relationship between cognitive background variables and language use, both from their investigation into the factors other than language ability that affect SLP and from their attempts at describing the nature of SL proficiency. Although this latter issue has stirred considerable controversy over the years,

1. Introduction

most recent models and theories of SLA (e.g., Dulay, Burt & Krashen, 1982; Ellis, 1985; Fillmore & Swain, 1984; Hatch, 1978; McLaughlin, 1987; Skehan, 1989) or models and theories of SL proficiency (e.g., Bachman, 1990; Bachman & Palmer, 1996; Canale, 1983; Canale & Swain, 1980; Carroll, 1981; Oller, 1979) acknowledge the importance of mental processing during the acquisition or use of a SL. A few language testers (e.g., Bachman, 1990; Bachman & Palmer, 1996; Carroll, 1981) have also proposed models of language ability in which cognitive factors play a fundamental role.

Although these recent advances are encouraging, language assessment researchers have just begun to investigate the interaction between mental processing and second language test performance (SLTP). In fact, only a handful of assessment researchers have considered the extensive body of literature in learner strategies and cognitive psychology for inspiration in investigating the role of mental processing in SLTP. Clearly, the interface of SL learner strategy studies, cognitive psychology and testing research could greatly augment our knowledge of mental processing and SL ability.

From a methodological perspective, most of the studies in the 1970s and 1980s investigating mental processing and SLP utilized observation (e.g., Rubin, 1981), verbal report protocols (e.g., Anderson, 1989; Cohen, 1984; Cohen & Aphek, 1981) or structured interviews (e.g., Gillette, 1987; Lennon, 1989; Wenden, 1987a). These studies generally reported the type, variety and frequency of strategies with low and high-ability students. Several others used questionnaires to examine learner strategies and SLP (e.g., Huang & Van Naerssen, 1985; Naiman, Fröhlich, Stern & Todesco, 1978; Oxford, 1986; Politzer & McGroarty, 1985; Reiss, 1983, 1985; Victori, 1992; Weinstein, Schulte & Cascallar, 1983; Zimmerman & Pons, 1986). However, only a few researchers (e.g., Oxford, 1986; Weinstein, Schulte & Cascallar, 1983) first investigated the psychometric characteristics of their questionnaires before relating them to SLP, and this was done primarily (1) by means of reliability analyses to examine the homogeneity of the strategy scales, so that items with low item-total correlations could be revised or eliminated, or (2) by means of exploratory factor analysis (e.g., Oxford, 1986; Oxford, Nyikos & Crookall, 1987) to identify the underlying factor clusters among several variables.

Skehan (1989) characterizes the research on strategy use and testing in the following way:

We are ready for (a) the first attempts at theorizing within the learner-strategies field which should account for the interrelationships between strategies, and the extent of their causal role in learning, and (b) the development of more replicable and public research techniques, including, perhaps, more examples of questionnaire measures (pp. 98–99).

Structural equation modeling

After the questionnaires in previously-mentioned strategy studies were analyzed, most researchers investigated the relationships between learner strategy use and SLP by means of frequency counts, correlations, ANOVA or T-tests; few used more sophisticated statistical procedures. In fact, to date, no study has used a structural equation modeling (SEM) approach to investigate the relationships between the mental characteristics of test-takers (i.e., learner strategies) and SLTP. Nor has any study empirically tested the assumption of variant differences between groups of successful and unsuccessful language learners. Nonetheless, SEM (also referred to as covariance structure analysis or causal modeling) is a more suitable statistical tool for investigating these relationships because it provides a means of representing the inter-relationships (1) between observed and latent variables and (2) among latent variables in an attempt to explain the links. In addition to specifying directional relationships, SEM allows for measurement error to be accounted for in the models, and it can also be used as a model-generating procedure in which models can be specified, tested, respecified and retested until a model with a statistical fit and meaningful interpretation is found. Finally, SEM can be used to perform simultaneous multiple-group analyses, where models of strategy use and SLTP can be investigated simultaneously across different groups (e.g. high-ability vs. low-ability or male vs. female). Therefore, SEM is clearly a more powerful statistical procedure than traditionally-used procedures (i.e., multiple regression analysis, path analysis) for investigating a variety of dependent and independent variables.

Purpose of the study

In the current study I examine the relationships between selected cognitive characteristics of test-takers and their performance on second or foreign language tests, in particular with regard to the influence that test-takers' self-reported cognitive and metacognitive strategy use might have on their performance. I first investigate the nature of cognitive and metacognitive strategy use as measured by two background questionnaires and the nature of SLTP as measured by the University of Cambridge Local Examinations Syndicate's (UCLES) *First Certificate of English (FCE) Anchor Test*. I then explore how the strategic processes relate to SLTP. Finally, I examine the effects of strategy use on SLTP across high and low-ability test-takers to determine if, in fact, the model of strategy use and performance for the high-ability group is substantively and statistically identical to the one posited for the low-ability group.

1. Introduction

Research questions

This study addresses the following research questions:

Single-group analyses

1. The nature of Cognitive Strategy Use (CSU)

What is the trait structure of cognitive strategy use as measured by the Cognitive Strategies Questionnaire? In other words, what is the relationship between the cognitive strategy item types (e.g., the "clarifying" strategy type) and the cognitive processes (e.g., comprehending, memory and retrieval). Also, what is the relationship among these processes?

2. The nature of Metacognitive Strategy Use (MSU)

What is the trait structure of metacognitive strategy use as measured by the Metacognitive Strategies Questionnaire? In other words, what is the relationship between the metacognitive strategy item types (e.g., the "monitoring" strategy type) and the metacognitive processes (e.g., goal-setting, planning, and assessment). Also, what is the relationship among these processes?

3. The nature of Second Language Test Performance (SLTP)

What is the trait structure of second or foreign language test performance as measured by the *FCE Anchor Test*?

4. The effects of Cognitive Strategy Use and Metacognitive Strategy Use on SLTP

What is the relationship between the test-takers' reported use of cognitive and metacognitive strategies and their performance on second or foreign language tests?

Multi-group analyses

5. The nature of SLTP across high and low-ability groups

Is the factorial structure of SLTP as measured by the *FCE Anchor Test* equivalent across high and low-ability groups? If not, what is the nature of these models?

6. The nature of Cognitive Strategy Use and Metacognitive Strategy Use across high and low-ability groups

Is the factorial structure of cognitive strategy use and metacognitive strategy use as measured by the two questionnaires equivalent across high and low-ability groups? If not, what is the nature of these differences?

7. The effects of Cognitive Strategy Use and Metacognitive Strategy Use on SLTP across high and low-ability groups

Is the structure of the relationships between the test-takers' cognitive and metacognitive strategy use and their performance on the language test equivalent across high and low-ability groups? If not, what is the nature of these differences?

Definition of key terms

This section defines several concepts in the study.

Test-taker characteristics

Bachman (1990) and Bachman and Palmer (1996) mention test-taker characteristics as one of the four categories of factors that influence performance on test scores and that generate sources of variation in language tests. Test-taker characteristics or personal attributes refer to background factors such as age or native language, social factors such as socio-economic status, and socio-cultural and socio-psychological factors such as attitude, motivation, aptitude or cognitive style. In this study, I limit my investigation of test-taker background characteristics to the test-takers' reported use of cognitive and metacognitive strategies.

Second Language Test Performance (SLTP)

Second language test performance has been defined in a number of ways; however, in the current study, SLTP is rooted in Bachman and Palmer's (1996) model of language ability. This model divides language ability into two components: language knowledge and strategic competence. Language knowledge consists of (1) organizational knowledge, or "how utterances or sentences and texts are organized," and (2) pragmatic knowledge, or "how utterances or sentences and texts are related to the communicative goals of the language user and to the features of the language use situation" (p. 68). Organizational knowledge is further subdivided into grammatical knowledge (i.e., morphology, syntax, lexis, phonology and graphology) and textual knowledge (i.e., cohesion, coherence and rhetorical or conversational organization).

In the present study, I examine Bachman and Palmer's (1996) notion of organizational knowledge as measured by the *FCE Anchor Test* since this test defines SLTP by means of morphology, syntax, lexis, cohesion, coherence and reading skills. SLTP in this study refers to both second and foreign language contexts.

1. Introduction

Metacognitive Strategy Use (MSU)

Brown, Bransford, Ferrara and Campione (1983) define metacognitive processing operationally as self-management strategies that learners use to oversee and manage their learning. For them, these strategies involve planning for, monitoring and evaluating a learning event. O'Malley and Chamot (1990) define metacognitive processing in terms of strategies that involve "thinking about or knowledge of the learning process, planning for learning, monitoring learning while it is taking place, or self evaluation of learning after the task has been completed" (p. 231). Wenden (1991) refers to metacognitive processing as self-management strategies with relation to processing time, distinguishing (1) between pre-planning and planning-in-action and (2) between monitoring (i.e., self-assessment during the act) and evaluating (i.e., self-assessment after the act). Faerch and Kasper (1983) refer to metacognitive processing in terms of metacognition. They relate metacognitive processing to SLP in their model of speech production, which involves a planning and execution phase used by an interlocutor during problematic communication. In this context, Faerch and Kasper (1983) limit their notion of metacognitive processing to the strategies invoked to repair communication that has broken down. Finally, Bachman and Palmer (1996) define metacognitive processing operationally in their model of language use as strategies that involve goal-setting (i.e., deciding what one is going to do in communication), assessment (i.e., taking stock of what is needed, what one has to work with, and how well one has communicated), and planning (i.e., deciding how to use the communication skills one has access to).

Drawing on these definitions, I define metacognitive processing, or in this study metacognitive strategy use (MSU), theoretically as a set of conscious or unconscious mental or behavioral activities which are directly or indirectly related to some specific stage of the overall process of language acquisition, use or testing. Operationally, I view metacognitive strategy use as strategies or processes that have a self-management or executive capacity.

Cognitive Strategy Use (CSU)

Unlike metacognitive strategy use, which can be applied to virtually all activities, cognitive strategy use relates to specific actions or behaviors that students invoke during learning, use or testing. In theory, metacognitive strategy use has an executive control over the cognitive strategy use. Brown and Palinscar (1982) define cognitive processing very generally as strategies involving the "manipulation or transformation" of material in a learning context. O'Malley and Chamot (1990), who were influenced predominantly by Anderson's (1982, 1985) cognitive theory of learning, define cognitive processing theoretically as strategies relating to human information processing. Operationally, they view cognitive processing as a set of behaviors that "involve mental manipulations or transformations of materials or tasks [that serve] to enhance comprehension, acquisition, or retention" (p. 229). Finally, Wenden (1991) defines cognitive processing in terms of strategies involving "mental steps or operations that learners use to process both linguistic and sociolinguistic content" (p. 19). Basing her definition on Hunt's (1982) model of human learning, Wenden (1991) relates cognitive strategy use directly to a four-stage model of human information processing.

In this study, I adopt Wenden's (1991) notion of cognitive processing, or cognitive strategy use as a set of strategies or processes which are related to behaviors associated with each stage of the learning process; however, instead of limiting cognitive strategy use to learning, I also see cognitive strategies as viable behaviors in language use and testing contexts. Therefore, in this study cognitive strategy use is defined as a set of conscious or unconscious mental or behavioral activities or operations which are directly or indirectly related to the comprehending, storing or retrieval of information during language acquisition, use or testing.

Strategies, processes and processing

A number of researchers have attempted to differentiate between strategies and processes and this has resulted in considerable confusion. Attempting to define intelligence, Sternberg (1980) refers to metacognitive, performance and knowledge-acquisition "processes," reserving "strategies" to describe higher-level executive functions or "cognitive steps" in problem-solving. Stern (1983) differentiates between "strategies" and "techniques." He defines "strategies" as general but somewhat intentional "approaches" to learning, while "techniques" constitute observable forms of language behaviors witnessed in particular areas of language learning such as vocabulary. Seliger (1984) refers to "strategies" as "universal, age and context-independent, and when engaged, are assumed to lead to long-term acquisition" (p. 38); he refers to "tactics" as devices used to meet the demands of a situation. For Seliger, (1983) "tactics" are "dependent on a wide variety of factors such as environment, age, personality, affective constraints, and the first language" (p. 38). Finally, Bialystok (1990) refers to "processes" as conscious or unconscious "mental steps taken to carry out a cognitive activity" (p. 15), and "strategies" as "techniques" (Seliger's "tactics") used to carry out these processes.

Following Bialystok's (1990) distinctions, I also delineate between "strategies" and "processes." However, in the current study, these notions relate specifically to the different levels of the variables in a model of cognitive or metacognitive strategy use. Operationally, "strategies" constitute the observable variables elicited by means of questionnaire items, where two

1. Introduction

or more items are typically designed to measure one strategy type (e.g., associating or monitoring). Theoretically, "strategies" are defined as conscious or unconscious techniques, behaviors or activities that an individual invokes in language learning, use or testing.

At a higher level, "processes" in this study refer to the individual latent variables underlying strategy use during language learning, use or testing. In other words, "processes" represent the individual stages of mental activity seen in models of human information processing (e.g., comprehending, storing, retrieval, assessment). A "process" is typically measured by one or more strategy-type variables. For example, the comprehending process is measured by both the "clarifying" strategies and the "analyzing inductively" strategies. Similarly, several strategy-type variables cluster to measure a stage of human information processing. In other words, the "clarifying" and the "analyzing inductively" strategies cluster to measure the comprehending stage of information processing. The specific distinctions between two levels as used in this study are displayed in Tables 4.2 and 4.6.

Finally, "cognitive processing," or in this study "cognitive strategy use," is a latent variable that represents all three cognitive stages of information processing (e.g., comprehending, storing, retrieval) measured by the Cognitive Strategies Questionnaire. Similarly, "metacognitive processing," or in this study "metacognitive strategy use", relates to the cumulative effect of using the metacognitive strategies.

Exploratory Factor Analysis (EFA)

Exploratory factor analysis is defined by Kim and Mueller (1978a, 1978b) as a set of statistical procedures designed to represent a set of variables in terms of a smaller number of hypothetical variables or underlying factors or traits. EFA is useful in that empirical data can be explored so as to discover characteristic features of the data and to examine inter-relationships among the factors without imposing a model on the data. Jöreskog and Sörbom (1989) refer to EFA as "a technique often used to detect and assess latent sources of variation and covariation in observed measurements" (p. 96).

In this study I use EFA as an initial step in identifying the latent factors in the questionnaires and in the language test data.

Structural Equation Modeling (SEM)

Structural equation modeling is a means of representing inter-relationships (1) between observed and latent variables (i.e., confirmatory factor analysis) and (2) also among latent variables based on substantive theory or previous empirical research. Each relationship in the model is defined by a set of mathematical equations, and the entire model is empirically tested for overall model data fit.

Although SEM is generally viewed as a means of testing a pre-determined theory about the relationships between theoretical constructs (Jöreskog, 1993), I use SEM in this study as a model-generating procedure in which an initial model is specified and tested, and in cases where the model does not fit the data, it is respecified and retested until a model with a statistical fit and meaningful interpretation is found.

Confirmatory Factor Analysis (CFA)

Confirmatory factor analysis, which is a special case of structural equation modeling, is a set of procedures in which substantive theory is used to generate a model which can explain or account for the data in terms of a limited number of parameters. Unlike exploratory factor analysis, CFA begins with a hypothesized model and sets out to confirm or disconfirm that model based on model data fit statistics and meaningful interpretation.

I use CFA in this study to examine the relationships between observed variables and the underlying latent variables. More specifically, I use it to analyze the underlying trait structure of the instruments used in the study.

Significance of the study

The investigation into the relationships between strategy use and SLTP has a number of far-reaching implications which could contribute theoretically, methodologically and pedagogically to the fields of SL assessment and SLA.

From a theoretical perspective, this study provides information on the underlying trait structure of the *FCE Anchor Test* produced by UCLES and used widely throughout the world. It also provides information on the trait structure of two questionnaires designed to measure the reported cognitive and metacognitive strategy use of test-takers. More importantly, this study attempts to answer questions raised by a number of language testing theorists relating to the relationships between the cognitive characteristics of test-takers and SLTP by examining how cognitive and metacognitive strategy use might impact performance on SL tests. However, this study does not attempt to replicate the research already carried out by strategy researchers such as Anderson (1989), Nevo (1988), Politzer and McGroarty (1985) or Zimmerman and Pons (1986), to name a few. Rather, it attempts to build on their work by embedding the notion of strategy use within a model of human information processing so that it can then be related to SLTP. In brief, the current study is firmly rooted in a model of human information processing, making the results more generally interpretable to a model of human learning. Thus, the current study can potentially inform language educators about those cognitive factors which influence the differential performance of individuals on language tests. The results of this study may have implications relating to

1. Introduction

the validity of test scores from which inferences are drawn and decisions about learners are made.

This study also provides information about how high and low-ability language learners invoke cognitive and metacognitive strategies in language learning, use or testing contexts. In this respect, it builds on the "good language learner" research that examined the strategies of successful and unsuccessful language learners (e.g., Abraham & Vann, 1987; Brown & Perry, 1991; Hosenfeld, 1984; Huang & Van Naerssen, 1985; Mangubhai, 1991; Naiman et al., 1978; Politzer & McGroarty, 1985; Reiss, 1985; Vann & Abraham, 1990). However, unlike those studies, the current one attempts to hypothesize and test models of the relationships between strategy use and SLTP across these different ability groups. From this, we can potentially learn how high-ability learners differ from low-ability learners in their use of strategies—results that have numerous implications for language educators. This information might ultimately be useful for language testers to discern how to control for variation in test scores due to strategy use, thereby reducing test bias and increasing test validity. Finally, the results of the current study have the potential to contribute theoretically to the formulation of a more comprehensive model of strategy use and SLTP.

Methodologically, the present study uses SEM as a primary analytic tool to investigate the relationships between selected cognitive characteristics of test-takers and SLTP. Up to now, several studies in language testing and SLA research have been performed in which SEM was used to investigate the relationships between selected background variables and performance (e.g., Gardner, Lalonde & Pierson, 1983; Kunnan, 1995; Purcell, 1983; Sasaki, 1991; Wang, 1988). However, only the study by Sasaki (1991) focused on the relationships between test-takers' cognitive characteristics and performance. In Sasaki's (1991) study, she focused on foreign language aptitude, two forms of intelligence (verbal intelligence and reasoning) and SL proficiency, finding that Oller's (1981) hypothesis of a general SL proficiency factor as the center of cognitive abilities was disconfirmed. No study, however, has utilized SEM to look at the relationships between strategy use and SLTP.

In addition to using SEM for single-group analyses as other studies have, SEM is used in the current study to perform simultaneous, multi-sample covariance structure analyses, where models of strategy use and SLTP are investigated simultaneously across different groups. Previous studies that investigated test-taker background characteristics and SLTP across multiple groups (e.g., Kunnan, 1995; Wang, 1988) used non-simultaneous, multi-group analyses, where separate, single-group analyses for each group of interest was modeled and the respective models as a whole were then compared. Simultaneous multi-group analysis, however, is a more appropriate procedure when analyses focus on certain types of multi-group comparisons

1. Introduction

and when specific cross-group parameters are compared (Byrne, 1994).

Finally, from a pedagogical perspective, the present study provides insights on the types of strategies test-takers report using during language acquisition, use and testing and how this might impact their performance on language tests. It also provides information on which strategy-type behaviors seem to be beneficial to "good" test performance and which do not, thereby complementing the research by Rubin and Thompson (1982), Wenden (1987) and Oxford (1990) and many others on behaviors related to successful and unsuccessful language learning. Finally, this study can ultimately provide language learners with information on how they use cognitive and metacognitive strategies to learn languages. These findings could then be used to provide students with individualized strategy instruction or to monitor their strategic growth. They could also be used to provide SL educators with an inventory of their students' cognitive and metacognitive behaviors, so that strategy training can be incorporated into their classroom materials and curricula.

Limitations of the study

There are several limitations in this study which may affect internal and external validity.

Self-report research

One concern in this study revolves around the question of whether mental processes are, in fact, conscious, intentional and observable and whether they can be validly elicited through self-report methods such as a questionnaire. A number of researchers have questioned the validity of self-report data. Seliger (1983), in particular, argues that self-report data cannot be independently confirmed and should, therefore, be treated with caution, stating that "introspections are conscious verbalizations of what we think we know" (p. 183) and "conscious verbal reports of learners about their own internal device cannot be taken as a direct representation of internal processing" (p. 189).

The current study makes no claim that the data elicited from the questionnaires are a "direct" reflection of mental processing. In this regard, this study recognizes that these self-report data present a constant threat to internal validity. For example, since all study participants are non-native speakers of English (presumably at the intermediate level of proficiency), it may be that some participants (1) lack the linguistic competence to respond to any number of questionnaire items, (2) misinterpret the intent of the item, (3) demonstrate a lack of self-awareness, or (4) attempt to provide socially desirable responses. However, in spite of these caveats, Ellis (1994), O'Malley and Chamot (1990), Skehan (1989) and many other researchers

1. Introduction

support the use of questionnaires as a viable elicitation procedure due to the degree of structure that such instruments afford.

To compensate for the potential threats to internal validity caused by questionnaire data, several researchers (e.g., Ellis, 1994; Mangubhai, 1991; O'Malley & Chamot, 1990) have advocated the use of multiple data collection procedures. In this way, information from one data elicitation method could be cross-validated with that of another. However, given the scope of this study (over 1,650 participants), the collection of data from multiple methods was not feasible and again, this may have compromised the results of this study.

The operationalization of strategy use

The strategy questionnaires were constructed according to Hunt's (1982) model of human learning and Gagné, Yekovich and Yekovich's (1993) model of human information processing. The stages of information processing were operationalized by several strategy types which were drawn from a survey of the literature on learning strategies; however, the questionnaires in this study make no claim at providing a comprehensive list of strategies for the test-taker to choose from and in so doing, might not be taking into account the actual strategy an individual would use in a particular situation.

The operationalization of second language test performance

Second language test performance in this study is measured by the UCLES *FCE Anchor Test*. This test presents two selected-response tasks which ask the test-takers to choose the appropriate responses and three limited-production tasks which require the test-takers to write anywhere from one word to a part of a sentence. No task eliciting a more extensive writing sample from the test-takers was given, nor were any tasks given that measured the students listening or speaking ability in English. Therefore, SLTP is defined with respect to these five tasks only, and the results of this study can only be generalized to the constructs measured by this test.

Population generalizability

The participants used in this study were selected because they were all presumably at an intermediate (or higher) level of English language proficiency, and they were all 15 years of age or older. All participants were students of English as a foreign language. Therefore, the results of this study can only generalize to populations that share these characteristics, and may not extend to other populations such as young children learning English as a SL or students at the beginning levels of proficiency.

Also, the students in this study were selected from different types of schools in three different countries based on my own personal contacts; no means were available to sample students more extensively from around the world. Therefore, the generalizability of the results to other populations must be made with extreme caution.

Competing models

Methodologically, there is the critical limitation that the models utilized in this study were underspecified. In other words, potentially influential variables such as the test-takers' motivation, attitudes or affect, which have been reported to have an impact on SLP, were not included in the study. However, since the present study claims to be neither exhaustive nor comprehensive, the results in this study can only support the best-fitting models posited in this study, given the variables that were measured. There remains the possibility that other models not proposed in this study would fit or explain the data as well or better than those posited.

2 Strategy use and second language performance: Theories and empirical research

Introduction

Most educators now accept the assumption that the use of learning strategies has become a guidepost for distinguishing high from low-skilled learners (Brown *et al.*, 1983). They also acknowledge that students can be taught to process information if they are also taught the strategies that facilitate information acquisition (Dansereau, McDonald, Collins, Garland, Holley, Diekhoff & Evans, 1979; McCombs, 1991; Wittrock, 1978). Similarly, several SLA researchers have also begun to recognize the influence that learning strategy use may have on the acquisition of a second or foreign language (e.g., Abraham & Vann, 1987; Chamot, 1987; Clahsen, 1987; Cohen, 1984, 1987; Cohen & Aphek, 1981; Hosenfeld, 1977b; Wenden 1991; Wenden & Rubin, 1987), and in a few studies, they have found strategies to be correlated with performance (e.g., Anderson, 1989; Bialystok, 1981; Huang & Van Naerssen, 1985; Jamieson & Chapelle, 1987; O'Malley, Chamot, Stewner-Manzanares, Küpper, & Russo, 1985; Politzer & McGroarty, 1985). These studies have begun to interest language assessment researchers since the results provide some evidence that strategy use plays an important role in how students learn a second language. Also, in cases where SLA is measured by performance on a language test, these results allude to the role strategy use might have in test score variation, or more interestingly, to the role it might have in how test-takers perform on language tests. Therefore, an examination of the relationships between strategy use and SLTP is a compelling area of investigation because of the potential implications it may have for the construct validation of language tests.

This chapter presents several strands of literature relevant to the current study. It first examines studies that attempt to characterize those factors which contribute to second and foreign language test performance. Then, it addresses more specifically the role of cognitive factors in theoretical models of SLTP. Next, it provides an in-depth review of the studies that examine learner strategies. This is followed by a discussion of the role of cognitive theory in second language strategy research. Finally, this chapter discusses the primary statistical procedures used in the study and reviews research that has also used these procedures to examine test-taker background characteristics and performance.

Factors that influence second language test performance

Language testers have long held an interest in the factors that affect SLTP, and several empirical studies have demonstrated that variation on language tests can be attributed to a number of underlying factors. Bachman (1990) has proposed a single framework for investigating the effects of these factors on test scores. This framework involves at least four factors: (1) communicative language ability (CLA), (2) the personal characteristics of test-takers, (3) test method factors, and (4) random factors. I will discuss each of these factors.

Bachman (1990) (and later Bachman & Palmer, 1996) argues that CLA is a central factor accounting for the variation of test scores in second language learners. In his model of CLA (or in the context of the current study, SLTP), Bachman (1990) divides CLA into three components: language competence, strategic competence and psycho-physiological mechanisms. Language competence includes the features of language responsible for communication through language; strategic competence refers to a set of executive functions, or more specifically a set of metacognitive strategies responsible for implementing language competence in language use contexts; and psycho-physiological mechanisms involve the neurological and psychological processes responsible for the actual execution of language. Bachman (1990) further divides language competence into (1) organizational competence involving grammatical and textual knowledge and (2) pragmatic competence involving illocutionary and sociolinguistic knowledge.

Traditionally, language testers have been most concerned with the assessment of organizational competence or, in other words, the syntactic, morphological, lexical, phonological and rhetorical features of the language, and although other areas of language knowledge (e.g., pragmatic knowledge) are crucial to CLA, the current study follows tradition and focuses on grammatical and textual knowledge.

Bachman's (1990) second set of factors that influence test scores—test-taker characteristics—includes the personal attributes of learners that potentially affect the differential performance of test takers on language tests. In this respect, test-takers vary on multiple dimensions relating to (1) background or demographic characteristics such as age, gender, native language, ethnic identity, educational background and socio-economic status, (2) socio-psychological or socio-cultural characteristics such as attitudes, motivation and effort expended, (3) personality characteristics such as self-esteem, anxiety and risk-taking and (4) cognitive characteristics such as aptitude, learning strategies, or cognitive style (i.e., introversion vs.

2. Strategy use and second language performance

extroversion, field dependence vs. independence). A number of studies have already been carried out in which researchers have examined the role of test-taker characteristics and SLTP (e.g., Clement & Kruidenier, 1985; Gardner, Lalonde & Pierson, 1983; Kunnan, 1995), and they have provided empirical evidence to support the notion that many of these attributes do indeed have a significant impact on differential performance.

Bachman's (1990) third category—test method factors—refers to the characteristics of the test tasks used to elicit test performance and the effects that they may have on test score variation. The role of test method factors in language tests stems from Bachman and Palmer's (1981, 1982) multi-trait multi-method studies in which they noticed that some variables loaded more heavily on the method factors than on the trait factors, demonstrating that performance on language tests may partially be a function of the test method or the characteristics of the elicitation devices. To examine these relationships more systematically, Bachman (1990) and Bachman and Palmer (1996) have proposed a framework of test task characteristics which provides a mechanism for specifying: (1) the test environment (e.g., the physical conditions, the time of testing); (2) the test rubric (e.g., the task organization, the task instructions); (3) the task input (e.g., the format, the nature of the language used in the input); (4) the expected response (e.g., the format, the nature of language used in the response); and (5) the interaction between the input and response. This framework also allows assessment specialists to compare tasks on any of the five dimensions. The initial research utilizing this framework (e.g., Bachman, Davidson & Milanovic, 1993; Bachman, Davidson, Ryan & Choi, 1993; Bachman, Kunnan, Vanniarajan & Lynch, 1988; Chapelle & Abraham, 1990) clearly shows that test method factors play a significant role in test score variation.

Bachman's (1990) final category involves random factors. This refers to the unsystematic variation of scores due to events during a test that might impact a test-taker's score. Random factors also refer to the interactions between and among the other task characteristics or to measurement error, which can also affect scores on tests.

In the current study, I examine two sets of factors in Bachman's (1990) framework: organizational knowledge as a component of CLA and test-takers' personal characteristics, or the strategies that test-takers report using in second language learning, use and testing. I also examine the inter-relationships between these two factors, or more specifically, the effects that strategy use might have on organizational competence.

Cognitive factors in models of second language proficiency

Language assessment researchers have also shown an interest in the cognitive factors of second language learning and use. This stems in part from their attempts to characterize second language proficiency and in part from their investigation into the factors other than CLA that affect test performance (Bachman, 1990). In this section, I examine the role that cognitive factors have played in the various models of second language proficiency proposed by SLA and second language assessment researchers.

In the models proposed by Lado (1961) and Carroll (1961, 1968), second language proficiency was viewed as a function of the four language skills (i.e., reading, writing, speaking, listening) and the components of language knowledge (i.e., structure, vocabulary, and phonology/graphology). Spolsky (1973) rejected the skills/components model of second language proficiency, claiming that it did not account for the creative and redundant characteristics of language. Rather, he asserted that second language proficiency tests should attempt to "go beyond the limitation of testing a sample of surface features, and seek rather to tap underlying linguistic competence" (p. 167).

In this study, Spolsky (1973) might have been alluding to an underlying cognitive component in discussing the "redundant" or "creative" aspects of language or in referring to an "underlying linguistic competence"; however, he never explicitly mentioned how cognitive factors may interact with language until much later, when he proposed a model of SLA based on preference rules (Spolsky, 1985).

In support of Spolsky's (1973) criticism of the skills/components model of second language proficiency, Oller (1979) explicitly argued for the inclusion of cognitive processes in language testing theory. He claimed that the ability to make guesses in context-reduced situations was an integral part of language competence since these situations led an interlocutor to process incoming input and predict future input. The idea of making guesses in context-reduced situations was the basis for Oller's (1979) "pragmatic expectancy grammar," which, he maintained, provided evidence for a general language factor or the idea that second language proficiency consisted of a single global trait (Oller's unitary trait hypothesis) that included cognitive processing, rather than several distinct traits as proposed earlier by Lado (1961) and Carroll (1961, 1968). Oller's (1979) claims generated several empirical studies on the nature of second language proficiency and eventually his notion of second language proficiency as a single unitary trait was disconfirmed in favor of a multi-componential view of second language proficiency proposed by Bachman & Palmer (1982, 1983).

In spite of the rejection of the unitary trait hypothesis, Oller's (1979)

2. Strategy use and second language performance

original notion of "pragmatic expectancy grammar" remains compelling because of the role it attributed to cognitive factors in second language proficiency. More specifically, Oller's (1983) notion of "pragmatic expectancy" was central to his theory of a "pragmatic expectancy grammar" since he claimed that "pragmatic expectancy" was responsible for invoking an individual's cognitive processes (i.e., his or her "pragmatic expectancy grammar") during language acquisition or use. Although Oller's (1983) "grammar" appeared on the surface to be limited to a series of predictions and inferences while negotiating meaning in learning or in communication, this theory was actually rooted in a system of perceptual processing proposed by Neisser (1967), which explained perceptual processing in listening in terms of "analysis-by-synthesis," where an interlocutor uses cognitive processes to decode input. More specifically, the receiver analyzes the input by creating syntheses of the intended meaning, which are later confirmed in the interaction to create meaning. Oller (1983) extended Neisser's (1967) processing system to include the idea of language production, thereby accounting for both reception and production in his "grammar."

Oller's (1983) efforts to base his "pragmatic expectancy grammar" on a model of cognitive processing demonstrated the importance of cognitive factors in understanding second language proficiency, and his work has led others to address cognitive processes in language assessments in years to come. Unfortunately, Oller did not describe the cognitive processes affecting SLA or SLTP in sufficient detail so as to provide a basis for empirical research. Nor did he explain how these processes could be incorporated into a comprehensive model of second language ability which could account for cognitive factors.

Volmer and Sang (1983) criticized Oller (1983) for having no theoretical justification for extending Neisser's (1967) model to include the processes of language production. They did agree, however, with Oller's (1983) call to account for cognitive factors in test performance and affirmed that regardless of the number of components or the inherent inter-relationships of the components, "cognition in general does play an important role in the learning and use of a language (L1 as well as L2)" and language assessment theorists must "understand and model those general cognitive processes that are implied in comprehending and producing language" (p. 40). Volmer and Sang (1983) conclude:

> *We have to increase our efforts to develop tests that are valid, and to prove the validity of the theoretical models and explications, we should not merely concentrate on the end products of language processing and how they relate to one another. We should equally stress the investigation of the underlying psycholinguistic processes leading to the comprehension and production of meaningful utterances in a foreign language (p. 70).*

2. Strategy use and second language performance

In addition to Oller, a number of other SLA researchers have recognized the importance of cognitive factors in SLA. Canale and Swain (1980), in examining the theoretical bases of language teaching and testing, proposed a model of second language proficiency which consisted of three major components of communicative competence: (1) grammatical competence (including syntax, lexis, phonology, morphology and semantics); (2) sociolinguistic competence (including sociocultural rules and the rules of discourse); and (3) strategic competence. Canale (1983) later revised this model to differentiate between sociolinguistic competence, seen as the sociocultural rules, and discourse competence, seen as cohesion and coherence. In Canale's (1983) revision, strategic competence refers to the verbal and nonverbal strategies that arise from difficulties in communication. These "communication strategies" are then invoked when learners attempt to overcome their lack of interlanguage resources in communication. This process of invoking communication strategies in interactive communication constituted the cognitive component of the model since these strategies were seen as manifestations of the cognitive processes learners used during reception of linguistic input and production of output.

The view that strategic knowledge constituted a cognitive component in Canale and Swain's (1980) and Canale's (1983) models was further explored in the work of Faerch and Kasper (1980, 1983, 1984), who located communication strategies within a general model of speech production. In Faerch and Kasper's (1984) model, communication strategies are again seen as behaviors that arise from problematic communication. However, their model relates communication strategies more generally to a psycholinguistic framework, where strategic processing involves a planning and execution phase and where an interlocutor utilizes specific communication strategies (e.g., avoidance strategies) to compensate for problems in designing or executing a plan during oral communication.

Canale and Swain's (1980) model of communicative competence was the first to mention strategies to repair communication breakdowns as a cognitive process involving strategic knowledge. However, their notion of strategic competence was severely limited since, unlike Faerch and Kasper (1984), they never explained exactly how communication strategies might function within a processing model and they never related strategic competence to a known model of cognition.

Influenced by Canale and Swain (1980), Fillmore and Swain (1984) proposed a framework for SLA in which the cognitive component also played an integral role. They claimed that the rate and level of learning stem from the interactions that occur between and among social, linguistic and cognitive processes, maintaining also that second language proficiency, or the ability to

2. Strategy use and second language performance

use the second language to achieve a social purpose, depends on the learner's ability to access the cognitive component in order to identify and learn linguistic elements. Fillmore and Swain (1984) address learning strategies in this model, arguing that strategies are primarily responsible for acquisition in children, while experiential factors account for learning in adults.

Finally, influenced by the work on communicative competence of Widdowson (1978), Hymes (1982), Canale and Swain (1980), Canale (1983) and several others, Bachman (1990) proposed a model of communicative language ability consisting of language competence, strategic competence and psycho-physiological mechanisms. In this framework, strategic processing plays a primary role; however, unlike Canale and Swain (1980), Bachman (1990) differentiated strategic competence from language competence, since, he explained, a high scorer on a test might report using a different set of test-taking strategies than a low scorer even though the underlying language competence of both might be the same. His views also differed from those of Canale and Swain (1980) by his characterization of strategic competence as a mechanism that controls cognitive processes in achieving a communicative goal. Bachman (1990) summarizes his position as follows:

Rather than considering strategic competence solely an aspect of language competence, I consider it more as a general ability, which enables an individual to make the most effective use of available abilities in carrying out a given task, whether that task be related to communicative language use or to non-verbal tasks such as creating a musical composition, painting or solving mathematical equations (p. 106).

In his work, Bachman (1990) acknowledged Tarone's (1981) and Faerch and Kasper's (1984) approaches to defining strategic competence; however, he also found them severely limited in some respects. First, he stated that both approaches restrict their definition of strategic competence to a component of speech production even though strategic competence occurs in all communicative language use—not just in compensatory situations in oral production. A second limitation related to Faerch and Kasper's (1984) definition of strategic processing as a planning and execution phase. This definition, according to Bachman (1990), failed to account for monitoring. As a result, in his own work, Bachman (1990) extended Faerch and Kasper's (1984) notion of strategic processing to include an assessment phase.

In sum, Bachman's (1990) model of CLA presented a clear accounting of the cognitive factors affecting competence. These factors are grouped under the rubric of strategic competence, which Bachman (1990) defined as metacognition rooted in an information-processing model of cognition. This

2. Strategy use and second language performance

model, however, left a number of questions unanswered regarding the precise nature of strategic competence as applied to second language acquisition, use and testing contexts.

In response to this shortcoming, Bachman and Palmer (1996), building on the work of Bachman (1990), produced a revised model of CLA in which language knowledge, metacognitive strategies and affect are shown to interact with each other during language use. Their model also shows an interaction between the components of CLA on the one hand and the characteristics of the language use context, the test task and other mental schemata on the other. In this model, Bachman and Palmer (1996) explored the notion of metacognition in communicative language use in much greater detail. For them, the metacognitive behaviors of communicative language use were described in terms of assessment, goal-setting and planning strategies.

Although Bachman's (1990) and Bachman and Palmer's (1996) notion of strategic competence as a set of metacognitive strategies is clearly more comprehensive and better articulated than previous conceptions, it still has some limitations. First and foremost, their depiction of metacognition is not based on empirical research and, therefore, remains hypothetical until this notion of metacognition can be operationalized and tested with data. Second, their hypothesized model views strategic competence only as a set of metacognitive strategies, while most strategy researchers (e.g., O'Malley & Chamot, 1990; O'Malley et al., 1987; Oxford, 1990; Wenden, 1991) agree that in second language acquisition and second language use situations, learners also invoke cognitive, social and affective strategies. Bachman and Palmer (1996) do state that metacognitive strategies interact with language knowledge and affect, but it remains unclear as to how affect might be operationalized and how it might interact with metacognitive strategies—or with the cognitive and social strategies—when learners are learning a second language, using it or taking a second language test.

In sum, language assessment theorists have only begun to explore how cognitive factors relate to SLTP. Oller (1979) discussed the cognitive processes of language comprehension and production. Canale and Swain (1980) identified strategic competence as a facet of language competence. Bachman (1990) and Bachman and Palmer (1996) defined strategic competence in terms of metacognitive strategies and related it to affect and language use. In short, all of these models have attempted to explain the nature of second language proficiency and all have explicitly addressed cognitive issues. These efforts have begun to produce more coherent theories to guide our research in language assessment. However, despite these encouraging advances, our understanding of how cognitive factors as a set of strategies influence SLTP remains in the early stages of investigation.

In the next section, I will review a number of empirical studies in the literature on learning strategies. This constitutes an attempt to demonstrate that the theoretical developments in learner strategy research can indeed contribute to our understanding of the role of cognition in language acquisition, use and testing.

Learning strategies and second language development

Whereas language assessment theorists have generally been influenced by the research in SLA theory, only a few have been inspired by the recent work in cognitive psychology, and even fewer have yet to capitalize on the empirical research carried out on learning strategies and the role that they play in learning another language. Nonetheless, recent developments in cognitive psychology and second language strategy research have far-reaching implications for language testers interested in investigating the cognitive factors involved in SLTP since the preeminent goal of many of these studies is to associate strategy use with success in learning or success in performance, which, in many instances, is measured by language assessments.

An overview of learning strategies research

Since the 1970s, an increasing number of SLA researchers have become more interested in how students learn rather than what they learn, thereby refocusing their investigations from the products to the processes of SLA. This shift has created an increased interest in the cognitive processes of SLA (e.g., Bialystok, 1978, 1981; Clahsen, 1987; Faerch & Kasper, 1983; McLaughlin, 1987; Pienemann, 1985), and many researchers have proposed models of SLA and second language proficiency which attempt to account for the cognitive factors of acquisition and performance (see previous section). This refocusing has produced numerous studies aimed at examining the strategies that students use when learning a second or foreign language or when using the new language in communicative contexts. In this section of review of research on learning strategies, I first discuss some of the problems researchers have encountered in providing a comprehensive, operational definition of learning strategies. This is followed by a set of descriptive studies that sought to identify the strategies that students invoke in language learning. After that, I review several studies which attempted to classify strategy use into taxonomies. Finally, I discuss a number of studies that endeavored to relate reported strategy use to SL acquisition or performance—some of which used descriptive accounts of the strategies that high and low-ability learners invoked and others which sought to find a statistical relationship between strategy use and performance.

2. Strategy use and second language performance

Defining learning strategies

All strategy researchers have endeavored to define "strategy," but few seem to agree on what a learning strategy actually is (Bialystok, 1983). This most likely stems from the fact that each researcher has defined strategy within the context of his or her own study. Nonetheless, these different notions of strategy have also resulted in considerable confusion. To illustrate, Chamot (cited in Ellis, 1994) refers to strategies as "techniques, approaches or deliberate actions" that learners invoke to facilitate learning and recall (p. 531), while Oxford (cited in Ellis, 1994) defines strategies as "behaviors or actions learners use to make language learning more successful, self-directed or enjoyable" (p. 531). Rubin's (1987) view of strategies relates more to how they might contribute directly to second language development, while Stern (1983), concerned more with the observability of strategies, describes a strategy as a general approach to learning by the individual learner and "techniques" as "particular forms of observable learning behaviors." Finally, relating strategy use to the encoding of information, Weinstein and Meyer (cited in Ellis, 1994) refer to strategies as "behaviors and thoughts that a learner engages in during learning that are intended to influence the learner's encoding process" (p. 531).

These definitions give rise to a number of issues associated with defining the term "strategy." The first concerns the precise nature of the behaviors that constitute a strategy. Are strategies actions? Activities? Behaviors? Operations? Techniques? Or tactics? Although these terms might seem interchangeable, I refer to strategies in the current study as specific actions, activities or behaviors that are directly related to some processing stage of language acquisition, use or testing. They do not refer to "general tendencies" or "approaches to learning," as Stern (1983) suggests, because those depictions typically relate to factors that affect strategy choice or to one's "learning style" (e.g., risk-taker).

A second problem in defining "strategy" relates to the issue of observability. Some researchers see strategies as essentially observable (e.g., Oxford, 1990; Stern, 1983), while others as both observable and unobservable (i.e., mental) (e.g., Weinstein & Mayer, 1986). In the current study, strategies are seen as both observable and unobservable, as I make no assumption that lack of observable behavior necessarily entails lack of mental processing.

A third concern revolves around intentionality, or whether strategies are conscious or subconscious behaviors. Chamot (1987) refers to strategies as "deliberate actions" or conscious behaviors in learning a language. Flavell (1979) and Lefebvre-Pinard (1983) claim that strategies are consciously deployed as a result of a problem in learning or communication. However, Faerch and Kasper (1983) and McLaughlin, Rossman and McLeod (1983) argue that learners may develop facilities with some strategies to the point

2. Strategy use and second language performance

where strategy use has become automatized or where strategy use remains a subconscious or potentially conscious behavior. In the current study, I view strategy use as conscious, potentially conscious, or subconscious, depending on the individual and the task at hand.

A final issue in defining "strategy" relates to directness, or whether strategy use implies a direct or indirect impact on learning or performance. Rubin (1987) asserts that both "cognitive and metacognitive strategies can contribute directly to language learning" (p. 27), while communication and social strategies contribute indirectly to learning. Chamot (1987) suggests that the cognitive strategies have a more direct impact on learning than do the metacognitive or social-affective strategies. Oxford (1990) claims that the memory, cognitive and compensation strategies are direct because they require mental processing of the language and provide direct support for language learning, while the metacognitive, affective and social strategies are indirect because they provide indirect support for language learning. Finally, several researchers (e.g., Bachman, 1990; Bachman & Palmer, 1996; Brown *et al.*, 1983; Faerch & Kasper, 1983; O'Malley & Chamot, 1990; Wenden, 1991) have claimed that the metacognitive strategies have a direct impact on the cognitive strategies in SLA or second language performance. All of these claims provide interesting hypotheses as to the relationships between strategy use and learning or performance; however, unfortunately, none of the above studies has been substantiated by empirical research of a confirmatory nature. In the current study, I use "directness" to refer to the impact that one variable may have on another. Directness is also characterized as having a positive or negative impact, which may or may not be statistically significant.

In sum, although strategy researchers remain divided over what a strategy actually is, they have each had to articulate their views on these issues in their work. This has contributed to more comprehensive and more precise operational definitions of "strategy" in recent years.

Identifying learner strategies: Descriptive studies

Many of the early studies on second language learning strategies have focused primarily on providing descriptive accounts of the behaviors that language learners were observed using or reported using. These studies provided lists of strategies, and little attempt was made at classifying them into typologies or relating them to a model of human information processing. Nonetheless, they were important in providing educators and researchers with a list of behaviors seen as strategic to learning.

Rubin (1975) was among the first to suggest that "good language learners" might warrant analysis, suspecting that "good language learners" might process information in such a way that might contribute to their success. As a result, she based her study on a set of working assumptions about learning and then used videotaped classroom observations of learners of mixed ages in classroom settings to identify seven strategy types that appeared to characterize "good" language learning behaviors.

In a subsequent study, Rubin (1981) examined the strategies of another group of young adults in classroom settings, but this time utilized observation along with self-reports and daily journal entries to observe learning strategies. She identified six strategy types: (1) clarification or verification, (2) monitoring, (3) memorization, (4) guessing or inductive inferencing, (5) deductive reasoning, and (6) independent practice. In this seminal study, Rubin (1981), somewhat controversially, delineates strategies that contribute both directly (e.g., classification or verification, guessing or inductive inferencing, deductive reasoning) and indirectly to the learning process (e.g., monitoring, memorization, and practice). These claims, although interesting, have not been supported by research of a confirmatory nature.

Wong-Fillmore (1976, 1979) investigated the learning strategies of five Mexican children when she noticed wide differences in communicative competence among the children over a nine-month period of time. In her study, she paired the five children off with five native English speaking children for an hour each week and recorded their interactions. An analysis of the tapes showed that the children were using three social and five cognitive strategies and that increased communicative competence seemed to be due to an increased use of the social strategies.

Also, looking at strategy use in children, Chesterfield and Chesterfield (1985) investigated how 14 Mexican-American children used different types of strategies as their knowledge of English developed during their first year of schooling. Using observation as a method of inquiry, they found that the children first used "receptive and self-contained" strategies (e.g., repetition, memorization and use of formulaic expressions), later used strategies based on interpersonal interaction (e.g., appeal for assistance, clarification) and, finally, used metacognitive strategies (e.g., monitoring). Similar to Rubin (1975, 1981) and Wong-Fillmore (1976, 1979), Chesterfield and Chesterfield (1985) simply compiled an inventory of strategies, making no attempt to classify them into a taxonomy of strategy use or relate them to a cognitive model of learning. Nonetheless, these lists provided rich descriptions of strategy use.

Classifying learning strategies

In addition to listing learning strategies, a few researchers have attempted to classify them into taxonomies and typologies. One of the most famous to date is that proposed by O'Malley and Chamot (1990). Their hierarchical framework of strategies distinguishes three major strategy types: metacognitive strategies, cognitive strategies and socio-affective strategies.

2. Strategy use and second language performance

Each strategy type is further represented by a number of individual strategies. For example, the metacognitive strategies include advance organizers, directed attention, selective attention, self-management, advance preparation, self-monitoring, delayed production and self-evaluation. O'Malley and Chamot's (1990) framework of strategies has considerable intuitive appeal and many practitioners have used this taxonomy in planning their teaching; however, O'Malley and Chamot have never examined the construct validity of their taxonomy. As a result, it is unclear if strategies such as "advance organizers," "directed attention" or "selected attention" constitute different enough behaviors to justify class time to teach students the subtle differences or to train them to use these three separate strategies. Or might it be that these three strategies all invoke a way of assessing the situation? More seriously, however, this taxonomy does not tell us the relative importance of each of these strategies in second language development. In other words, do all of these metacognitive strategies influence development equally as depicted in the taxonomy, or do some have a statistically significant impact on second language learning, while others have no significant impact at all. Until such analyses are performed, one must use this framework with caution.

Oxford (1986) has also endeavored to propose a taxonomy of language learning strategies. Building on earlier classifications, she constructed a questionnaire entitled the "Strategy Inventory for Language Learning" (SILL) in which 64 strategies were the basis for generating items. She then categorized these strategies into primary and secondary strategy types. After performing a number of statistical analyses on the SILL, Oxford (1990) presented a revised framework of strategies in which she classified learning strategies as having a direct or an indirect impact on learning a language. Each strategy type was further represented by three subtypes which were then represented by a number of individual strategies. Oxford's (1990) taxonomy is interesting for a number of reasons. It is the first to explicitly indicate directionality in terms of impact on learning and to provide a hierarchical organization of strategies into levels, making it more than just a list. Second, this taxonomy is extremely comprehensive and again intuitively appealing. Unfortunately, it still remains unclear how this taxonomy relates to a model of human information processing or if the posited relationships to learning are statistically significant or not. Finally, Oxford's (1990) taxonomy is unique in that it made no distinction between strategies that were invoked in both language learning and language use—a point that Ellis (1994) strangely criticized as a shortcoming. I might only add that these strategies could also be invoked in language assessment situations, or even in situations involving learning, use or assessment in other content areas.

2. Strategy use and second language performance

Relating learning strategies to SLA

Implicit in the studies that attempted simply to identify the strategies that learners used is the notion that there exists a set of strategies which strongly promote acquisition. As a result, a number of researchers have examined the differential strategy use of successful and unsuccessful language learners. In these "good language learner" studies, students were grouped according to some external criterion as being "successful" or "unsuccessful" and a descriptive account of their strategy use was investigated or their strategy use was examined and the type, variety and frequency of strategies were reported for the different groups. A second set of studies carried this research beyond description. These studies looked at the relationships between strategy use and performance by means of statistical procedures in an effort to determine which strategies produced statistically significant correlations with performance.

The "successful/unsuccessful language learner" studies

Investigating "good language learners," Naiman et al. (1978) utilized semi-structured interviews with 34 "successful" graduate students, many of whom were multilingual, to investigate the strategies that seemed common to all "good" language learners. They found that these learners (1) had an active task approach, (2) viewed language as a system, (3) treated language as a means of communication and interaction, (4) knew how to manage the affective demands of learning a language, and (5) monitored their second language performance. They also found that each of these strategy types was associated with a number of specific substrategies. These findings are interesting in that they provided a wide range of strategy types occurring during learning. However, the claims made in this study cannot be fully supported since Naiman et al. (1978) interviewed only successful students, leaving it unclear if those strategies were any different from those used by the unsuccessful students.

In response to this criticism, a number of researchers examined the behaviors of both unsuccessful and successful learners (e.g., Abraham & Vann, 1987; Chamot & Küpper, 1989; Hosenfeld, 1984; Huang & Van Naerssen, 1985; Reiss, 1983; Vann & Abraham, 1990). These researchers sought to describe and compare patterns of behaviors that served as predictors of success (or lack thereof).

Focusing predominantly on unsuccessful learners, Abraham and Vann (1987) used think-aloud protocols to investigate the performance of two Saudi women who had completed four test activities. They found that unsuccessful learners do not lack strategies to perform tasks, but rather, their problems stem from the inappropriate use of strategies.

2. Strategy use and second language performance

Examining strategy use with both successful and unsuccessful learners, Wesche (1987) investigated the learning behaviors of 37 students studying French in the Canadian Civil Service. Using videotaped observation and in-depth structured interviews, she identified strategies that were similar to those listed in Rubin's (1975) work, finding also that learners who made quick progress used a greater variety and quantity of strategies. More interestingly, Wesche (1987) found that since many of the learned behaviors occur together in complexes of strategies, rather than individually, these complexes could potentially serve as criteria for characterizing a learner.

In a very interesting study of the differential strategy use observed with beginning and intermediate ESL students, O'Malley, Chamot, Stewner-Manzanares, Küpper and Russo (1985) used student and teacher interviews along with classroom observations to determine the range, type and frequency of learning strategies of these groups. They found that the students as a group used more cognitive than metacognitive strategies, but saw that the intermediate students reported using more metacognitive strategies than the beginning students. They concluded that greater target language proficiency depends on metacognitive strategy use.

One of the most comprehensive "good language learner" studies to date was carried out by Chamot, Küpper and Impink-Hernandez (1988), who investigated strategy use and performance in a study involving beginning, intermediate and advanced students of Spanish and Russian, over a period of four semesters. They first asked teachers to classify learners as "effective" and "ineffective" and then analyzed their strategy use and performance over time. They found that the "effective" students used a larger range of strategies and made more appropriate strategy choices for particular tasks than did the "ineffective" students. Also, they seemed more goal-oriented than the "ineffective" students. Finally, the "effective" learners displayed a greater degree of "comprehension monitoring" than "production monitoring" (i.e., attention to discrete linguistic features) and made better use of their general world knowledge and their second language linguistic knowledge than did the "ineffective" ones.

Finally, in a study specifically geared toward strategy use and SLTP, Anderson (1989) used immediate retrospective report protocols with 28 ESL students to investigate the relationship between reading strategy use and performance on a standardized ESL test. He found that of the 47 strategies recorded, no single set of strategies promoted success, but rather, concurring with Vann and Abraham (1990) and Chamot *et al.* (1988), concluded that success is more contingent on "effective" strategy use than on knowledge of strategy use.

In the next section, I will discuss studies that use statistical techniques to relate strategy use to high and low English language performance.

2. Strategy use and second language performance

Strategy use and performance: The correlational studies

Moving beyond qualitative methods, several researchers have investigated the relationships between strategy use and performance by means of statistical procedures. One of the most interesting studies was that of Politzer and McGroarty (1985), who examined the strategy use and performance of 37 Asian and Hispanic students enrolled in an eight-week ESL course at an American university. Politzer and McGroarty (1985) elicited strategy use by means of a questionnaire designed to measure three scales: classroom behavior, individual study and non-classroom interactions. They measured the students' performance by means of three pre- and post-course proficiency tests, each consisting of an aural comprehension subtest, a grammar subtest and a communicative competence subtest. They then calculated gain scores from the pre- and post-tests and correlated the results with the strategy use scales. They found first that the reliability (i.e., the internal consistency) of the questionnaire scales was relatively low, ranging from 0.23 to 0.45, and that very few statistically significant correlations were observed between the questionnaire scales and the performance measures. They further observed that the questionnaire items related differently to the respective measures of proficiency, echoing the claims made by Wesche (1987) and O'Malley *et al.* (1985) that strategy use and the task are inextricably related. Then questioning the construct validity of their questionnaire, they noticed that the interpretation of the questionnaire items seemed to vary according to the respondent, a serious flaw in their study. Finally, Politzer and McGroarty (1985) uncovered several interactions between learning strategy use and ethnic background, suggesting that certain learning strategies might be culture-dependent, a very vital area of inquiry at present (see Oxford, 1996). Although Politzer and McGroarty's (1985) attempt to establish a statistical relationship between strategy use and performance was unsuccessful, their study is exemplary in that it provides invaluable information for those interested in examining the relationships between learning strategies and proficiency using a questionnaire format.

In addition to Politzer and McGroarty, Bialystok (1981, 1983) also attempted to investigate the statistical relationships between strategy use and performance. Using questionnaires to elicit strategy use, she examined the relationships between two communication strategies ("functional practice" and "inferencing") and two conscious learning strategies ("formal practice" and "monitoring") on the one hand, and second language performance using an oral and a written task on the other. Surprisingly she found no relationship between inferencing and proficiency, and then found a significant correlation between functional practice and proficiency—but only with the 10th graders. Finally, functional practice, formal practice and monitoring correlated with

2. Strategy use and second language performance

proficiency only in the 12th grade, another result that lacks any plausible explanation. Although Bialystok's studies failed to establish a statistical relationship between strategy use and performance, her results served to provide insights on her Model of Second Language Learning (Bialystok, 1978), which generated further empirical research for this type.

Somewhat more successful was the study by Huang and Van Naerssen (1985) who utilized Bialystok's (1978) Model of Second Language Learning to study the top and bottom thirds of a group of 65 students whose performance was based on an oral skills test, to examine the similarities and differences of strategy use in successful and unsuccessful learners. Using questionnaires along with in-depth interviews to investigate differential performance, they focused on formal practice, functional practice and monitoring in non-classroom situations and found similar results to those reported in Bialystok (1978). They found no significant differences between the high and low achievers with regard to formal practice and monitoring, but did find significant differences for some functional practice strategies. Aside from these findings, this study leads us to question whether greater strategy use fosters higher levels of proficiency or whether high levels of proficiency promote increased strategy use.

Finally, in a more recent study, Mangubhai (1991) studied the strategies used by five adult beginning second language learners of Hindi with Total Physical Response (Asher, 1977) as a means of instruction. Strategies were derived from concurrent think-aloud protocols, immediate retrospective reports and discussions following each lesson, and performance was based on a test consisting of three tasks. Mangubhai (1991) identified three sets of strategies depending on whether the learners were focusing on form, meaning or memory (retrieval and storage). Although this study was limited in nature, he found that the high achievers appeared to use more memory strategies, resorted less to translation, and practiced more than the low achievers.

In sum, the majority of the studies relating learner strategies to SLA were descriptive in nature and although many of them lacked interpretability within a model of human information processing or even within a model of SLA, they have been useful in generating classification schemes for cognitive, metacognitive and social/affective strategies from learner-generated data and in providing a basis for studying which strategies appear effective in promoting learning. These studies have also begun to show the differential strategic behaviors of successful and unsuccessful learners, where in a few cases, these behaviors were found to correlate with performance. In the next section, I will discuss the role that cognitive theory has played in learner strategy research.

Second language strategy research and cognitive theory

Although most of the studies in the previous section inherently claimed that strategy use is a metaphor for mental processing, the majority of those mentioned were not rooted in any explicit theory of cognition. As a result, the findings from those studies lack a certain generalizability, since they cannot be interpreted within a model of human information processing. These studies notwithstanding, there have been a number of very credible attempts to relate the process of second language learning (i.e., strategy use) to theory and research in cognitive psychology that examine human memory and learning. In the following section, I will first review a number of cognitive theories which have had the greatest impact on second language strategy researchers and then discuss the role that cognitive theory has played, thus far in second language strategy research.

Cognitive theories: Human information processing

Since the 1970s, second language strategy researchers have been influenced by several cognitive psychologists who have attempted to explain how humans process information. In this regard, most theories revolved around the nature of human memory and the role it has played in the acquisition of information. Although numerous educational and cognitive psychologists have proposed theories of human information processing, only a few have gained the attention of those investigating language learning.

Atkinson and Shiffrin (1968) proposed the multistore model of memory, which built on the work in mnemonic devices. This model attributed a major role to subject-controlled processes such as retrieving and encoding. Craik and Lockhart (1972), also concerned with how information was transformed during learning and remembering, posited a model based on "depth of processing." Anderson (1980, 1983, 1985) proposed his "spread of activation" theory, where he attempts to explain the underlying competencies of complex cognitive skill acquisition by describing production systems, or processes by which procedural knowledge is stored in human memory. Weinstein and Mayer (1986) proposed a four-stage encoding process designed to explain information acquisition through (1) selection, (2) acquisition, (3) construction and (4) integration. Hunt (1982) and Klatsky (1980) synthesized information-processing into coherent models of human learning. Finally, Gagné, Yekovich and Yekovich (1993) described the basic components of human information processing in which they included both the cognitive stages of input storage and retrieval and the metacognitive function of system management.

Of particular interest for the purposes of the current study is the model of human information processing proposed by Gagné, Yekovich and Yekovich (1993). In this system, two theoretical components are postulated: (1) a structural component, which consists of sensory receptors, short and long-term memory, and (2) a functional component, which describes the operations or strategies occurring at the specific stages of the process of information acquisition (Swanson, 1985). As seen in Figure 2.1, information or input is said to enter the structural system through receptors and is passed along to immediate memory. Some input is attended to through selective perception processes (i.e., selecting strategies), while the input not attended to is lost or forgotten. The selected input then moves along to working memory, where storage processes (i.e., comprehending strategies and memory/storing strategies) act upon the input for assimilation into long-term memory (LTM). In the information retrieval process, information is retrieved from LTM through working memory by means of retrieval processes (i.e., retrieval strategies) and is readied for output by means of response organization processes (i.e., psycho-physiological mechanisms). Each of these cognitive activities in the process is said to be managed or regulated by a set of metacognitive processes (depicted in Figure 2.1 as control processes). Thus, the metacognitive processes aid in the planning and self-assessment of learning. A graphic representation of this model is seen in Figure 2.1.

Figure 2.1

Basic Elements of the Human Information Processing System

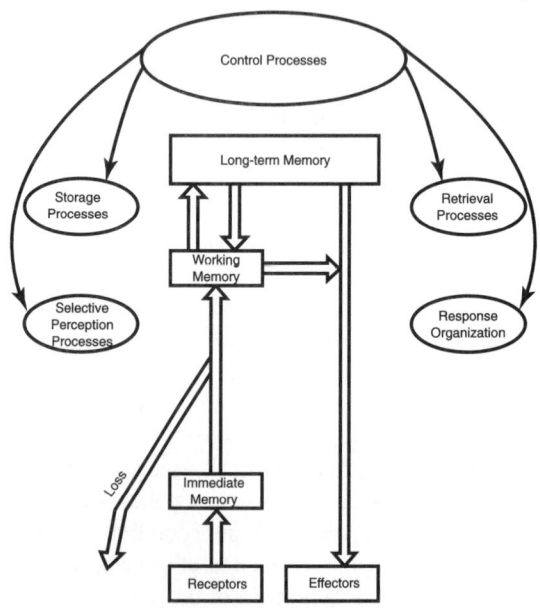

(Gagné, Yekovich & Yekovich, *The cognitive psychology of school learning*, (c) 1993, p. 40. Reprinted by permission of Scott Foresman, Glenview, IL.)

Cognitive theory in first and second language development

Each of the previous theories of learning presumed that a set of strategies would be used to render explicit the behaviors that constitute strategic knowledge. In other words, cognitive processing was operationalized by strategies. This was also seen in the studies I reviewed that looked at the mental processes of first and second language learners. Each referred to the "strategies" the learners used to accomplish their tasks.

With regard to the first language studies, Sternberg and Powell (1983) investigated reading by means of "strategies" on the metacognitive, performance and knowledge levels. Campione and Brown (1978) and later Borkowski (1985) postulated a model of intelligence in which "rules and strategies" were used to operationalize control processes. Similarly, Van Dijk and Kintsch (1983) explored the notion of first language discourse comprehension using "strategies" across several discourse levels.

Several second language strategy researchers also referred to learner "strategies" to describe mental behaviors inherent in the process of learning a second language. For example, Hosenfeld (1976, 1977a, 1977b) looked at strategies for grammar and second language skill tasks; O'Malley, Chamot and Küpper (1989) for listening tasks; Cohen and Hosenfeld (1981) and N. J. Anderson (1989) for reading tasks; Cohen (1984) and Grotjahn and Stemmer (1985) for test-taking tasks; and finally Poulisse, Bongaerts and Kellerman (1987) examined strategies in speaking tasks.

Aside from using strategies to represent human learning behaviors, several other SLA researchers made explicit attempts at relating the process of learning to a specific model or theory of learning. Of these, McLaughlin (1987) is one of the most convincing. He argued that learning a language is a complex cognitive skill, where "various aspects of the task must be practiced and integrated into fluent performance" (p. 133). This is done by thought processes which regulate and guide language performance. In this information-processing model, McLaughlin maintained that learning involves the use of the learner's cognitive system to store and retrieve information, and the degree to which a learner can process the information and achieve automaticity depends on the cognitive requirements of the task on the one hand, and the learner's ability to restructure knowledge schemata when cognitive representations change on the other.

Adding to McLaughlin's approach, Pintrich (1988) stated that:

The relevance of the information-processing approach lies in the assumption that it is not just the amount or quantity of knowledge that a student possesses, but also the qualitative organization and structure of that knowledge that is important for future performance (p. 67).

2. Strategy use and second language performance

Although McLaughlin (1987) believed that "learning a second language does involve the acquisition of a complex cognitive skill," he also cautioned that "it involves the acquisition of a complex linguistic skill as well" (p. 150). As a result, McLaughlin (1987) asserted that a model of language acquisition or use should draw not only on information from cognitive theories, but also on information from linguistic theories, such as markedness theory or universal grammar. Unfortunately, McLaughlin (1987) proposed no such model himself.

O'Malley and Chamot (1990) were also inspired by information processing as a theoretical model to explain strategy use. To this end, they proposed a framework of learning strategies in SLA based on Anderson's (1981, 1983, 1985) theoretical model of language processing in cognitive psychology. Anderson's (1983, 1985) theory of learning describes how information is represented in memory. In this view, he distinguishes between (1) declarative and (2) procedural knowledge, and described the process of skill acquisition as consisting of (1) a cognitive stage, (2) an associative stage and (3) an autonomous stage. Anderson (1983, 1985) also described the process of language production and comprehension. In his language production model, he referred to (1) a construction stage, where goal setting and planning take place, (2) a transformation stage, where language rules are applied to formulate meanings and (3) an execution stage, where the message is expressed. His language comprehension model consists of perceptual processing, parsing and utilization. O'Malley and Chamot (1990) applied Anderson's (1981, 1983, 1985) conceptual model to the field of SLA and, drawing also on the research of Naiman *et al.* (1978), Rubin (1981) and Brown *et al.* (1983), they proposed a system for categorizing learning behaviors into metacognitive, cognitive and social/affective strategies. The subcategories for each strategy type were generated from empirical studies in which O'Malley and Chamot used a variety of methods to investigate learning strategies. Their taxonomy of learning strategies consisted of a wide range of learning behaviors and provided one of the more coherent, categorizational schemes in the second language strategy literature.

However, as mentioned earlier, O'Malley and Chamot's (1990) taxonomy is not without its problems. The relationship between this taxonomy and Anderson's (1981, 1983, 1985) information-processing models of production and comprehension is not readily obvious, thereby making it impossible to relate strategy use to Anderson's theory. Furthermore, the subcategories of strategies listed under each of the three rubrics are not based on a processing framework (i.e., storing, retrieval), so that differences between the strategies in the learning process are not obvious. Finally, although the substrategies were generated from empirical studies, no research has been conducted on the validity of these categories or on the relationship of the individual behaviors to the three strategy types. Hence, until further empirical research is conducted, this taxonomy can only be regarded as an organized list of strategies. In spite of these shortcomings, O'Malley and Chamot's (1990) taxonomy has been a source of great inspiration for the current study.

Also influenced by information-processing models of learning, Rubin (cited in Wenden, 1991) proposed a system of strategies for "cognitive" learning in which cognitive strategies are divided into (1) the getting process, (2) the storing process and (3) the retrieval or using process. Each process is further divided into specific strategy types. For example, the getting process consists of (1) clarification or verification, (2) guessing or inductive inferencing, (3) deductive reasoning and (4) resourcing. Finally, each strategy type is characterized by one or more behaviors. Although the classification of some behaviors within this framework seems confusing at times, Rubin's typology clearly demonstrates how cognitive strategies might be related to a model of human learning. It was also a great source of inspiration for the current study.

In an excellent validation study, Stemmer (1991) drew on cognitive psychology, language testing and learner strategy research to examine test-takers' mental processes while taking a cloze test. She used think-aloud and immediate-retrospective report protocols to analyze the strategies used by test-takers and related them both to the characteristics and organization of memory as a component of the human information process and to theories of problem solving. In addition, Stemmer (1991) performed a task analysis on the data, which involved an item analysis and a text analysis, and found that specific cloze tasks determine the types of strategies measured, and this varied according to the individual facets of the test method. In other words, "a low number of cohesive ties in the text requires the subject to make more inferences" (p. 327); moreover, with greater text difficulty, the subjects tended to retrieve items by use of association strategies (p. 329). Stemmer (1991) concluded that the types of cloze tasks utilized in her study required that students identify a greater number of functional rather than propositional units, thereby suggesting that the cloze test invokes lower level processing, similar to recall, rather than a higher level processing of text comprehension.

Drawing explicitly on Hunt's (1982) information-processing model of human learning, Wenden (1991) described cognitive strategies as a process that involved (1) selecting information from incoming data, (2) comprehending and storing the information and (3) retrieving the information. Within this framework, she identified a number of strategies that typified each stage in the information process. Then, with regard to the self-management strategies, Wenden (1991) described metacognitive strategies in terms of planning, monitoring and evaluating, claiming that planning involved pre-planning or planning-in-action, monitoring involved self-

2. Strategy use and second language performance

assessment during the act, and evaluating occurred when a learner self-assessed the "outcome of a particular attempt to learn or use a strategy" (p. 28). Although Wenden's (1991) notion of self-management strategies was not related to any particular model of information-processing, it was rooted in the work of Lefebvre-Pinard (1983) and Flavell (1979), and had a significant impact on the thinking that led to the current study.

In addition to Oxford's (1990), O'Malley and Chamot's (1990) and Wenden's (1991) work on metacognitive strategies, the current study was also influenced by the self-management and execution models of metacognition proposed by Faerch and Kasper (1983), Bachman (1990) and Bachman and Palmer (1996).

Faerch and Kasper (1983) related metacognition to second language performance in their psycholinguistic model of speech production, which suggested that "communication strategies" are invoked as a result of problematic communication. This model divides metacognition into a planning phase and an execution phase. The planning phase involves the determination of communication goals, the assessment of linguistic resources available to the speaker, and an assessment of the communicative situation, while the execution phase refers to the neurological and physiological processes that result during language use. Faerch and Kasper's (1983) "simplified model of the principles behind goal-related intellectual behavior" was an attempt to explain the metacognitive strategies second language learners utilize during problematic oral communication.

Bachman (1990) and Bachman and Palmer (1996), elaborating on Faerch and Kasper's (1983) work, proposed a model of language use in which a metacognitive component including goal-setting, planning and assessment was explicitly articulated as a factor affecting second language learning and performance. They related these self-managing strategies to specific learner behaviors during language learning and use.

In sum, the study of learning strategies holds considerable promise for investigating the processes used in learning; however, the work done to date has essentially been descriptive in nature, with the majority of effort being devoted to identifying and describing strategies and proposing taxonomies and frameworks. Only a few studies have drawn on the research and theory in cognitive psychology to anchor the notion of strategies within an information processing framework, while those that have attempted to do just that have only been marginally successful. From a methodological perspective, the majority of studies seen thus far have relied on learner self-reports involving questionnaires, diaries, interviews, think-aloud protocols and observations. These methods of inquiry have provided rich information on learner strategies. Finally, the assumption implicit in all of these studies is that there is a causal relationship between strategy use and performance, but to date, no

2. Strategy use and second language performance

such study has provided empirical evidence to support this claim.

In the final section of this review, I will discuss the various methods that have been used to examine the relationships between strategy use and performance.

Methods for investigating strategy use and SLTP

From a methodological perspective, the majority of the studies in the 1980s aimed at investigating cognitive processes and performance were done by means of observation (e.g., Chesterfield & Chesterfield, 1985; Rubin, 1981), verbal report protocols (e.g., Anderson, 1989; Cohen, 1984; Cohen & Aphek, 1981) or structured interviews (e.g., Gillette, 1987; Lennon, 1989; Wenden, 1987). Most other researchers utilized questionnaires to investigate learner strategies and performance (e.g., Bialystok, 1978; Oxford, 1986; Politzer & McGroarty, 1985; Victori, 1992; Weinstein, Schulte & Cascallar, 1983; Zimmerman & Pons, 1986).

Most of these studies compiled lists of strategies reported by the different learners and reported the frequency of strategy use for individuals or for specific groups of interest. Some studies also used t-tests or ANOVA to compare groups, and others did correlation analyses. For the most part, however, the analyses were limited to descriptive procedures.

To provide evidence of reliability, a few studies reported the inter-observer agreement rate of the strategy codings (e.g., O'Malley *et al.*, 1985), and a few others did formal reliability analyses of the questionnaires to assess scale homogeneity (e.g., Politzer & McGroarty, 1985). Of the studies using questionnaires, only a few used exploratory factor analysis (EFA) to determine the underlying factor structure of the questionnaires. EFA is a set of statistical procedures designed to represent a set of variables in terms of a smaller number of hypothetical variables or factors (Kim & Mueller, 1978a) (a more detailed discussion of EFA is presented in Chapter 3). Of those studies, Oxford (1986) used EFA to identify the underlying factor clusters of the 64 strategies included in the SILL. She was able to reduce the 64 variables to eight clusters of variables or eight factors. Subsequent EFAs of the SILL using a larger sample size yielded four factors (Oxford, Nyikos & Crookall, 1987). In this study, EFA proved effective in trimming variables and identifying underlying factors in the data.

Following Oxford (1986), the current study utilizes EFA to investigate the clusterings of questionnaire items so that those items best measuring the underlying constructs could be identified and retained. It also used EFA to explore the criterion measures of SLTP. The factor structures of the questionnaires and the language tests were then used as preliminary models for analyses using structural equation modeling (SEM).

2. Strategy use and second language performance

SEM, also referred to as covariance structure analysis or causal modeling, is another set of multivariate, analytic procedures that have been used to investigate the relationships between background variables and criterion variables. The usefulness of SEM to investigate models of SLA and SLTP is well-documented (Clement & Kruidenier, 1985; Fouly, 1985; Gardner, 1983, 1985; Gardner, Lalonde, Moorcroft & Evans, 1987; Kunnan, 1995; Purcell, 1983; Sasaki, 1991; Wang, 1988) as SEM is a means of representing inter-relationships (1) between observed and latent variables (CFA) and (2) among latent variables based on substantive theory or previous empirical research. Once these models have been represented, they can be assessed for statistical viability and substantive interpretability. The main advantage of SEM over EFA is that SEM is able to test models that have already been formulated (a more detailed discussion of SEM is presented in Chapter 3).

Of the studies in applied linguistics that have used SEM, Purcell (1983) was among the first to utilize it as a means of investigating alternative hypotheses of SLP. He examined the effects of 11 predictor variables on pronunciation accuracy and found that pronunciation accuracy is not explained by a single factor (based on Oller's (1979) unitary trait hypothesis) as he had expected, but rather, a two-factor orthogonal model fit the data better. Although Purcell's study had some serious methodological problems (i.e., a small sample size given the number of variables and a lack of nesting in the comparisons), it was ground-breaking in that it was one of the earliest studies in the SLA research to use the statistical package, LISREL, to solve empirical, substantive, data-analytic problems by means of SEM.

Gardner (1983, 1985) also used an SEM approach to investigate SLP, positing models of SLP in which motivation played an essential role. This research generated his "Socio-Educational Model," which showed that language aptitude and motivation, consisting of attitudinal variables, had a direct impact on SLP. In a subsequent study, Gardner et al. (1987) used 98 students in 12th-grade French to re-examine Gardner's (1983, 1985) socio-educational model. Their results showed that language attitudes influence motivation, but have no direct impact on achievement. However, motivation has a direct effect on both language use and achievement at time one, and both language use and time-one achievement directly influence achievement at time two. Although these results appear informative, they have been criticized for both substantive and technical flaws (Bachman et.al., 1988; Kunnan, 1995).

In addition to the work on motivation, two studies in the second language testing literature have specifically investigated the relationships between background characteristics of second or foreign language test-takers and performance on language tests. Kunnan (1995) examined the impact of test-taker characteristics on SLTP by exploring the structural relationships between (1) test-taker responses to a 45-item questionnaire relating to exposure in three different settings and self-monitoring during language use on the one hand, and (2) test-taker performance on a battery of language tests on the other. Using 985 students from eight countries, he found that in modeling both the test-taker characteristics and test performance, the data supported an "equal influence factors model," where the factors have equal status, and an "intervening factors model," where the factors are not equal and at least one factor is an intervening factor (p. xiv). Kunnan (1995) also found this relationship to be replicated when modeling both the non-Indo-European and the Indo-European language groups.

Finally, Sasaki (1991) used both SEM and verbal report protocols to investigate the relationships between foreign language aptitude, intelligence and SLTP with 160 Japanese university students. She found that her data supported two models: one with correlated specific trait factors and one with specific trait factors related to a higher-order general SLTP factor. Furthermore, the results from her protocol analysis complemented her statistical results, revealing differences in information-processing between the high and low-ability students and suggesting that the high-ability group differed from the low-ability group in the variety of strategies they used to memorize items and in their ability to respond correctly to cloze items that were more context-reduced in nature.

Summary

In this section, I have discussed the general factors that contribute to SLTP, focusing more specifically on the role of strategy use factors in SLTP. To this end, I have endeavored to describe the role of strategy use in models of language ability. I have also reviewed several strands of research on learning strategies, some of which simply described the strategies students report using or were observed using; others which attempted to relate learning strategies to differential success; and still others which detailed how learning strategies related to a theory of information-processing. Finally, I have discussed the methods used for investigating strategy use on the one hand and the relationships between strategy use and SLTP on the other. From this review, one can see that there is a fairly extensive body of literature in each of these strands of literature, but that there is also a need to pursue further research as a number of questions still remain to be answered.

The current study aims to contribute to the literature on strategy use and SLTP. To this end, I have utilized research procedures and tools that have allowed me (1) to investigate numerous relationships between predictor and criterion variables which have not been examined empirically and (2) to approach the issues of strategy use and SLTP from a model-oriented

2. Strategy use and second language performance

perspective, where models of these patterns of behavior can be generated and tested for their statistical and substantive viability prior to making recommendations about learning or training.

3 The structural equation modeling approach: Single and multi-group procedures

Introduction

As seen in the previous chapter, most of the statistical studies aimed at relating strategy use to performance used simple univariate correlations to assess the degree of inter-relatedness between these constructs. In the current study, I used an ex post-facto correlational research design with exploratory factor analysis (EFA) and structural equation modeling (SEM) as primary analytic techniques to examine these relationships. I utilized EFA in the construction and construct validation of the strategy questionnaires in the preliminary analyses, and again used it to identify composite variables from the item-level data and to generate baseline models for subsequent analysis. SEM was used to assess the statistical and interpretative quality of these models.

Although I used procedures in this study which allow for a confirmatory approach to model analysis, this study remains essentially exploratory in nature. This is because no study prior to the current one has used EFA and SEM to investigate the relationships between the reported cognitive and metacognitive strategy use of test-takers and their performance on language tests. Consequently, in the single-group analyses, I was not able to confirm any prior baseline model of strategy use and SLTP. In sum, I used an approach in this study which allowed me to posit and test models iteratively until a model was found that both fit the data statistically and had substantive viability.

Once the base-line model for strategic use and performance for the entire group was established, I was then able to examine the degree to which this model held for the high and low-ability groups. In this respect, the multi-groups analyzed were more confirmatory in nature.

This chapter discusses the procedures used throughout the study.

Study participants

I collected the original data for this study from 17 different test centers in three countries. This involved 1,660 students of English as a Foreign Language (also referred to as "test-takers"). These data were then reduced to

3. The structural equation modeling approach

1,382 cases due to missing information (for further information on data reduction, see the section on "Data Preparation" in this chapter). Theoretically, the sampling procedure was designed to reflect the characteristics of the candidates from the University of Cambridge Local Examinations Syndicate (UCLES) who intend to sit for the *First Certificate in English (FCE)*;[1] however, as the participants in this study were arranged through my own personal contacts, I was unable to include a true cross-sampling of *FCE* participants from around the world and consequently, I make no claim in this study to generalize to the entire *FCE* candidature. In the end, I collected the data at two sites in the Czech Republic (Kralupy and Liberac, comprising 9.6% of the participants), one site in Spain (Barcelona, comprising 16.3% of the participants) and five sites in Turkey (Ankara, Istanbul, Izmir, Kayseri, and Tekirdat, comprising 74.2% of the participants). The breakdown of participants by country and test centre is shown in Appendix A.

With regard to gender, the majority of participants in the study were female (N = 878), representing 63.5% of the population, while 36.5% were male (N = 504). Also, the vast majority of participants (92.1%) were 25 years of age or under. The average age was approximately 18, with the youngest participant being 14 and the oldest being 53. The median age was 16. Finally, approximately 60% of the students were enrolled in high school, while the other 40% were enrolled in English classes at the university or at a Bi-national center.[2]

With regard to language proficiency, the participants in this study were limited to those enrolled in high-beginning level English classes or above. Students at the low-beginning proficiency levels were not included since their proficiency in English may have prevented them from completing the strategy questionnaires without extensive linguistic assistance. As the designations "beginning" and "intermediate" sometimes do not refer to the similar levels of proficiency in different contexts around the world, I used the students' textbooks as well as their ability to understand the strategy questionnaires as criteria for determining whether they were at the minimum level of proficiency required for this study. In two cases (the school in Badalona, Spain and the one in Kayseri, Turkey), the students were using an "intermediate" textbook in their courses, but were still unable to make sense of the questionnaire. As a result, I did not administer the language test to those students and the questionnaire data were not used in this study. A breakdown of students by course level is shown in Appendix B.

Similar to the *FCE* candidature, the test-takers represented a wide variety of native languages, the majority of whom obviously reported Catalan, Czech, Spanish and Turkish to be their native language. Appendix C shows the test-takers by native language.

3. The structural equation modeling approach

Finally, the students in this study were asked if they had ever studied English in an English-speaking country and 91.4% responded that they had not.

Measurement instruments

Two types of instruments were used in this study: (1) strategy use questionnaires designed to collect data on the test-takers' reported cognitive and metacognitive strategy use and (2) a language proficiency test. These measures are described below.

Background of the strategy use questionnaires

In designing the strategy use questionnaires, I (in conjunction with Lyle Bachman and Sara Cushing Weigle from UCLA and the EFL Division of UCLES) initially intended to develop instruments that would allow test-takers to report the cognitive and metacognitive strategies they thought they used in second or foreign languages testing situations, so that I could investigate the role of strategic competence in Bachman's (1990) and Bachman and Palmer's (1996) models of communication language ability. However, in attempting to operationalize areas of strategic competence for test-taking only, we soon realized that strategic competence in testing could not be dissociated from strategic competence in second language use and acquisition, and that strategy use affects test performance directly in some circumstances and indirectly in others (Bachman, Cushing & Purpura, 1993). For example, the cognitive strategy "linking with prior knowledge" could be invoked in SLA, second language use and also in second language test-taking situations. As a result, I did not attempt to differentiate strategy use in these three contexts.

Furthermore, "strategy use" or "cognitive processing" was operationalized by means of "strategies," which refer to conscious or unconscious mental or behavioral activities, related directly or indirectly to human information processing in the context of SLA, second language use or second language testing. I decided to adopt this characterization because nearly all the studies looking at the mental processes of learners referred to the "strategies" that learners used to accomplish their tasks (Borkowski, 1985; Campione & Brown, 1978; Sternberg & Powell, 1983; Van Dijk & Kintsch, 1983). Also, all the studies I reviewed in the SLA literature used "strategies" to describe the mental behaviors inherent in the process of learning a second language (e.g., N. J. Anderson, 1989; Cohen, 1984; Cohen & Hosenfeld, 1981; Grotjahn & Stemmer, 1985; Hosenfeld, 1976, 1977a, 1977b; O'Malley, Chamot & Küpper, 1989; Poulisse, Bongaerts & Kellerman, 1987).

A third goal in developing the questionnaires for this study was to ensure that they were both firmly embedded in a model of human information processing. In this regard, I was influenced by Wenden (1991), who based her

3. The structural equation modeling approach

work specifically on Hunt's (1982) model of human information processing (see Figure 3.1). Hunt (1982) divides learning into four stages: (1) the "selecting" stage, where incoming information is selected for processing; (2) the "comprehending" stage, where it is decoded; (3) the "storing" stage, where it is elaborated in order to be remembered; and finally (4) the "retrieval" stage, where information is retrieved from memory for use. Hunt's (1982) model was particularly useful in helping to shape my thinking in the design of the Cognitive Strategy Questionnaire.

Figure 3.1

A Flow Chart of the Human Memory System

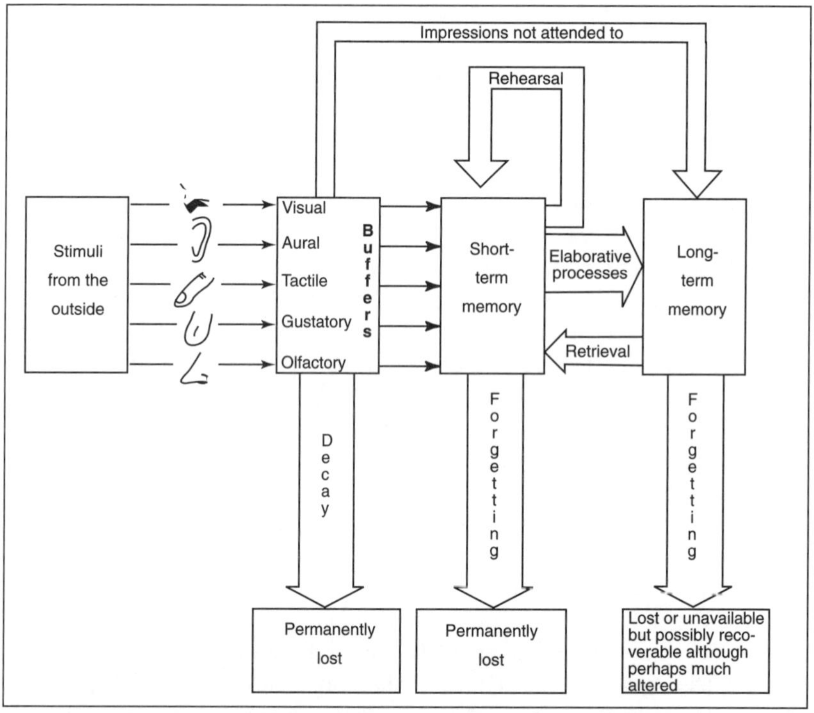

(Hunt, cited in Wenden, *Learner strategies for learner autonomy*, (c) 1993, p. 19. Reprinted by permission of Prentice Hall, Upper Saddle River, New Jersey.)

In developing the Metacognitive Strategies Questionnaire, I was influenced by the taxonomies proposed by O'Malley and Chamot (1990), Oxford (1990) and Wenden (1991) and by the self-management and execution models of metacognition proposed by Faerch and Kasper (1983) and elaborated upon by Bachman (1990) and Bachman and Palmer (1996).

In the end, I based the current study on Gagné, Yekovich and Yekovich's

3. The structural equation modeling approach

(1993) model of human information processing which, unlike Hunt's (1982) model, accounted for both cognitive and metacognitive processing in one single model. Gagné, Yekovich and Yekovich's (1993) model of the basic elements of human learning is presented in the Figure 3.2.

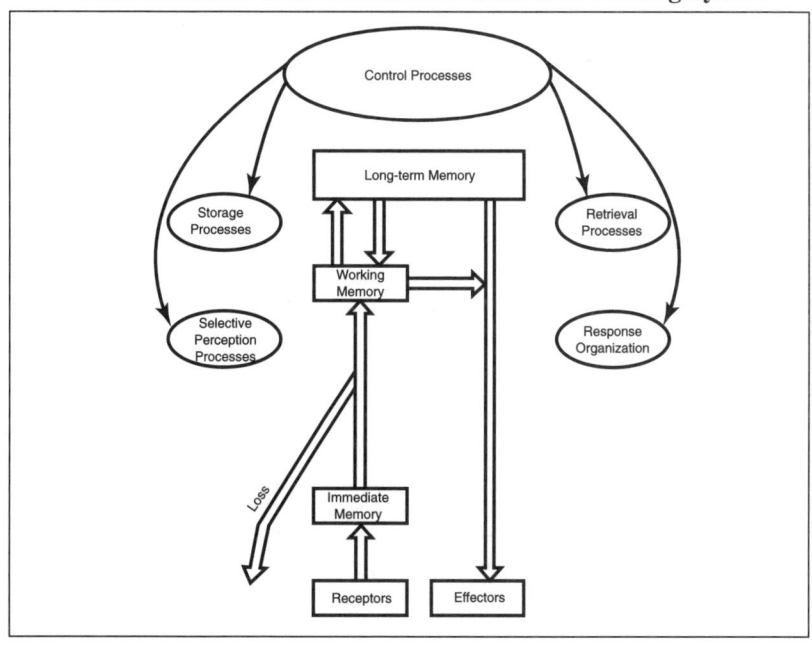

Figure 3.2

Basic Elements of the Human Information Processing System

(Gagné, Yekovich & Yekovich, 1993, *The cognitive psychology of school learning,* p. 40. Reprinted by permission of Scott Foresman, Glenview, IL.)

I might clarify that in the present study, I did not adopt verbatim the specific ways of operationalizing cognitive processing that were proposed by Rubin (1987), O'Malley and Chamot (1990) and Wenden (1991), or the taxonomies put forth by Oxford (1986, 1990) and Weinstein (1987). Similarly, with regard to metacognitive processing, I did not follow to the letter the models proposed by Faerch and Kasper (1983), Bachman (1990), Bachman and Palmer (1996) and Gagné, *et al.* (1993). These studies did, however, serve as a basis for the thinking in the current study.

Finally, unlike most of the prior studies on strategy use, the current one hypothesizes a theoretical model in which cognitive and metacognitive processing are said to have direct substantive and statistical relationships with each other as well as with SLTP. It views cognitive processing as

3. The structural equation modeling approach

multifaceted, hierarchically-organized and closely associated with the structural and control components of the information-processing system and postulates a strong relationship between the metacognitive and cognitive processes, whereby the integration of metacognitive knowledge with cognitive behaviors would result in better SLTP.

In the following sections, I describe each instrument separately.

The Cognitive Strategies Questionnaire

Klatsky (1980), Hunt (1982) and Gagné et al. (1993) all describe human learning as involving stages in a process. With regard to the cognitive strategies, this process consists of (1) a selecting or attending stage, where information is identified or isolated from other input for processing; (2) a comprehending stage, where information is held in short-term memory long enough to be transformed into meaningful symbols; (3) a storing or memory stage, where information is elaborated so that a learner can recognize patterns, make associations, relate to previous knowledge structures, etc. in order to store the information in long-term memory; and (4) a using or retrieval stage, where information is drawn from long-term memory for use when needed.

Influenced by these models of human learning and by several learner strategy studies, Bachman, Cushing and Purpura (1993) designed the first version of the Cognitive Strategies Questionnaire to include items that measured all four stages of the information process. We drew on first and second language research to compile a list of cognitive strategies for inclusion in the questionnaire and wrote operational definitions for each strategy type. We then classified the strategies in the processing framework and developed items to measure each one. To do this, we adapted a number of items from Oxford's (1990) Strategy Inventory for Language Learning (SILL), and Weinstein's (1987) Learning and Study Strategies Inventory (LASSI), and we wrote several items of our own.

This questionnaire was initially designed as one component of the University of Cambridge Language Learning Questionnaires developed by Bachman, Cushing and Purpura (1993) as part of a joint venture by the EFL Division of UCLES and the Language Assessment Group in the Department of TESL/Applied Linguistics at UCLA to investigate the background characteristics of Cambridge EFL Examination candidates and the relationship of these characteristics to test performance. It consisted of 71 items designed to measure the four stages of the learning process. Then, with the goal of assessing the construct validity of this questionnaire, I, along with Sara Cushing Weigle, administered the instrument to 301 ESL/EFL students. The results of a reliability analysis showed that a number of items yielded low item–total correlations. In such cases, the items were dropped from the scales. Also, the "selecting" strategy items yielded a relatively low alpha (0.46), and this scale was subsequently dropped from the questionnaire, resulting in a three-stage rather than a four-stage operationalization of a model of human learning. In further analyses using EFA, Purpura (1998) found that the wording of a number of items caused them to cluster with more than one scale or with a scale other than the one they had originally been intended to measure. In these cases, items were either dropped or reclassified. This study resulted in a revised questionnaire that contained 51 items as measures of the underlying factors.

Of these 51 items, the 40 that showed the strongest factor loadings were selected for inclusion in the version of the Cognitive Strategies Questionnaire utilized in the current study (See Appendix D). Table 3.1 presents a taxonomy of the cognitive strategy use variables and strategy type variables.

Table 3.1
A Taxonomy of the Cognitive Strategies Questionnaire (40 items)

			Items used
1. Comprehending Processes (COMP)			
•Analyzing Contrastively (AC)		3 items	5, 16, 17
•Analyzing Inductively (AI)		3 items	36, 39, 40
•Clarifying/Verifying (CLAR)		4 items	3, 4, 20, 38
•Inferencing (INF)		2 items	34, 37
•Translating (TRL)		2 items	9, 14
	Subtotal	14 items	
2. Storing/Memory Processes (MEM)			
•Associating (ASSOC)		4 items	10, 11, 12, 13
•Linking with Prior Knowledge (LPK)		3 items	1, 2, 6
•Repeating/Rehearsing (REP)		4 items	27, 28, 29, 30
•Summarizing (SUMM)		2 items	7, 33
	Subtotal	13 items	
3. Using/Retrieval Processes (RET)			
•Applying Rules (APR)		5 items	8, 18, 22, 31, 32
•Practicing Naturalistically (PN)		5 items	21, 23, 25, 27, 35
•Transferring (TRF)		3 items	15, 19, 24
	Subtotal	13 items	
	Total	**40 items**	

Appendix E lists the cognitive strategy use items according to their respective strategy types.

The Metacognitive Strategies Questionnaire

Faerch and Kasper (1983) related metacognition to second language performance in their psycholinguistic model of speech production, dividing metacognition into a planning and execution phase. Bachman and Palmer (1996) proposed a model of language use in which the metacognitive component included goal-setting, planning and assessment. O'Malley and Chamot (1990) described metacognitive behaviors as planning, directed attention, selective attention, self-management, self-monitoring, problem

3. The structural equation modeling approach

identification and self-evaluation, while Wenden (1991) viewed metacognitive strategies as planning (pre- and post), monitoring and evaluating.

Drawing on the work of these researchers, Bachman, Cushing and Purpura (1993) developed the Metacognitive Strategies Questionnaire, another component of the University of Cambridge Language Learning Questionnaires, to contain 68 items designed to measure (1) goal-setting, (2) assessment, consisting of strategies designed to "assess the situation," "self-monitor" and "self-evaluate," and (3) planning, where items measured strategies to "formulate a plan" and to "learn to learn."

Again, with the goal of assessing the construct validity of this instrument, I, along with Sara Cushing Weigle, administered the questionnaire to 227 students. In a construct validity study of this questionnaire, Purpura (1994) found that a number of items yielded low item-total correlations and again these items were dropped from the scales. Also, the EFA of this questionnaire again showed that the wording of several items caused them to cluster with more than one scale or with a scale other than the one they had originally been designed for. This was observed most with items designed to measure "monitoring" and "evaluating," two very similar assessment strategies. In these cases, items were again either dropped or reclassified, resulting in a revised questionnaire that contained 60 items as measures of the underlying factors.

Of these items, the 40 that showed the strongest factor loadings were selected for inclusion in the version of the Metacognitive Strategies Questionnaire used in the current study (See Appendix F). Table 3.2 presents a taxonomy of the metacognitive strategy use variables and strategy types.

Table 3.2
Taxonomy of the Metacognitive Strategies Questionnaire (40 items)

			Items used
1. Goal-Setting Processes (GS)			
•Setting Goals (GS)		5 items	43, 53, 54, 56, 80
	Subtotal	5 items	
2. Assessment Processes (ASSESS)			
•Assessing the Situation (ASSIT)		8 items	41, 42, 58, 63, 65, 66, 67, 72
•Monitoring (MON)		9 items	44, 47, 49, 52, 55, 57, 60, 68, 75
•Evaluating (EVAL)		10 items	46, 50, 51, 61, 62, 69, 71, 73, 74, 76
	Subtotal	27 items	
3. Planning Processes (PLAN)			
•Formulating a Plan (FPL)		5 items	48, 59, 64, 78, 79
•Learning to Learn (LLRN)		3 items	45, 70, 77
	Subtotal	8 items	
	Total	**40 items**	

Appendix G lists the metacognitive strategy use items according to their respective strategy types.

The *FCE Anchor Test*

The *First Certificate in English (FCE)*, a proficiency test developed by UCLES, is the third level exam in the UCLES suite of five exams designed for different proficiency levels. This particular exam is geared toward intermediate-level students. The *FCE Anchor Test* is one of a series of measures used in an on-going project organised by UCLES to monitor the difficulty of EFL examinations over time.[3]

The individual components of the *Anchor Test* for the *FCE* (referred to here as the *FCE Anchor Test* – see Appendix H) are the criterion measures used in the current study and are designed to gauge the students' second or foreign language performance levels in the different areas of language ability. Following UCLES procedures, the *FCE Anchor Test* takes one hour and thirty minutes to complete and consists of two sections as outlined in Table 3.3.

Table 3.3

Description of the *FCE Anchor Test* (70 items)

Section A:	The Reading Comprehension Section
Part 1:	Grammar and Vocabulary (GV) (20 items)
Part 2:	Passage Comprehension (PC) (2 passages: 10 items)
Section B:	**The Use of English Section**
Part 1:	Word Formation (WF) (10 items)
Part 2:	Cloze (CLZ) (20 items)
Part 3:	Sentence Formation (SF) (10 items)

The Reading Comprehension Section contains 30 selected-response items and tests the students' ability to understand written English. More specifically, the Grammar and Vocabulary (GV) part of the Reading Comprehension Section contains 20 discrete-point multiple-choice items designed to measure the test-takers' (1) use of grammatical rules and constraints, (2) semantic sets and collocations and (3) phrasal verbs (EFL Division of UCLES, 1994).

The Passage Comprehension (PC) part of this section presents test-takers with two passages and ten multiple-choice questions (five per passage). These questions aim to measure the students' ability to read a passage in English for details, synonymy and inferences. Each passage is 250–550 words long, giving an approximate total of 800–1,000 words in the PC section. The passage presents examples of expository writing (EFL Division of UCLES, 1994).

The second section of the *Anchor Test*, the Use of English Section, contains 40 limited-production items and tests the students' ability to use English at the word and sentence levels. Each section is scored by means of a scoring rubric, where some items have one and only one correct answer, while others allow for a number of answer possibilities. (For further information on UCLES scoring criteria and the criteria for correctness used in this study, see the section on "Scoring the *FCE Anchor Test*" in this chapter.)

The Word Formation (WF) part of this Section contains ten discrete items, where test-takers are required to transform the root of a word into a related word form based on how the word is used in a sentence (e.g., hand -> handful). They then have to write the word in the blank.

The Cloze (CLZ) part of this section consists of a modified cloze procedure with 20 item-gaps for students to fill in. The Cloze is based on a single text and is designed to test structural and lexical appropriacy.

Finally, the Sentence Formation (SF) part contains six discrete sentences. Here, test-takers are asked to write a sentence similar in meaning to the one provided based on a short prompt.

Study variables

The procedure for operationalizing the variables used in this study is described in this section. This study contains three sets of variables: the cognitive processing variables (measured by 40 questionnaire items), the metacognitive processing variables (measured by 40 questionnaire items) and the SLTP variables (measured by 70 test items). The first two types of variables represent the strategy use variables, and the third, the test-performance variables.

The cognitive strategy use variables

The Cognitive Strategies Questionnaire consists of 40 items—with each item measuring only one strategy-type variable. For example, item 28 measures the "repeating/rehearsing" strategy type. Each strategy-type variable is represented by at least two questionnaire items. To derive variables that represent the different strategy types, an average of all the items representing that strategy type was computed. For example, the strategy type "linking with prior knowledge" is an averaged composite of items 1, 3 and 6. This study contained 12 such cognitive strategy-type variables and they formed the 12 observed variables of the cognitive strategy use component. The observed strategy variables and the items used to form the composites are displayed in Table 3.1.

The 12 strategy-type variables were hypothesized to measure three latent variables referred to as the "process-type" variables. These three variables included the comprehending processes, the memory processes and the retrieval processes. In theory, each of the 12 strategy-type variables measured only one process-type variable. For example, the strategy-type variable, "associating," was hypothesized to represent the memory (or storing) process.

A complete taxonomy of the cognitive strategy items, types and processes

3. The structural equation modeling approach

is presented in Table 3.1. A description of each cognitive strategy variable in the study follows.

A: Cognitive strategy-type variables

The following twelve variables are the observed variables, measured by the Cognitive Strategies Questionnaire.

Comprehending processes

1. Analyzing Contrastively (AC)

This variable is designed to measure the extent to which the test-takers seek to understand by noticing what is similar or different between two or more language elements, whether they be of a phonologic, lexical, syntactic or discourse nature. These new elements could be compared with those in the first language or with those in another language the learner might be familiar with.

2. Analyzing Inductively (AI)

This variable is designed to measure the extent to which the test-takers seek to understand by analyzing input so as to formulate hypotheses and make generalizations.

3. Clarifying/Verifying (CLAR)

This variable is designed to measure the extent to which the test-takers seek to understand by asking themselves or others for explanatory or clarifying information or by asking themselves or others for verification or confirmation of what a test-taker has understood to be correct.

4. Inferencing (INF)

This variable is designed to measure the extent to which the test-takers seek to understand by using contextual information to interpret meanings. Inferencing might involve behaviors such as guessing words, predicting outcomes, supplying missing information, providing an interpretation of a reading or listening passage, or determining the author's attitude or tone.

5. Translating (TRL)

This variable is designed to measure the extent to which the test-takers seek to understand by translating from one language to another.

Storing or memory processes

6. Associating (ASSOC)

This variable is designed to measure the extent to which the test-takers seek to remember information by classifying input into meaningful groups or categories or by making semantic connections between entities.

7. Linking with Prior Knowledge (LPK)

This variable is designed to measure the extent to which the test-takers seek to remember information by making connections between what is already

3. The structural equation modeling approach

known (e.g., topical, linguistic or procedural knowledge) and what is about to be learned, remembered or used.

8. Repeating or Rehearsing (REP)
This variable is designed to measure the extent to which the test-takers seek to remember information by repeating it or rehearsing it.

9. Summarizing (SUMM)
This variable is designed to measure the extent to which the test-takers seek to remember information by making mental, oral or written summaries of the target information.

Using or retrieval processes

10. Applying Rules (APR)
This variable is designed to measure the extent to which the test-takers seek to retrieve or use language knowledge by consciously applying rules.

11. Practicing Naturalistically (PN)
This variable is designed to measure the extent to which the test-takers seek to retrieve or use language knowledge by communicating with an intended (e.g., in writing) or an actual interlocutor.

12. Transferring (TRF)
This variable is designed to measure the extent to which the test-takers seek to retrieve or use language knowledge by utilizing previous linguistic or procedural knowledge in order to facilitate use of this knowledge in a new or different situation.

B: Cognitive process-type variables

The following three variables constitute the latent variables representing the three stages in human information processing. Each variable is composed of the two or more strategy-type variables, as seen in Table 3.1.

13. Comprehending Processes (COMP)
This variable represents the comprehending component of cognitive strategy use. In theory, it consists of the following strategy types: analyzing contrastively, analyzing inductively, clarifying, translating and inferencing.

14. Storing or Memory Processes (MEM)
This variable represents the storing or memory component of cognitive strategy use. In theory, it is related to the associating, linking with prior knowledge, repeating or rehearsing and summarizing strategies.

15. Using or Retrieval Processes (RET)
This variable is designed to measure the using or retrieval component of cognitive strategy use. In theory, it is related to applying rules, practicing naturalistically and transferring.

3. The structural equation modeling approach

The metacognitive strategy use variables

The Metacognitive Strategies Questionnaire consists of 40 strategy items. Again, each strategy item belongs theoretically to one strategy type. For example, item 65 represents "assessing the situation." Also, each strategy-type variable is composed of two or more questionnaire items. Again, to derive composite variables of the strategy types, an average of all the items representing that strategy type was computed. For example, the metacognitive strategy type "assessing the situation" consisted of the average of all the questionnaire items that were used to measure it. This study contained five metacognitive strategy types, forming the five observed variables of the metacognitive strategy use component. The strategy-type variables and the items used to form the composites are displayed in Table 3.2.

Again these five strategy-type variables were hypothesized to measure one of three latent variables relating to metacognitive strategy use. These three metacognitive strategy use variables included goal-setting, assessment and planning. For example, "monitoring" was identified as one of the variables measuring the "assessment processes."

A complete taxonomy of the metacognitive strategy items, types and processes is presented in Table 3.2. A description of each metacognitive strategy use variable follows.

A: Metacognitive strategy-type variables:

Goal-setting processes

1. Setting Goals (GS)

This variable is designed to measure the extent to which the test-takers feel they use the higher-order executive function of identifying and choosing specific goals and objectives before or during an activity.

Assessment processes

2. Assessing the Situation (ASSIT)

This variable is designed to measure the extent to which the test-takers feel they use the higher-order executive function of taking stock of conditions surrounding a language task by assessing one's own knowledge, one's available internal and external resources and the constraints of the situation before they engage in the activity.

3. Monitoring (MON)

This variable is designed to measure the extent to which the test-takers feel they use the higher-order executive function of determining the effectiveness of one's own or another's performance of a task while engaging in the activity.

4. Evaluating (EVAL)

This variable is designed to measure the extent to which the test-takers feel

3. The structural equation modeling approach

they use the higher-order executive function of determining the effectiveness of one's own or another's performance after engaging in the activity.

Planning processes

5. Formulating a Plan (FPL)
This variable is designed to measure the extent to which the test-takers feel they use the higher-order executive function of generating an overall plan of action before attempting a language task or changing/adapting a plan of action while completing a task.

6. Learning to Learn (LLRN)
This variable is designed to measure the extent to which the test-takers feel they understand and arrange for the presence of the conditions that help them successfully accomplish language tasks and also find out how language learning, use and testing work.

B: Metacognitive process-type variables:

The following three variables constitute the latent variables of metacognitive strategy use. Each variable is composed of one or more strategy-type variables, as seen in Table 3.2.

7. Goal-Setting Processes (GOALS)
This variable is designed to measure the goal-setting component of metacognitive strategy use and is related to the "setting goals" strategies.

8. Planning Processes (PLAN)
This variable is designed to measure the planning component of the metacognitive strategy use and is related to "formulating a plan" and "learning to learn."

9. Assessing Processes (ASSESS)
This variable is designed to measure the assessment component of metacognitive strategy use. It includes "assessing the situation," "monitoring" and "evaluating."

The SL Test Performance (SLTP) variables

These five performance variables (generally referred to as SLTP variables) constitute the five observed variables of the language test.

1. Grammar and Vocabulary (GV).
This variable is designed to measure the test-takers' ability in the use of grammatical rules and constraints, semantic sets and collocations, and phrasal verbs.[4]

2. Passage Comprehension (PC)
This variable is designed to measure the test-takers' ability to measure the students' ability to read a passage in English for details, synonymy and inferences.

3. The structural equation modeling approach

3. Word Formation (WF)
This variable is designed to measure the test-takers' ability to use English morphology to transform the root of a word into a related word form according to how the word is used in a sentence.

4. Cloze (CLZ)
This variable is designed to measure the test-takers' ability in structural and lexical appropriacy.

5. Sentence Formation (SF)
This variable is designed to measure the test-takers' ability to generate synonymous sentences.

Data collection and scoring

Administration of instruments

I administered the questionnaires and test to all study participants using the same procedures. I distributed the test materials to the students and briefly explained the purpose of the study.[5] I then read the directions aloud as the students read along. Questions relating to the test instructions were answered. The students were then asked to complete the questionnaires and encouraged to ask questions about any vocabulary they did not understand. In those cases, translations or explanations were provided.[6] They were given as long as they needed to complete the questionnaire (no one needed more than one hour). Once the students had finished, we collected the questionnaires and proceeded with the test.

We first distributed the *FCE Anchor Test* answer sheets (See Appendix I). We then gave them their test packet and read aloud the general instructions, followed by the specific instructions for each test section. All questions about the instructions were answered. We gave the test-takers exactly one-and-a-half hours to finish the test.

Scanning the questionnaire answer sheets

The completed answer sheets were scanned using an NCS optical scanner. This provided raw data, along with a report indicating the number of participants choosing each of the five choices on the answer sheet as well as the number who did not respond or who responded twice. Following the scanning, each piece of data flagged as missing or double-marked was checked for possible scanning errors and corrected accordingly.

Scoring of the *FCE Anchor Test*

When the questionnaire and test were collected, an identification number was assigned to both instruments. If a participant did not complete either the

3. The structural equation modeling approach

questionnaire or the test, the case was not included in the study.

UCLES provides a scoring key and a set of guidelines for scoring the *FCE Anchor Test*, as presented in Appendix J. All items were scored "right/wrong." A key was provided for the multiple-choice parts (Grammar/Vocabulary; Passage Comprehension), and a scoring rubric with correct answer possibilities was provided for the limited-production items (Word Formation; Cloze; Sentence Formation).

As the *FCE Anchor Test* scoring rubric was devised by speakers of British English, I revised the scoring rubric to include answer choices that were also correct in American English. To verify the accuracy of the scoring rubric for speakers of American English, I gave the Anchor Test to five native speakers of American English. None of the native speakers (NSs) got a perfect score and many provided answers that were not on the UCLES rubric. In these cases, two other NSs were asked to assess correctness and the rubric was changed accordingly. Appendix J presents those items in which a discrepancy was seen between the UCLES rubric and the responses provided by the NSs of American English. It also displays any modifications to the scoring rubric based on these discrepancies.

Once the rubric was modified, I scored all 1,660 exams. In a number of instances, the test-takers provided answers that also appeared to be plausible choices. A log of these possibilities was kept during the scoring.

When all 1,660 papers were scored, two NSs were asked to judge the student-provided answer choices supplied for correctness. The rubric was again revised and the exams were scored a second time. Appendix J shows these "Additional TT Choices" in the "Rubric Modifications" column.

Data preparation

In a study such as this, a number of procedures need to be followed in order to prepare the data for analysis. First, since this study involved both test and questionnaire data, the two types of data were input in separate files on the computer and each data set was examined for missing values. The issue of missing values is an important one since structural equation modeling procedures require a fully-crossed data set (i.e., all individuals must have responses to all items).

In this study, the *FCE Anchor Test* was inspected first and as expected, I found a considerable number of missing data. However, to determine whether these data should be treated as "missing" or "wrong," I established the following procedures. First, if a participant made a "reasonable" attempt at answering the questions in a test section, the questions left unanswered were treated as "wrong" (i.e., scored zero). However, if a student left an entire section blank or if three questions or fewer (especially the first couple of items) were answered in any particular section, the data were treated as "missing," and the participant was dropped from the study. Following this

3. The structural equation modeling approach

procedure, 278 cases were dropped from the study, leaving a total sample size of 1,382 to be used in the current study.

The second data set involved the questionnaire items. Again these data were examined for missing values using the missing data protocol in EQS. Surprisingly, only 18 questionnaire items were left unanswered from the two questionnaires; eight from the Cognitive Strategies Questionnaire and ten from the Metacognitive Strategies Questionnaire. In order to be able to use these 18 cases in the study, I decided to complete each individual's data set by imputing the missing piece of data from other items in the data. This decision was taken because (1) only 18 cases were involved (out of 1,382) and (2) in each case, no more than one questionnaire item was found to be missing. Nonetheless, I recognize that data imputation is a controversial procedure and must be used with extreme caution.

To impute these data, I used a multiple regression approach. In this approach, predictor variables are used as a means of estimating the scores of a dependent variable. The predictor variables for each item were based on the other items in its respective strategy scale after preliminary item-level factor analyses were performed. In this approach, EQS uses the estimated beta weights and scores of subjects on the predictor variables to compute the imputed dependent variable score (Bentler & Wu, 1995). To illustrate, person 546 did not respond to item 4 (a clarifying strategy) on the questionnaire. As a result, item 4 was imputed from predictor items 27, 28, 29 and 30, which also belonged to the "clarifying strategy" scale. These specific items were chosen as predictors since they were from the same scale and seemed, therefore, to be the best predictors of the missing item.

Once the item-level data sets for both the *FCE Anchor Test* and the strategy questionnaires were complete, I then prepared composite variables for use in the study. To form composite variables for the *FCE Anchor Test*, I simply added the scores for each item in the same test section and got a total score for that variable. For example, the scores for each of the ten items measuring sentence formation were totaled to form the sentence formation variable.

The formation of composite variables for the strategy items, however, was not based on a total score of each item measuring that scale. Rather, in order to keep the strategy scores on a 0 to 5 scale, the scores from each item measuring a scale were averaged to form the composite variable. For example, the scores from each item measuring "summarizing" were averaged to form a composite "summarizing" variable. For further information on the procedures used to form composite variables in this study, see Chapter 4.

Once the composite variables were formed, I matched and merged the data sets by test-taker identification number. The final data set was fully-crossed and contained 1,382 cases.

3. The structural equation modeling approach

Statistical procedures

Computer equipment and software

Microsoft EXCEL for the MAC Version 5.0 (Microsoft Corporation, 1995) was used to input the data. These data were then exported to the other statistical programs. SPSS Version 4.0.4 for the MAC (SPSS Inc., 1990) was used to compute descriptive statistics and perform both reliability analyses and exploratory factor analyses. PRELIS 2 (Jöreskog & Sörbom, 1993) on the IBM was used to compute tetrachoric correlations from the dichotomously-scored data. Finally, EQS for the MAC Version 5.0 (Bentler & Wu, 1995) was used to perform missing data analyses, impute data, compute descriptive statistics and perform both confirmatory factor analyses and covariance structure analyses.

Overview of statistical procedures

The following statistical procedures were used in this study. A flow chart of these procedures is seen in Figure 3.3.

1. **Descriptive statistics:** I first calculated descriptive statistics and checked assumptions regarding normality. To this end, I examined the means, standard deviations, skewness and kurtosis of each variable. A normally-distributed variable has a skewness and a kurtosis near zero (SPSS Inc., 1988). The majority of variables in this study were found to be normally distributed.

2. **Reliability analyses:** I then computed internal consistency reliability estimates (i.e., coefficient alpha) of the variables for all the strategy variables and for all parts of the *FCE Anchor Test* except the Cloze. Reliability for this section was based on Guttman's split-half procedure, since cloze tests may violate the assumption of independence (Bachman, 1990).

3. **Exploratory factor analysis:** I used item-level exploratory factor analyses to examine the factor structures of the Cognitive Strategies Questionnaire, the Metacognitive Strategies Questionnaire and the *FCE Anchor Test*. These item-level analyses were performed as a preliminary step in understanding the clusterings of the items. Based on these analyses, composite variables were formed, which were used in subsequent analyses. (A detailed discussion of the exploratory factor analysis is provided later in this chapter.)

4. **Single-group structural equation modeling:** Subsequent to the EFAs, I followed the structural equation modeling analytic procedures outlined by Jöreskog (1993) to posit and test models for the entire group. (A detailed discussion of the methods used for these analyses is also provided later in this chapter.)

3. The structural equation modeling approach

    a. **Confirmatory factor analysis:** I used EQS to examine the trait structure of the individual measurement models. I did separate confirmatory factor analyses relating to cognitive strategy use, metacognitive strategy use and second language test performance.

    b. **Structural equation modeling:** I used EQS to examine the relationships among all observed and latent variables in the model.

5. **Multi-group structural equation modeling:** Subsequent to the single-group analyses, I posited and tested models of strategy use and second language test performance for both the high and low-ability groups. These procedures were based on Bentler (1992), Byrne (1994) and Byrne, Shavelson and Muthén (1989). (A detailed discussion of the procedures used for these analyses is provided in chapter 6.)

    a. **Separate group analyses:** I used EQS to perform separate analyses of the relationships between strategy use and second language test performance with both the high and low-ability groups.

    b. **Simultaneous group analyses:** I used EQS to perform simultaneous analyses of the relationships between strategy use and second language test performance with both the high and low-ability groups and to test hypotheses related to cross-group equivalence.

Figure 3.3

A Flow Chart of Statistical Procedures Used in this Study

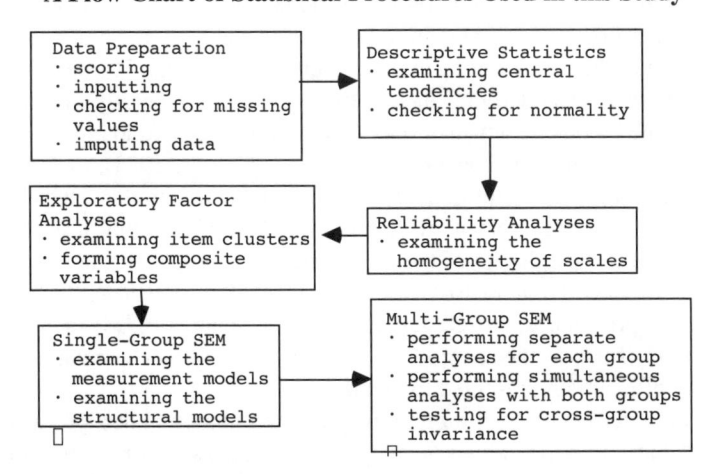

```
┌─────────────────────────┐     ┌─────────────────────────┐
│ Data Preparation        │     │ Descriptive Statistics  │
│  · scoring              │────▶│  · examining central    │
│  · inputting            │     │    tendencies           │
│  · checking for missing │     │  · checking for         │
│    values               │     │    normality            │
│  · imputing data        │     └─────────────────────────┘
└─────────────────────────┘                 │
                                            ▼
┌─────────────────────────┐     ┌─────────────────────────┐
│ Exploratory Factor      │     │ Reliability Analyses    │
│ Analyses                │◀────│  · examining the        │
│  · examining item       │     │    homogeneity of scales│
│    clusters             │     └─────────────────────────┘
│  · forming composite    │
│    variables            │
└─────────────────────────┘
                                ┌─────────────────────────┐
┌─────────────────────────┐     │ Multi-Group SEM         │
│ Single-Group SEM        │     │  · performing separate  │
│  · examining the        │     │    analyses for each    │
│    measurement models   │────▶│    group                │
│  · examining the        │     │  · performing simultaneous│
│    structural models    │     │    analyses with both groups│
│                         │     │  · testing for cross-group│
└─────────────────────────┘     │    invariance           │
                                └─────────────────────────┘
```

Exploratory factor analysis

EFA is a set of statistical procedures designed to represent a set of variables

59

3. The structural equation modeling approach

in terms of a smaller number of hypothetical variables or factors (Kim & Mueller, 1978a).

Using SPSS Version 4.0.4 for the MAC, I performed an EFA in order to examine the patterns of correlations among the items within and across each cognitive strategy scale. In other words, I used EFA to determine both if the items in each set of strategies were measuring the same underlying strategy variable and if each set of strategies represented an independent latent variable within that stage of the information process. I then performed similar EFAs with the Metacognitive Strategies Questionnaire and the *FCE Anchor Test*. The results of these item-level analyses are reported in Chapter 4.

Following Kim and Mueller (1978a, 1978b), I utilized three steps in performing the EFAs: (1) preparation of the matrix to be analyzed, (2) extraction of the initial factors and (3) rotation and interpretation.

First, for the questionnaire data, I generated a matrix of product–moment correlations among the various strategy items to be analyzed so that the appropriateness of these data for factor analysis could be evaluated. However, for the *FCE Anchor Test*, I generated a matrix of tetrachoric correlations among the various items due to the dichotomous nature of the variables. Following this, I based specific decisions regarding appropriateness of the data for factor analysis on (1) Bartlett's test of sphericity, used to test the hypothesis that the correlation matrix is an identity matrix, (2) the Kaiser-Meyer-Olkin (KMO) measure of sampling adequacy and (3) the determinant of the correlation matrix.

With regard to the extraction, initial principal axes were extracted with squared multiple correlations on the diagonal. In each case, I examined the eigenvalues obtained from the initial extraction and the scree plot as an initial indication of the number of factors represented by the data. The determination of the number of underlying factors to be extracted generally involved two criteria: the "roots greater than one" criterion, that is, extracting the number of eigenvalues greater than or equal to one (Carroll, 1983), and the "one above and one below the number of factors indicated on the 'elbow' of the scree plot" criterion (Carroll, 1985, 1993). This information, used together with the theoretical design of the measures, served to determine the ultimate number of underlying factors to be extracted. Subsequent to these initial extraction procedures, I used generalized least squares (GLS) or maximum likelihood (ML) as the method of extraction for further estimation of the number of factors represented by the data.

After determining the minimum and maximum number of factors to extract, the extractions were rotated to an orthogonal solution using a varimax rotation (Kaiser, 1958) and to an oblique solution using a direct oblimin rotation. For substantive reasons, it was expected that the strategies within a process would be correlated with each other, suggesting that the oblique solution might provide better simple structure and enhance interpretability of the data. To confirm this hypothesis, however, inter-factor correlation matrices were inspected in each case. In sum, I based the final determination regarding the best number of factors to extract on simple structure of the factors and meaningful interpretation.

Since this study was the first to examine the statistical relationships between the strategy use and SLTP, the results of these EFAs served as the baseline models from which to test these relationships in subsequent full group covariance structure analyses.

Structural equation modeling

Bentler (1992) describes linear structural equation modeling as a "useful methodology for specifying, estimating and testing hypothesized inter-relationships among a set of substantively meaningful variables" (p. ix). To be more specific, SEM (also referred to as covariance structure analysis) is a multivariate analytic procedure for representing and testing (1) hypothesized inter-relationships between observed and latent variables and (2) hypothesized inter-relationships among latent variables, based on substantive theory or previous empirical research. The procedures for testing the hypothesis of linkages between observed variables and their underlying latent variables are referred to as confirmatory factor analysis (CFA) and within the context of SEM, CFA is considered to represent the *measurement model*. Then, the procedures for testing the hypotheses of linkages among latent variables are referred to in SEM as the *structural model*. The analysis of both the measurement and structural models together is called the *full latent variable model*. When SEM is used to estimate models across groups this is referred to as multi-group SEM (see Chapter 6). I utilized all of these models in the current study.

Therefore, SEM involves both a measurement model and/or a structural model. The measurement model describes how the latent variable is measured in terms of the observed variables and describes the measurement properties (i.e., reliabilities and validities) of these variables. For example, in this study, SLTP is measured in terms of the separate parts of the *FCE Anchor Test*, whereas metacognitive processing is measured in terms of the metacognitive strategy scales. The structural model in SEM describes how the hypothesized latent variables relate. In the present study, this answers the question of how cognitive and metacognitive strategy use might relate to each other and how they each might relate to SLTP.

Generally speaking, the purpose and process of statistical modeling are the following. Based on theory or empirical research, a researcher hypothesizes a series of relationships among measured and latent variables. Each of these relationships in the model is then defined by a set of mathematical equations.

3. The structural equation modeling approach

The researcher then tests the plausibility of this model with specific data. This is done by assessing the goodness of fit between the hypothesized model and the observed data. The goal is for the hypothesized model to "fit" the data, thereby providing evidence of model validity. The discrepancy between the hypothesized model and the observed data is called the *residual*. The smaller the residual, the better the model fit.

In the current study, the SEM approach was used as a model-generating procedure in which an initial model was specified and tested. Then, if this model did not fit the data, it was modified and retested until a model with a statistical fit and meaningful interpretation was found.

SEM was utilized as the primary tool for statistical analysis in this study because it offers a number of advantages over previous multivariate procedures. First, although it is capable of taking an exploratory approach to data analysis, it generally takes a more confirmatory one, thereby facilitating the analysis of data for inferential purposes. Then, unlike regression analysis, path analysis or EFA, SEM is equipped both to assess and account for measurement error, providing explicit estimates of this parameter. Finally, SEM allows for the simultaneous analysis of both observed and latent variables in single-group analyses (Byrne, 1994) and it allows for the simultaneous analysis of multiple groups in multi-sample analyses.

The following describes the general EQS Model.

EQS terms and notation

One-way arrows from a factor to an observed variable represent regression coefficients or factor loadings, indicating the degree to which an underlying factor is measured by the variables. One-way arrows from one factor to another factor represent regression coefficients or path coefficients and indicate the impact of one variable on another. A one-way arrow from an error term to a variable represents the error associated with that variable. Curved two-way arrows represent covariances or correlations.

To illustrate, Figure 5.1 contains 11 measured variables (V2 to V12), three latent factors (F1, F2, F3) and 11 error terms (E2 to E12). A one-way arrow leads from F1 (the comprehending process factor) to V2 through V5, indicating that F1 can be explained by these four measured variables. One-way arrows also lead from the 11 error terms to the 11 measured variables. These represent the error associated with the respective variable. Finally, a two-way arrow goes between the factor 1 and factor 2 and between factor 1 and factor 3. These two-way arrows represent covariances or correlations between the factors—or the correlation between comprehending process factor and the memory process factor and between the comprehending process factor and the retrieval process factor.

3. The structural equation modeling approach

The Bentler-Weeks representation system

EQS uses the Bentler-Weeks Representation System (Bentler & Weeks, 1979, 1980) to transpose data into parameters of the mathematical model. This system categorizes all variables as either dependent or independent. A dependent variable is any variable that has a unidirectional arrow pointing toward it, while an independent variable has no unidirectional arrow pointing toward it. The main parameters of concern in this model include (1) the path coefficients or factor loadings, (2) the variances of the independent variables and (3) the covariances of the independent variables (Bentler, 1992). The dependent variables are expressed mathematically in terms of equations representing a structural regression function of other variables.

Statistical identification of the model

Identification refers to the notion of whether there is a unique set of parameter values specified in the model that are consistent with the data (Bollen, 1989; Byrne, 1994). More specifically, "a structural equation model is identified when all the unknown parameters in the implied covariance matrix (e.g., variances and covariances among the latent factors) are uniquely determined by the known values in the population covariance matrix of the observed variables" (Sasaki, 1991). If the model is not identified, only some of the parameters will be estimated and the model will not be testable. The aim regarding identification in SEM is to have an "overidentified" model or one in which the number of data points (i.e., the variances and covariances of the observed variables) exceeds the number of free parameters. This situation provides a positive number of degrees of freedom and unlike a just-identified model, allows for the model to be rejected (Byrne, 1994).

EQS indicates identification problems by providing error messages stating that linear dependencies exist among parameters. This is interpreted as an unidentified model (Chou & Bentler, 1995). Therefore, if the models in EQS run successfully, they are assumed to be overidentified.

Estimation methods

Once the models are specified, EQS estimates the unknown or free parameters in the model (i.e., the regression coefficients and the variances and covariances of the independent variables) from a set of observed data. Although a number of estimation methods are available on EQS, the present study utilizes the maximum likelihood (ML) and the ML Robust methods. ML estimation assumes that the data meet the distributional assumption of multivariate normality; however, a small number of variables in this study were not found to meet this assumption exactly (see Chapters 4 and 5). Therefore, ML Robust estimation was also used. This estimation method provides a robust chi-square (χ^2) statistic referred to as the Satorra-Bentler

3. The structural equation modeling approach

scaled statistic, S-Bχ^2, (Satorra & Bentler, 1988a, 1988b; 1994) and robust standard errors (Bentler & Dijkstra, 1985) that correct for the nonnormality in large samples.

However, Byrne (1994) cites three caveats with regard to the ML Robust estimation method: (1) robust statistics must be computed from raw data; (2) they are not available with multi-group input files; and (3) they are computationally very demanding and should be used in the final states of analysis.

Assessment of overall model fit

The focal point in SEM revolves around the degree to which a hypothesized model describes or "fits" the sample data. To assess model fit, a number of indices are available, each with advantages and disadvantages. The most commonly used index of goodness of model fit is the chi-square statistic; however, Bollen and Long (1993) recommended that "no single measure of overall fit should be relied on exclusively" (p. 6). Therefore, to determine if a model within a class of models fits the data well statistically and provides a substantively meaningful interpretation for all estimated parameters, the following indices were used.

1. The chi-square statistic was used as one measure of overall goodness of fit. This statistic tests the specified model against the unconstrained or null model and measures the distance between the sample covariance matrix and the fitted covariance matrix (Jöreskog & Sörbom, 1989). Bentler (1992) summarizes this statistic as follows:

   The given χ^2 statistic and tables values of the $\chi^2(df)$ distribution are used to determine the probability of obtaining a χ^2 value as large or larger than the value actually obtained, given that the model is correct. This is printed out as the probability value for the χ^2 statistic. When the null hypothesis is true, the model should fit the data well and this probability should exceed a standard cut-off in the χ^2 distribution (such as .05 or .01). Thus, in a very well fitting model, the probability will be large. In a poorly fitting model, the probability will be below the standard cut-off (pp. 92–93).

2. The Satorra-Bentler scaled statistic, S-Bχ^2, (Satorra & Bentler, 1988a, 1988b; 1994) was used in this study given the multivariate nonnormality of some of the distributions. This statistic provides a scaling correction for the chi-square statistic when the distributional assumption of multivariate normality is violated. Furthermore, this robust statistic has been shown to be the most reliable statistic for assessing covariance structural models with different distributions and sample sizes (Byrne, 1994).

3. The structural equation modeling approach

3. The Comparative Fit Index (CFI) (Bentler, 1990) was also used as a goodness-of-fit index. This index is based on the comparison of a hypothesized model with a null model and provides a measure of complete covariance in the data. Bentler (1992) states that this index is perhaps more useful than other indices (e.g., the Normed Fit Index or the Non-Normed Fit Index) in that it is not dependent on sample size. Based on a 0 to 1.0 scale, Bentler (1990) suggests that values of 0.90 and above are considered acceptable indices of model fit. Given the size of the sample in this study, the CFI was used as the primary index of goodness of fit.

Model modification

In the case of model misfit, a number of procedures are available in EQS to help identify misspecification problems and to indicate how the model could be improved to fit the data better statistically. Two such procedures are discussed below.

1. The Lagrange Multiplier (LM) Test was used to test the degree to which the restrictions in the model were statistically viable. In other words, the LM test was used to identify which fixed parameters would provide a significantly better model fit if they were set free or added to the model. Ultimately, the results of the LM test in addition to a supporting theoretical rationale were used before the constraints in the model were relaxed.

2. The Wald Test (Wald, 1943) was another test used to identify model misfit. Unlike the LM Test, the Wald Test assesses the degree to which hypothesized paths are redundant in a model and should be removed. One way of identifying these paths is to examine individually the z statistics associated with the structural parameter estimates for nonsignificance. This procedure, however, represents a univariate test of significance, while the Wald Test provides a multivariate test of statistical significance for determining redundant paths.

Summary

This chapter detailed the methodology that was used in the various parts of the study. It described the participants in the study, the measurement instruments, the variables, the methods used to collect and score the data, the preparation of the data and statistical procedures used to analyze the data. Chapter 4 will discuss the results of the item-level analyses performed on the questionnaires and the *FCE Anchor Test* before composite variables were formed.

3. The structural equation modeling approach

End notes

1. According to the *UCLES First Certificate in English Handbook* (EFL Division of UCLES, 1994), the *FCE* is designed for EFL students at the intermediate level of English language proficiency. The *FCE* candidature typically includes students from throughout the world with the majority of these test-takers from Europe or South America. UCLES reports that approximately 75% of the candidates are under 25 with a mean age of 22, except in some countries where the average age is 17. UCLES also reports that approximately 65% of the test-takers are female and that most are of a student status.
2. A Bi-National Center is an establishment outside the United States whose mission is to promote cross-cultural understanding between the United States and the host national country. Bi-National Centers are non-profit organizations that typically offer courses in English as a Foreign Language and/or in American Studies. They also offer a variety of cultural activities from both countries ranging from art exhibits to political debates. Bi-National Centers have usually had some formal association with the US government.
3. In lieu of administering a separate anchor test, UCLES also embeds anchor items in the new version of the *FCE* pretest for linking purposes.
4. As indicated in *FCE Handbook* (EFL Division of UCLES, 1994), the GV section of the test aims to measure (1) use of grammatical rules and constraints, (2) semantic sets and collocations, (3) adverbial phrases and connectives and (4) phrasal verbs; however, the current *FCE Anchor Test* contained only three question types. It did not measure adverbial phrases and connectives.
5. In all cases, actual class time was taken to administer the *FCE Anchor Test* and fill out the questionnaires. Permission was granted from the school principals, the heads of the English Departments or the Director of the School and the teachers involved. Results of the test scores were sent to some of the schools.
6. Some students did not understand a couple of words in the questionnaire. These words were explained or translated. In one case, Center 17, involving approximately 175 students in Badalona, Spain, the students were unable to understand the instructions for completing the background information. Given the low proficiency level of the students, I decided to end the test administration. A similar situation occurred in Kayseri, Turkey.

4 Item-level analysis

Introduction

Prior to modeling the relationships between strategy use and second language test performance, a number of item-level analyses were carried out. The purpose of these analyses was to validate the taxonomies proposed in Chapter 3. In this regard, I examined how the items in each instrument related to their respective design. In other words, even though items 5, 16 and 17 were designed to measure "analyzing contrastively," I had no evidence that these items were congruent with the observed patterns of behavior exhibited by the test-takers. These analyses also served to provide empirical information from which to formulate composite variables from the individual items. In other words, should the "analyzing contrastively" scale consist of items 5, 16 and 17, or should this strategy type have a different composition of items?

First, a series of internal consistency reliability analyses was performed on the data so that the homogeneity of the items within each strategy scale could be inspected. For example, the reliability of the "analyzing contrastively" strategy scale, which included items 5, 16 and 17, was examined. The internal consistency reliability of each section of the test was also examined.

A second set of item-level analyses sought to determine the factorial structure of the two questionnaires and the language test. This involved a series of item-level factor analyses to assess how the questionnaire and test items clustered, and how these clusterings related to the original taxonomies, seen in Chapter 3. For example, when all the cognitive strategy items were factor analyzed together, did the items cluster to form discrete strategy types as proposed in the taxonomy in Table 3.1, or did the items cluster in a different fashion? Similarly, did the items in the grammar and vocabulary section, for example, cluster to form one underlying lexico-grammatical factor or did they cluster to form separate grammar and vocabulary factors?

The results from these analyses provided empirical information regarding the substantive nature of each variable in the study. Based on this information, I was able to generate empirically-based, composite variables, which could then be used to posit a model of strategy use and SLTP.

In this chapter I describe the results of these different item-level analyses.

4. Item-level analysis

The Cognitive Strategies Questionnaire

Distributions and reliabilities

I first analyzed the item-level data from the Cognitive Strategies Questionnaire based on all 1,382 test-takers. The descriptive statistics for the 40 items are presented in Table 4.1. The means ranged from 1.68 to 3.69 and the standard deviations from 1.12 to 1.63. The medians ranged from 1 to 4. All values for skewness and kurtosis were within the accepted limits, indicating that the items appeared to be normally distributed.

Table 4.1

Distributions for the Cognitive Strategies

Variable	Mean	Std.dev	Kurtosis	Skewness	Median	Mode
COG1	3.27	1.24	-0.86	-0.21	3.00	4.00
COG2	3.18	1.26	-0.53	-0.33	3.00	4.00
COG3	3.21	1.30	-0.84	-0.26	3.00	4.00
COG4	3.38	1.42	-0.74	-0.54	4.00	5.00
COG5	2.69	1.51	-1.04	-0.04	3.00	2.00
COG6	3.42	1.31	-0.56	-0.51	4.00	4.00
COG7	2.20	1.46	-0.83	0.31	2.00	2.00
COG8	3.65	1.29	0.03	-0.83	4.00	5.00
COG9	2.89	1.58	-1.11	-0.19	3.00	2.00
COG10	2.13	1.38	-0.75	0.20	2.00	2.00
COG11	2.85	1.48	-0.89	-0.26	3.00	4.00
COG12	2.09	1.50	-0.96	0.22	2.00	2.00
COG13	2.48	1.40	-0.85	0.03	2.00	2.00
COG14	3.40	1.51	-0.63	-0.66	4.00	5.00
COG15	1.68	1.58	-0.76	0.62	1.00	0.00
COG16	2.04	1.50	-0.90	0.33	2.00	2.00
COG17	3.02	1.26	-0.49	-0.32	3.00	4.00
COG18	3.40	1.31	-0.29	-0.63	4.00	4.00
COG19	1.81	1.46	-0.57	0.54	2.00	2.00
COG20	2.66	1.41	-0.80	-0.04	3.00	2.00
COG21	2.43	1.43	-0.87	0.23	2.00	2.00
COG22	3.08	1.12	-0.37	-0.14	3.00	3.00
COG23	3.42	1.31	-0.78	-0.40	4.00	5.00
COG24	2.16	1.35	-0.72	0.20	2.00	2.00
COG25	3.20	1.46	-0.95	-0.36	3.00	5.00
COG26	2.55	1.63	-1.20	0.06	2.00	2.00
COG27	2.96	1.41	-0.88	-0.23	3.00	4.00
COG28	3.20	1.38	-0.74	-0.37	3.00	4.00
COG29	3.30	1.34	-0.64	-0.45	3.00	4.00
COG30	2.93	1.32	-0.76	-0.12	3.00	3.00
COG31	2.76	1.25	-0.52	-0.13	3.00	3.00
COG32	3.50	1.22	-0.22	-0.60	4.00	4.00
COG33	2.55	1.40	-0.77	0.05	2.00	2.00
COG34	3.48	1.28	-0.25	-0.66	4.00	4.00
COG35	3.69	1.28	-0.32	-0.74	4.00	5.00
COG36	2.60	1.30	-0.57	-0.10	3.00	3.00
COG37	3.67	1.14	0.12	-0.74	4.00	4.00
COG38	2.49	1.54	-1.05	0.05	2.00	2.00
COG39	2.67	1.34	-0.70	-0.10	3.00	2.00
COG40	2.56	1.28	-0.63	-0.07	3.00	2.00

4. Item-level analysis

Table 4.2 shows the original scales of the Cognitive Strategy Questionnaire along with the individual items designed to measure these scales. It also presents the reliability estimates for internal consistency for the 12 strategy-type variables, the three process-type variables and the overall questionnaire. The strategy-type reliabilities ranged from a low 0.35 for the "analyzing contrastively" scale to a relatively high 0.76 for the "repeating/rehearsing" scale. Generally speaking, the reliability estimates were mixed: some scales were relatively high (AI, INF, REP, PN), others were somewhat low (AI, CLAR and ASSOC), and the rest were moderate (SUMM, TRL).

Table 4.2

Reliability Estimates for the Cognitive Strategies

	No.	Items used	Reliability estimates
1. Comprehending Processes (COMP)			
• Analyzing Contrastively (AC)	3	5, 16, 17	0.35
• Analyzing Inductively (AI)	3	36, 39, 40	0.73
• Clarifying/Verifying (CLAR)	4	3, 4, 20, 38	0.47
• Inferencing (INF)	2	34, 37	0.59
• Translating (TRL)	2	9, 14	0.71
Subtotal	14		0.60
2. Storing or Memory Processes (MEM)			
• Associating (ASSOC)	4	10, 11, 12, 13	0.49
• Linking w/Prior Knowledge (LPK)	3	1, 2, 6	0.52
• Repeating/Rehearsing (REP)	4	27, 28, 29, 30	0.76
• Summarizing (SUMM)	2	7, 33	0.56
Subtotal	13		0.74
3. Using or Retrieval Processes (RET)			
• Applying Rules (APR)	5	8, 18, 22, 31, 32	0.58
• Practicing Naturalistically (PN)	5	21, 23, 25, 27, 35	0.70
• Transferring (TRF)	3	15, 19, 24	0.63
Subtotal	13		0.66
Total	**40**		**0.84**

Item-level EFAs for the Cognitive Strategies Questionnaire

To investigate how the cognitive strategies items clustered with their respective scales, a matrix of product–moment correlations was generated using all 40 items, and a series of EFAs was performed according to the procedures detailed in the last chapter.

4. Item-level analysis

The results showed that an 11-factor varimax solution seemed to maximize parsimony and interpretability, in spite of the fact that 12 factors, each representing one of the strategy types, was expected. The strategy type variable not accounted for in the clusterings was the "analyzing contrastively" scale, as this scale produced two items that loaded with the "transferring from L1 to L2" scale (COG5 and COG16) and one that loaded with the "associating" scale (COG17). These mixed loadings came as no surprise given both the low alpha for "analyzing contrastively" seen in the reliability analysis results and the substantive relatedness between the L1–L2 transferring strategy and the L1–L2 contrasting strategy. Thus, the "analyzing contrastively" scale was dropped, and COG5 and COG17 were deleted from the other scales due to low loadings, while COG16 was recoded as a "transferring" item.

Four other items did not load with their respective scales: COG4, COG22, COG3 and COG31. COG3 and COG31 were eventually deleted due to low or uninterpretable loadings; COG4 was recoded as "repeating/rehearsing"; and COG22 as "linking with prior knowledge," after the substantive plausibility of these recodings had been examined. These changes left 36 items in the Cognitive Strategies Questionnaire from which to make the 11 composite variables.

I then reanalzyed the 36-item questionnaire. The initial factor extraction yielded 11 eigenvalues greater than 1.0, accounting for 57% of the variance. Table 4.3 presents the 11-factor varimax solution. Factors 1, 5, 8 and 10 represent the comprehending processes, factors 2, 4, 6 and 11 the memory processes, and factors 3, 7 and 9 represent the retrieval processes. An inspection of the inter-factor correlation matrix indicated that the majority of the factors were not highly correlated.

Table 4.3
Results of EFA for Cognitive Strategies Questionnaire: Varimax Rotation

	MEM REP F1	RET PN F2	COMP AI F3	RET TRF F4	COMP TRL F5	MEM ASSOC F6	MEM LPK F7	RET APR F8	COMP INF F9	MEM SUMM F10	COMP CLAR F11
COG29 REP	**.73756**	.09669	.08150	.05304	.02042	.09458	.07226	.03812	.12227	.10216	.04529
COG28 REP	**.71923**	.22143	.08696	.04591	-.04570	.07327	.06777	.11640	.07978	.00522	.00841
COG27 REP	**.56196**	.10933	.03446	.04072	.09262	.03341	.08953	.02759	.10368	.15027	.05015
COG30 REP	**.49293**	.21774	.12119	-.01398	-.00900	.11547	.11471	.09474	.01836	.08284	.12343
COG4 REP	**.37554**	.10027	.04746	.00176	-.00210	-.00588	.17023	-.14807	.15330	.10422	.03384
COG25 PN	.14721	**.59321**	.07081	-.04203	.05185	.08819	.00359	.08368	-.01459	.02313	.01130
COG26 PN	.22751	**.57145**	.08315	-.01947	-.03097	-.01847	.10803	-.03370	.03317	.17014	-.00881
COG21 PN	.13906	**.51412**	.05203	-.06992	-.14763	.11145	-.04282	.01153	.04829	.00108	.08203
COG35 PN	.08315	**.51172**	.15248	-.07270	-.12033	.05504	-.13290	.23343	.17816	.04072	.13143
COG23 PN	.19105	**.40665**	.03059	-.06378	-.15485	.32085	.04886	.11454	.19327	.04604	.01711
COG40 AI	.15357	.11435	**.95566**	.00696	-.05613	.12224	.08988	.07469	.07070	.09330	.05957
COG39 AI	.16233	.16038	**.55680**	-.00537	-.05033	.08173	.07136	.07507	.15445	.11615	.30170
COG36 AI	.08589	.24152	**.37434**	.02751	-.10514	.17630	.08111	.15430	.01463	.23807	.08310
COG16 TRF	.02828	.04125	.00126	**.70862**	.12758	.04610	.06854	-.01245	.01735	.01475	.02957
COG15 TRF	.01934	.11454	-.02696	**.68891**	.10858	-.02835	.14394	-.05140	-.02357	.04156	.00279
COG19 TRF	.09135	.06289	.06133	**.41462**	.17199	-.05817	.36110	-.07036	.02339	.12117	.10719
COG24 TRF	.05566	.06282	.07174	**.36830**	.28834	.05314	.30561	-.00188	.03541	.08632	.04569
COG14 TRL	.02815	.08824	-.06934	.15803	**.77853**	.01329	.02762	-.04622	.14013	.05469	.02938
COG9 TRL	.02331	.11162	-.05316	.19692	**.63588**	-.02485	.11374	-.08734	.01909	.01792	-.01356
COG1 LPK	.07198	.07756	.08844	.02079	-.04404	**.57825**	.06905	.07975	.02175	.04593	.06679
COG2 LPK	.00560	.05288	.02795	-.02327	.03663	**.47082**	.07687	.10821	.03422	.07728	.03054
COG6 LPK	.08475	.05532	.06463	.03683	.03270	**.41175**	.08813	.09357	.09147	.02622	-.02161
COG22 LPK	.16500	.26709	.06912	-.04821	-.15362	**.34279**	.09623	.07333	.25006	.07322	-.02171

4. Item-level analysis

Table 4.3 (cont.)
Results of EFA for Cognitive Strategies Questionnaire: Varimax Rotation

		MEM REP F1	RET PN F2	COMP AI F3	RET TRF F4	COMP TRL F5	MEM ASSOC F6	MEM LPK F7	RET APR F8	COMP INF F9	MEM SUMM F10	COMP CLAR F11
COG10	ASSOC	.10167	.02983	-.00876	.09932	-.00430	.06874	**.51508**	.04003	.05185	.11089	.02996
COG13	ASSOC	.08871	.03516	.06768	.12809	.05518	.11202	**.49701**	.05383	.00288	.04766	.04581
COG12	ASSOC	.04471	.02214	.06045	.10094	.04771	.16522	**.28829**	.00996	-.02271	.07108	.03455
COG11	ASSOC	.16683	.01506	.05296	.02817	.02070	.10890	**.28601**	-.05063	.17809	.03922	-.00425
COG34	INF	.05681	.05804	.07947	-.06378	-.06778	.09722	.03778	**.62883**	.04087	.00265	.00663
COG37	INF	.03364	.11242	.04603	-.01368	-.04626	.19410	-.00162	**.61377**	.08944	.01210	.04204
COG18	APR	.21118	.07428	.04671	-.09554	.07838	.14741	-.00227	.03973	**.52818**	.09667	.00474
COG8	APR	.05632	.03417	.02182	.06638	.07489	-.02267	.04856	.01231	**.50582**	.01166	.07795
COG32	APR	.12786	.09004	.13139	.03692	.02506	.14900	.08518	.20427	**.43238**	.15704	.02013
COG33	SUMM	.13617	.05262	.13075	.04725	.02182	.06205	.16212	.07240	.11799	**.64649**	.08433
COG7	SUMM	.16526	.07663	.06737	.07134	-.03906	.09876	.09260	-.09234	.07376	**.49535**	.01783
COG38	CLAR	.07608	.07384	.16433	.05147	-.00870	.06954	.05934	.05556	.05681	.05620	**.73173**
COG20	CLAR	.16315	.07150	.06399	.06294	.09753	-.02413	.30642	-.03059	.05516	.07774	**.33253**

INTER-FACTOR CORRELATION MATRIX

		MEM F1	RET F2	COMP F3	RET F4	COMP F5	MEM F6	MEM F7	RET F8	COMP F9	MEM F10	COMP F11
MEM	F1	1.00000										
RET	F2	.29846	1.00000									
COMP	F3	.04643	.04500	1.00000								
RET	F4	.22332	.04414	-.08146	1.00000							
COMP	F5	.10308	-.01358	-.39005	.14226	1.00000						
MEM	F6	.32955	.18316	.11579	.08028	-.05313	1.00000					
MEM	F7	.34176	.33572	.15513	.00334	-.03794	.18482	1.00000				
RET	F8	.30242	.39270	-.11967	.20311	.21222	.17172	.18611	1.00000			
COMP	F9	.26887	.21102	-.00269	.31317	.07378	.05781	.18526	.25698	1.00000		
MEM	F10	.19381	.34066	-.01160	.11208	-.06990	.12284	.20577	.18390	.21484	1.00000	
COMP	F11	.19413	.30787	.33826	-.03977	-.19603	.19936	.32936	.07526	.23127	.13458	1.00000

4. Item-level analysis

The factor solution in Table 4.3 was used to form the 11 cognitive strategy composite variables to be used in subsequent analyses. Table 4.4 provides a summary of the items used in the composites for each strategy type scale.

Table 4.4

Composites for the Cognitive Strategy Use Variables (36 items)

	No.	Items used
1. Comprehending Processes (COMP)		
•Analyzing Inductively (AI)	3 items	36, 39, 40
•Clarifying/Verifying (CLAR)	2 items	20, 38
•Inferencing (INF)	2 items	34, 37
•Translating (TRL)	2 items	9, 14
Subtotal		9 items
2. Storing/Memory Processes (MEM)		
•Associating (ASSOC)	4 items	10, 11, 12, 13
•Linking with Prior Knowledge (LPK)	4 items	1, 2, 6, 22
•Repeating/Rehearsing (REP)	5 items	4, 27, 28, 29, 30
•Summarizing (SUMM)	2 items	7, 33
Subtotal		15 items
3. Using/Retrieval Processes (RET)		
•Applying Rules (APR)	3 items	8, 18, 32
•Practicing Naturalistically (PN)	5 items	21, 23, 25, 26, 35
•Transferring (TRF)	4 items	15, 16, 19, 24
Subtotal	12 items	
Total	**36 items**	

The Metacognitive Strategies Questionnaire

Distributions and reliabilities

I then analyzed the item-level data from the Metacognitive Strategies Questionnaire based on all 1,382 test-takers. The descriptive statistics for the 40 items are presented in Table 4.5. The means ranged from 2.89 to a high 4.34 (compared with a range of 1.68 to 3.69 for the cognitive strategies), and the standard deviations ranged from 0.97 to 1.64 (compared with a range of 1.12 to 1.63 for the cognitive strategies). The medians ranged from 3 to 5 (compared with a range of 1 to 4 for the cognitive strategies). Then, except for MET59, with a kurtosis of 3.62, all values for skewness and kurtosis were within the acceptable limits, indicating that the items appeared to be reasonably normally distributed.

Comparing these results with those of the cognitive strategies, we see that

4. Item-level analysis

the test-takers reported using the metacognitive strategies much more frequently than the cognitive strategies. Also, the test-takers displayed a slightly larger degree of variability (based on the standard deviations) in their use of the metacognitive strategies than they did in their use of the cognitive strategies.

Table 4.5

Distributions for the Metacognitive Strategies

Variable	Mean	Std dev	Kurtosis	Skewness	Median	Mode
MET41	2.91	1.51	-0.93	-0.27	3.00	4.00
MET42	2.99	1.64	-1.05	-0.38	3.00	5.00
MET43	3.55	1.35	-0.14	-0.78	4.00	5.00
MET44	3.30	1.11	-0.31	-0.37	3.00	4.00
MET45	3.66	1.29	-0.01	-0.83	4.00	5.00
MET46	3.32	1.29	-0.41	-0.51	4.00	4.00
MET47	3.63	1.33	-0.27	-0.75	4.00	5.00
MET48	3.66	1.14	-0.05	-0.67	4.00	4.00
MET49	3.57	1.25	-0.42	-0.58	4.00	5.00
MET50	3.16	1.15	-0.40	-0.26	3.00	3.00
MET51	3.29	1.16	-0.32	-0.41	3.00	4.00
MET52	3.57	1.15	-0.22	-0.59	4.00	4.00
MET53	3.08	1.33	-0.50	-0.30	3.00	3.00
MET54	3.33	1.20	-0.29	-0.38	3.00	3.00
MET55	3.12	1.39	-0.62	-0.45	3.00	4.00
MET56	3.85	1.24	0.83	1.12	4.00	5.00
MET57	3.31	1.23	-0.26	-0.50	3.00	4.00
MET58	2.94	1.49	-0.78	-0.37	3.00	4.00
MET59	4.34	0.97	0.62	1.80	5.00	5.00
MET60	3.46	1.19	-0.04	-0.69	4.00	4.00
MET61	3.78	1.15	0.47	-0.88	4.00	4.00
MET62	3.85	1.08	0.83	-0.92	4.00	4.00
MET63	3.28	1.40	-0.36	-0.64	4.00	4.00
MET64	4.25	1.00	2.40	1.52	5.00	5.00
MET65	3.13	1.29	-0.20	-0.57	3.00	4.00
MET66	3.48	1.35	-0.14	-0.75	4.00	4.00
MET67	3.07	1.35	-0.48	-0.40	3.00	3.00
MET68	3.36	1.23	-0.34	-0.50	4.00	4.00
MET69	3.76	1.13	0.32	-0.83	4.00	4.00
MET70	3.18	1.22	-0.36	-0.40	3.00	4.00
MET71	3.61	1.16	-0.12	-0.64	4.00	4.00
MET72	2.89	1.32	-0.53	-0.31	3.00	3.00
MET73	3.83	1.15	0.11	-0.84	4.00	5.00
MET74	3.63	1.14	0.00	-0.64	4.00	4.00
MET75	3.29	1.18	-0.09	-0.54	3.00	4.00
MET76	3.53	1.14	-0.30	-0.49	4.00	4.00
MET77	3.36	1.20	-0.12	-0.60	4.00	4.00
MET78	3.25	1.33	-0.48	-0.46	3.00	4.00
MET79	3.78	1.28	0.22	-0.95	4.00	5.00
MET80	3.38	1.34	-0.48	-0.56	4.00	4.00

Table 4.6 shows the original scales of the Metacognitive Strategy Questionnaire along with the individual items designed to measure these scales. It also presents the reliability estimates for internal consistency for the six strategy variables, the three process-type variables and the overall

questionnaire. The strategy-type reliabilities ranged from a low 0.40 for the "learning to learn" scale to a high 0.82 for the "evaluating" scale. Generally speaking, the estimates for reliability were moderate for the "learning to learn," "goal-setting" and "formulating a plan," while those for the other scales were relatively high.

Table 4.6

Reliability Estimates for the Metacognitive Strategies

	No.	Items used	Reliability estimates
1. Goal-Setting Processes (GS)			
• Setting Goals (GS)	5	43, 53, 54, 56, 80	0.60
Subtotal	5		0.60
2. Assessment Processes (ASSESS)			
• Assessing the Situation (ASSIT)	8	41, 42, 58, 63, 65, 66, 67, 72	0.72
• Monitoring (MON)	9	44, 47, 49, 52, 55, 57, 60, 68, 75	0.67
• Evaluating (EVAL)	10	46, 50, 51, 61, 62, 69, 71, 73, 74, 76	0.82
Subtotal	27		0.85
3. Planning Processes (PLAN)			
• Formulating a Plan (FPL)	5	48, 59, 64, 78, 79	0.57
• Learning to Learn (LLRN)	3	45, 70, 77	0.40
Subtotal	8		0.65
Total	**40**		**0.89**

Item-level EFAs for the Metacognitive Strategies Questionnaire

To investigate the clustering of the metacognitive strategies items, a matrix of product–moment correlations was generated using all 40 items and a series of EFAs was performed.

The initial EFA yielded a clustering that differed considerably from the originally-hypothesized scales; however, the final analysis showed that a 4-factor oblimin solution seemed to maximize parsimony and interpretability in spite of the fact that 6 factors, each representing one of the strategy types, was expected. To summarize, the "goal-setting" strategy scale (MET43, MET53, MET54, MET56, MET80) was deleted from the questionnaire, as these items consistently loaded with several scales in the various analyses. This does not necessarily mean that goal-setting is not a part of metacognitive strategy use; it simply means that this particular set of items did not cluster given these data. This finding suggests perhaps that goal-setting might be characterized as a complex cognitive task represented by several strategy types, rather than one unique strategy. For

4. Item-level analysis

example, when one sets goals, one is also making a series of assessments and plans. This factor complexity might also explain why the test-takers reported using "goal-setting" (and "assessing the situation") less frequently than the other strategies, as seen by the low item means of these two strategies.

Furthermore, the "learning-to-learn" strategies consistently loaded with the "evaluating" items. Upon further examination, these items, along with this group of evaluating items, seemed to represent a "self-testing" (ST) strategy type, where learners evaluate how much they have learned by quizzing themselves **after** the learning or use event. For example, Item 76 states: "After I learn something in English, I test myself to make sure I have really learned it." In theory, these "self-testing" strategy items seem different from both the "assessing the situation" items and the "monitoring" items in that "assessing the situation" might be characterized as describing metacognitive practices **before** the event, while "monitoring" might describe them **during** the event. This characterization of metacognitive strategy use supports Wenden's (1991) view of metacognitive strategies as a function of processing time.

Next, several of the items representing strategies for "formulating a plan" and "evaluating" consistently loaded together. Again, this finding might suggest that goal-setting and formulating a plan are not discrete behaviors, but rather are intrinsically associated with the other assessment strategies.

Upon further inspection, the clustering of the "formulating a plan" and "evaluating" strategy items seemed to represent a "self-evaluating" (SE) strategy type, where learners evaluate what they know or how they performed, so that they can plan for further learning or make changes in their language practices. An example of this is seen in Item 69, which states: "After I finish a conversation in English, I think about how I could say things better." Similar to the self-testing strategy types, the self-evaluating strategy types seem to elicit assessment practices after the language learning or language use event, again supporting Wenden's (1991) processing time depiction of metacognitive strategy use.

Based on these interpretations, a number of items changed scales and were recoded. Also, some items were deleted due to low, complex or uninterpretable loadings. These changes left 30 items in the Metacognitive Strategies Questionnaire from which to make the composites for further analyses.

I then reanalyzed the 30-item questionnaire. The initial factor extraction yielded seven eigenvalues greater than 1.0, accounting for 48.4% of the variance. Table 4.7 presents the 4-factor oblimin solution. Factor 1 represents the "self-testing" strategies, factor 2 the "assessing the situation" strategies, factor 3 the "self-evaluating" strategies and factor 4 represents the "monitoring" strategies. An inspection of the inter-factor correlation matrix indicated that the majority of these factors were moderately correlated.

Table 4.7

Results of EFA for the Metacognitive Processing Variables: Oblimin Rotation

		ST F1	ASSIT F2	SE F3	MON F4	RECODED TO
MET74 EVAL		**0.68454**	-0.07410	0.11394	-0.10536	ST
MET76 EVAL		**0.68020**	-0.07313	0.11324	-0.07721	ST
MET46 EVAL		**0.65952**	0.07633	-0.08865	-0.05161	ST
MET50 EVAL		**0.59211**	-0.05420	-0.01122	0.17462	ST
MET51 EVAL		**0.56860**	-0.08558	0.02037	0.25241	ST
MET70 LLRN		**0.38341**	0.08508	0.06132	-0.03686	ST
MET45 LLRN		**0.37778**	0.19751	-0.02654	0.03054	ST
MET61 EVAL		**0.28410**	0.16843	0.15635	0.09684	ST
MET63 ASSIT		-0.01068	**0.59363**	-0.05864	0.15862	
MET42 ASSIT		-0.14189	**0.52950**	-0.00307	0.04771	
MET67 ASSIT		0.05064	**0.50774**	0.09552	-0.09969	
MET58 ASSIT		0.03152	**0.50120**	-0.10472	0.12820	
MET41 ASSIT		0.05835	**0.44239**	0.06655	-0.09562	
MET66 ASSIT		0.06427	**0.43151**	0.10115	0.04185	
MET72 ASSIT		0.08075	**0.43031**	0.05682	-0.04526	
MET65 ASSIT		0.11950	**0.38285**	0.19538	-0.09750	
MET64 FPL		0.02839	-0.13331	**0.52355**	0.11216	SE
MET73 EVAL		0.03087	0.14258	**0.51796**	-0.07438	SE
MET71 EVAL		0.04189	0.06291	**0.49303**	0.02880	SE
MET69 EVAL		0.09679	0.02528	**0.48504**	-0.00734	SE
MET59 FPL		0.03488	-0.01930	**0.47082**	0.08474	SE
MET62 EVAL		0.01826	-0.05574	**0.46545**	0.13215	SE
MET78 FPL		-0.05670	0.12358	**0.38514**	-0.09387	SE
MET49 MON		-0.02363	-0.00491	**0.34909**	0.24507	SE
MET79 FPL		0.21097	0.08730	**0.29532**	-0.11898	SE
MET47 MON		0.09408	0.01716	**0.24428**	0.10798	SE
MET52 MON		0.04308	0.03777	0.10355	**0.46890**	
MET60 MON		-0.03917	0.12894	0.12411	**0.41182**	
MET57 MON		0.20430	0.11292	0.09093	**0.37253**	
MET68 MON		0.18190	0.02474	0.20133	**0.24251**	
Inter-Factor Correlation Matrix						
		ST F1	ASSIT F2	SE F3	MON F4	
ST	F1	1.00000				
ASSIT	F2	0.29162	1.00000			
SE	F3	0.51912	0.36976	1.00000		
MON	F4	0.20578	0.09425	0.30161	1.00000	

This solution was used to form the four metacognitive strategy composite variables to be used in subsequent analyses. Table 4.8 shows the items used to form the composites for each strategy type.

4. Item-level analysis

Table 4.8

Composites for the Metacognitive Strategy Use Variables (30 items)

	No.	Items used
1. On-Line Assessment Processes (OL-ASSESS)		
•Assessing the situation (ASSIT)	8 items	41, 42, 58, 63,
(before the event)		65, 66, 67, 72
•Monitoring (MON)		
(during the event)	4 items	52, 57, 60, 68
Subtotal	12 items	
2. Post-Assessment Processes (P-ASSESS)		
•Self-Evaluating (SE)	10 items	47, 49, 59, 62, 64,
(after the event)		69, 71, 73, 78, 79
•Self-Testing (ST)	8 items	45, 46, 50, 51,
(after the event)		61, 70, 74, 76
Subtotal	18 items	
Total	**30 items**	

The *FCE Anchor Test*

Distributions and reliabilities

I first analyzed the item-level data from the *FCE Anchor Test* based on all 1,382 test-takers. The descriptive statistics for the 70 items by test section are presented in Table 4.9.

The means for the Grammar and Vocabulary (GV) part ranged from 0.20 to 0.88, suggesting a wide range of item-difficulty levels. The standard deviations ranged from 0.32 to 0.50. Except for Item 2 with a kurtosis of 3.68, all values for skewness and kurtosis were within the limits, indicating that the items in this section appeared to be reasonably normal. Item 20 was dropped from further analyses since two answers were possible (see Appendix J).

The means for the Passage Comprehension (PC) section ranged from 0.28 to 0.86, again suggesting a wide range of item-difficulty levels, and the standard deviations ranged from 0.35 to 0.50. All values for skewness and kurtosis were again within the limits, indicating univariate normality. Item 25 was also dropped from further analyses due to two correct answers (see Appendix J).

The means for the Word Formation (WF) section ranged from 0.11 to 0.65, suggesting that this section of the test was more difficult than the previous two. The standard deviations ranged from 0.31 to 0.49. All values for skewness and kurtosis were within the limits, except for items 39 and 40 with a kurtosis of 4.36 and 3.43 respectively.

The means for the Cloze (CLZ) section ranged from a low 0.04 to 0.79. In

4. Item-level analysis

fact, five items had means of less than 0.10, and four had means of less than 0.20, indicating that students found this section to be extremely challenging. These results are corroborated by the performance of the NSs who took this test, since the cloze section posed the most problems for them (see Appendix J). The standard deviations ranged from 0.19 to 0.50. Six items had a kurtosis beyond +/-3 (Item 41, Item 42, Item 52, Item 55, Item 59 and Item 60) and four had a skewness greater than 3 (Item 41, Item 42, Item 52, and Item 60), suggesting that if these items were retained, the scores for this section might be non-normally distributed.

Finally, the means for the Sentence Formation (SF) section ranged from 0.10 to 0.64, similar to that of the Word Formation section and the standard deviations extended from 0.30 to 0.48. Two items had a kurtosis beyond +/-3 (Item 65, Item 67).

Table 4.9

Distributions of the *FCE Anchor Test*

Section 1: Grammar/Vocabulary (GV)

Variable	Mean	Std Dev	Kurtosis	Skewness
ITEM1	0.68	0.47	-1.41	-0.77
ITEM2	0.88	0.32	3.68	-2.38
ITEM3	0.39	0.49	-1.79	0.46
ITEM4	0.69	0.46	-1.33	-0.82
ITEM5	0.60	0.49	-1.85	-0.40
ITEM6	0.46	0.50	-1.97	0.18
ITEM7	0.30	0.46	-1.24	0.87
ITEM8	0.35	0.48	-1.59	0.64
ITEM9	0.38	0.49	-1.76	0.49
ITEM10	0.50	0.50	-2.00	-0.02
ITEM11	0.26	0.44	-0.83	1.08
ITEM12	0.22	0.41	-0.13	1.37
ITEM13	0.28	0.45	-1.05	0.98
ITEM14	0.42	0.49	-1.90	0.32
ITEM15	0.26	0.44	-0.75	1.12
ITEM16	0.52	0.50	-2.00	-0.09
ITEM17	0.32	0.46	-1.37	0.79
ITEM18	0.20	0.40	0.21	1.49
ITEM19	0.26	0.44	-0.76	1.11
ITEM20	0.27	0.45	-0.97	1.02

Section 2: Passage Comprehension (PC)

Variable	Mean	Std Dev	Kurtosis	Skewness
ITEM21	0.32	0.47	-1.42	0.76
ITEM22	0.86	0.35	2.12	-2.03
ITEM23	0.51	0.50	-2.00	-0.05
ITEM24	0.47	0.50	-1.99	0.13
ITEM25	0.28	0.45	-1.04	0.98
ITEM26	0.41	0.49	-1.86	0.38
ITEM27	0.51	0.50	-2.00	-0.02
ITEM28	0.49	0.50	-2.00	0.03
ITEM29	0.35	0.48	-1.59	0.65
ITEM30	0.47	0.50	-1.99	0.10

4. Item-level analysis

Section 3: Word Formation (WF)

Variable	Mean	Std Dev	Kurtosis	Skewness
ITEM31	0.37	0.48	-1.72	0.53
ITEM32	0.39	0.49	-1.79	0.46
ITEM33	0.24	0.43	-0.52	1.22
ITEM34	0.61	0.49	-1.78	-0.47
ITEM35	0.65	0.48	-1.59	-0.64
ITEM36	0.22	0.41	-0.14	1.36
ITEM37	0.17	0.37	1.24	1.80
ITEM38	0.34	0.47	-1.55	0.67
ITEM39	0.11	0.31	4.36	2.52
ITEM40	0.12	0.33	3.43	2.33

Section 4: Cloze (CLZ)

Variable	Mean	Std Dev	Kurtosis	Skewness
ITEM41	0.05	0.23	13.29	3.91
ITEM42	0.05	0.21	16.05	4.25
ITEM43	0.36	0.48	-1.67	0.57
ITEM44	0.52	0.50	-2.00	-0.08
ITEM45	0.24	0.43	-0.56	1.20
ITEM46	0.23	0.42	-0.26	1.32
ITEM47	0.21	0.41	0.04	1.43
ITEM48	0.62	0.49	-1.75	-0.50
ITEM49	0.45	0.50	-1.96	0.22
ITEM50	0.13	0.34	2.76	2.18
ITEM51	0.34	0.47	-1.53	0.69
ITEM52	0.07	0.25	9.66	3.41
ITEM53	0.17	0.38	1.07	1.75
ITEM54	0.43	0.49	-1.92	0.30
ITEM55	0.08	0.28	7.04	3.00
ITEM56	0.16	0.37	1.51	1.87
ITEM57	0.79	0.41	-0.07	-1.39
ITEM58	0.13	0.33	2.97	2.23
ITEM59	0.11	0.32	4.06	2.46
ITEM60	0.04	0.19	20.71	4.76

Section 5: Sentence Formation (SF)

Variable	Mean	Std Dev	Kurtosis	Skewness
ITEM61	0.33	0.47	-1.48	0.72
ITEM62	0.64	0.48	-1.69	-0.56
ITEM63	0.16	0.37	1.45	1.86
ITEM64	0.26	0.44	-0.85	1.07
ITEM65	0.12	0.33	3.24	2.29
ITEM66	0.28	0.45	-1.00	1.00
ITEM67	0.10	0.30	4.80	2.61
ITEM68	0.25	0.43	-0.61	1.18
ITEM69	0.24	0.43	-0.47	1.24
ITEM70	0.27	0.44	-0.92	1.04

Table 4.10 presents the reliability estimates for internal consistency (Cronbach's alpha) for all test sections but the Cloze. Reliability for the Cloze section was calculated by the Guttman split half procedure. All parts of the test produced reasonably high reliability estimates.

Table 4.10

Reliability Estimates for the *FCE Anchor Test* (68 items)*

	No.	Reliability estimates
Section A: The Reading Comprehension Section		
Part 1: Grammar and Vocabulary (GV)	19 items	0.81
Part 2: Passage Comprehension (PC)	9 items	0.63
Subtotal	28 items	0.85
Section B: The Use of English Section		
Part 1: Word Formation (WF)	10 items	0.83
Part 2: Cloze (CLZ)*	20 items	0.83
Part 3: Sentence Formation (SF)	10 items	0.76
Subtotal	40 items	0.92
Total	**68 items**	**0.94**

* Items 20 and 25 were removed from the analyses; reliability estimates for the CLZ is a Guttman split-half estimate.

Item-Level EFAs for the *FCE Anchor Test*

To investigate the factorial structure of the *FCE Anchor Test*, a matrix of tetrachoric correlations using all 68 items was generated in PRELIS2 and exported to SPSS. Then, a series of EFAs was performed on each section of the test. The following presents a summary of the findings.

I first performed EFAs on the 19 items in the Grammar and Vocabulary part of the test. These analyses produced a 2-factor oblimin solution that seemed to maximize parsimony and interpretability in spite of the fact that three factors, each representing one of the three categories identified in the test content specifications, were expected. This discrepancy is due to the fact that this version of the *Anchor Test* presented only one item dealing with phrasal verbs, and it loaded with the other grammar items, thereby producing a two-factor solution.

Also, in the course of these analyses, two items (Item 2 and Item 18) were dropped due to extremely low factor loadings. The GV section ended up with 17 items to measure the two underlying factors.

I then reanalyzed the test, and the initial factor extraction yielded two eigenvalues greater than 1.0, accounting for 32.7% of the variance. As seen in Table 4.11, this solution produced (1) an underlying vocabulary factor (VOC), which included items dealing with semantic sets and collocations and (2) a grammar factor (GRAM), which consisted of items relating to grammatical rules and constraints and the phrasal verb item (Item 9). An inspection of the inter-factor

4. Item-level analysis

correlation matrix indicated that the two factors were moderately correlated.

Based on these analyses, 17 items were used to form the individual GRAM and VOC composite variables for subsequent analyses.

Table 4.11
EFA Results of GV Section: Oblimin Rotation

		F1 VOC	F2 GRAM	Correct Answer Choices
ITEM12	SSC*	**0.60258**	-0.01743	charge (for cleaning)
ITEM7	SSC	**0.50363**	0.15189	brought up (by grandparents)
ITEM15	SSC	**0.48066**	0.16156	judgment
ITEM11	SSC	**0.46146**	0.17006	runs (that shop)
ITEM3	SSC	**0.45654**	0.18178	way (of life)
ITEM8	SSC	**0.42047**	-0.17268	notice (of what I said)
ITEM6	SSC	**0.37683**	0.05255	hold (handlebars)
ITEM13	SSC	**0.36801**	0.14367	do (some drawings)
ITEM14	SSC	**0.32420**	0.20527	determined
ITEM16	SSC	**0.32054**	0.12188	available
ITEM19	SSC	**0.30268**	0.13583	charged (with murder)
ITEM1	GRC**	-0.06508	**0.48199**	solution (to)
ITEM9	PV***	0.17476	**0.47684**	(get) rid (of)
ITEM5	GRC	0.11210	**0.39842**	expected (the taxi to)
ITEM17	GRC	0.06133	**0.37669**	(no) hesitation (in)
ITEM4	GRC	0.14348	**0.34835**	(is) supposed (to)
ITEM10	GRC	0.16236	**0.26996**	will have left

SSC* Semantic Sets & Collocations; GRC** Gram Rules & Constraints; PV*** Phrasal Verbs

		Inter-Factor Correlation Matrix	
		F2 VOC	F1 GRAM
VOC	F1	1.00000	
GRAM	F2	0.54744	1.00000

I then performed EFAs on the nine items in the Passage Comprehension part of the test. These analyses again produced a 2-factor oblimin solution which maximized parsimony and interpretability, as seen in Table 4.12.

The initial factor extraction yielded two eigenvalues greater than 1.0, accounting for 36.9% of the variance. The 2-factor solution produced a "reading for explicit information" (REI) factor, where students were asked questions about specific information in the text (details) or were asked questions that required them to understand synonymous words or sentences (synonymy). This factor seemed to invoke the lower-level process of reading, where decoding of lexical or syntactic information is performed (Grabe,

1997). Seven of the items loaded under this factor. The second factor represented "reading for inferential information" (RII), where students were required to infer meaning not explicitly stated in the text (inferencing), such as the author's attitude. Unlike reading for explicit information, this factor invokes a higher-level processing of information (Grabe, 1997). Only two of the items loaded under the reading for inferential information factor. An inspection of the inter-factor correlation matrix showed that these two factors were moderately correlated with a correlation coefficient of -.5027. Since, substantively, these two processes seem to be inextricably related in the reading process, I decided to combine these factors to form one composite variable based on the nine items to be used in the modeling. In sum, the passage comprehension composite variable measured the test-takers' ability to read for both explicit and inferential information.

Table 4.12

EFA Results of PC Section: Oblimin Rotation

		F1 (Rdg for Explicit Info)	F2 (Rdg for Inferential Info)
ITEM23	SYN*	**0.51707**	0.01095
ITEM27	DET**	**0.45169**	-0.11143
ITEM22	DET	**0.39419**	0.11714
ITEM21	SYN	**0.39373**	-0.05115
ITEM28	SYN	**0.36733**	-0.05381
ITEM26	DET	**0.28725**	-0.10628
ITEM24	DET	**0.24157**	-0.10479
ITEM29	INF***	0.01087	**-0.68397**
ITEM30	INF	0.09605	**-0.33509**

SYN* = Rdg for synonyms; DET** = Rdg for details; INF*** = Rdg for inferences

Inter-Factor Correlation Matrix			
		F1 REI	F2 RII
REI	F1	1.00000	
RII	F2	-0.50270	1.00000

Next, I performed EFAs on the ten items in the Word Formation part of the test. As seen in Table 4.13, the initial factor extraction yielded one eigenvalue greater than 1.0, accounting for 41.1% of the variance. This solution produced a "word formation" factor, where students were asked to transform words from one syntactic form to another based on its use in a sentence (e.g., generous -> generosity).

4. Item-level analysis

All ten items were used to form the WF composite variable for the modeling.

Table 4.13

EFA Results of the Word Formation Section

	F1 WF
ITEM38	0.74344
ITEM31	0.73952
ITEM36	0.72988
ITEM37	0.64143
ITEM32	0.56313
ITEM40	0.52255
ITEM39	0.49135
ITEM35	0.47719
ITEM33	0.45166
ITEM34	0.44984

After that, I performed EFAs on the 20 items in the Cloze. These analyses produced a 2-factor oblimin solution, with one factor representing the content words (including prepositions carrying meaning) (CW) and one representing the function words (FW).

In the course of these analyses, five items were flagged for removal. Initially, two items (Item 49 and Item 51) produced loadings greater than 0.30 on more than one factor and were subsequently dropped due to this factorial complexity. Interestingly, Item 49, a logical connector (once), had a loading of 0.32 on the function words and 0.31 on the content words, thereby capturing the syntactic and semantic quality of the logical connectors. Similarly, Item 51, a modal auxiliary (might/could) had a loading of 0.37 on the function words and a loading of 0.35 on the content words, again capturing the syntactic and semantic quality of this category of auxiliaries. Then, one item (Item 54: best/ideal/perfect), a content word, loaded with the function words and was dropped. Finally, two items (Item 47: essential/necessary; and Item 56: through/via) were removed due to extremely low loadings, thereby leaving 15 items in the Cloze section from which to form the cloze composite variable for the subsequent analyses.

Table 4.14 presents the results from the final analysis of the 15-item Cloze section. The initial factor extraction yielded two eigenvalues greater than 1.0, accounting for 38.8% of the variance. Factor 1 represents the content words and factor 2 the function words.

An inspection of the inter-factor correlation matrix showed that these two factors were highly correlated with one another ($r = 0.6216$).

Similar to the PC composite variable, I decided to combine the content

4. Item-level analysis

and function word factors to form one composite CLZ variable because again, the content words and function words are inextricably related to each other within a passage. Therefore, all 15 items were used to form the CLZ composite variables. Substantively, however, the CLZ composite variable measured the test-takers' ability to supply both content and function words in a passage.

Table 4.14

EFA Results of Cloze Section: Oblimin Rotation

	CONTENT WORDS F1	FUNCTION WORDS F2	
ITEM 59	**0.72694**	-0.04575	nothing
ITEM 53	**0.71283**	0.07365	without
ITEM 55	**0.69353**	-0.06650	puts
ITEM 58	**0.61094**	0.02731	during
ITEM 60	**0.51066**	-0.01436	extent
ITEM 42	**0.50155**	-0.03410	members
ITEM 45	**0.46738**	0.19723	sight
ITEM 46	**0.39843**	0.18096	despite
ITEM 50	**0.39175**	0.23936	so (as not to)
ITEM 52	**0.33517**	-0.03925	(clue) to
ITEM 41	**0.31475**	0.04854	usual
ITEM 44	0.02494	**0.56871**	those (who)
ITEM 43	0.02404	**0.50667**	being (seen)
ITEM 57	-0.03639	**0.42651**	who
ITEM 48	0.04603	**0.27769**	a

Factor Correlation Matrix

		CW F1	FW F2
CW	F1	1.00000	
FW	F2	.62160	1.00000

Finally, I performed EFAs on the ten items in the Sentence Formation part of the test. As seen in Table 4.15, the initial analyses produced a factor extraction with two eigenvalues greater than 1.0, accounting for 44.3% of the variance. However, a 1-factor solution was substantively more interpretable.

All ten items were used to form the sentence formation composite variable in the modeling.

4. Item-level analysis

Table 4.15

EFA Results of Sentence Formation Section

	Factor Matrix
	SF
	F1
ITEM66	0.74471
ITEM64	0.66117
ITEM65	0.62325
ITEM61	0.60522
ITEM63	0.56079
ITEM67	0.43903
ITEM69	0.43436
ITEM70	0.34314
ITEM68	0.28539
ITEM62	0.25806

Table 4.16 presents a summary of the items used to form the composite variables for each test task.

Table 4.16

Composites for the *FCE Anchor Test* (61 items)

	No.	Items used
1. Grammar and Vocabulary Section (GV)		
• Grammar composite (GR)	6 items	1, 4, 5, 9, 10, 17
• Vocabulary composite (VOC)	11 items	3, 6, 7, 8, 11, 12,13, 14, 15, 16, 19
2. Passage Comprehension Section (PC)		
• Rdg for Explicit Information (REI)	7 items	21, 22, 23, 24, 26, 27, 28
• Rdg for Implicit Information (RII)	2 items	29, 30
• PC composite	9 items	
2. Word Formation Section (WF)		
• Word Formation (WF) composite	10 items	31 to 40
4. Cloze Section (CLZ)		
• Content Words (CW)	11 items	41, 42, 45, 46, 50, 52, 53, 55, 58, 59, 60
• Function Words (FW)	4 items	43, 44, 48, 57
• CLZ composite	15 items	
5. Sentence Formation Section (SF)		
• Sentence Formation (SF) composite	10 items	61 to 70

Summary

This chapter served to describe the process used in determining the factorial structure of both the questionnaires and the language test, using reliability analysis and exploratory factor analyses. More specifically, these item-level analyses on the two questionnaires and the language test allowed me to examine the factorial structure of cognitive and metacognitive strategy use, as measured by the respective questionnaires, and second language test performance as measured by the *FCE Anchor Test*. From these exploratory analyses, 11 cognitive strategy use variables were identified and composites were constructed. These 11 variables were hypothesized to measure the three stages of the information process (comprehending, memory and retrieval). Similarly, four metacognitive strategy use variables were identified, and composites formed, and these strategy types were hypothesized to measure two underlying processes, the on-line assessment processes and the post-assessment processes. Finally, six Second Language Test Performance variables were identified and corresponding composites created. Given the *FCE Anchor Test* design, these subtests were hypothesized to measure two factors: reading comprehension and use of English.

Based on these analyses, three measurement models were posited regarding the nature of cognitive strategy use, metacognitive strategy use and second language test performance. In the next chapter, I will test these hypotheses statistically in a more confirmatory mode using SEM procedures. Subsequent to that, I will use the substantive literature in SLA and SL assessment to propose models of the inter-relationships between the 11 cognitive and four metacognitive strategy types on the one hand and between these strategy–use variables and SLTP on the other. In the following chapter, I will examine these models to see if they hold across different ability-level groups.

5 Modeling strategy use and test performance: Findings and discussion[1]

Introduction

As seen in Chapter 4, I factor-analyzed the measurement instruments in the study prior to modeling the relationships between strategy use and second language test performance. More specifically, I examined the factorial structure of each measure and found that the Cognitive Strategy Questionnaire produced 11 strategy-type factors, the Metacognitive Strategy Questionnaire yielded four, and the *FCE Anchor Test* produced six underlying factors. These item-level analyses served as a basis for generating composite variables and provided invaluable information on the substantive characteristics of each composite variable.

Based on these analyses and the substantive literature in SLA and second language assessment, I was able to posit and test a number of competing models regarding the nature of cognitive strategy use (CSU), metacognitive strategy use (MSU) and second language test performance (SLTP). This was done by means of a series of separate CFAs. Then, once the linkages between the observed and the latent variables in each measurement model were examined, I began to explore the relationships among the underlying constructs by means of latent structure analysis. This was done by positing models and testing them for statistical and substantive plausibility. Chapter 5 describes the results of these analyses.

The cognitive processes

Distributions and reliabilities

Based on the results of the EFAs in Chapter 4, I created 11 composite cognitive strategy use variables (see Table 4.4). Table 5.1 presents the summary descriptive statistics for each of them. The means ranged from a low 1.92 for the reported use of the "transferring" strategies to a moderately high 3.57 for the "inferencing" strategies. The standard deviations ranged from 0.81 to 1.36. All values for variable skewness and kurtosis were within the limits, indicating that these strategy-type variables appeared to be normally distributed.

5. Findings and discussion

Table 5.1
Distributions for the Cognitive Strategy Use Variables

Variable	Mean	Std Dev	Kurtosis	Skewness	Minimum	Maximum
AI	2.61	1.05	-0.37	-0.11	0.00	5.00
CLAR	2.57	1.19	-0.62	-0.03	0.00	5.00
INF	3.57	1.02	-0.34	-0.51	0.00	5.00
TRL	3.14	1.36	-0.65	-0.43	0.00	5.00
ASSOC	2.39	0.91	-0.29	0.00	0.00	5.00
LPK	3.24	0.81	-0.08	-0.28	0.25	5.00
REP	3.15	0.98	-0.40	-0.34	0.20	5.00
SUMM	2.37	1.19	-0.60	0.11	0.00	5.00
APR	3.52	0.91	0.10	-0.57	0.00	5.00
PN	3.06	0.96	-0.61	-0.11	0.20	5.00
TRF	1.92	1.07	-0.60	0.29	0.00	5.00

CSU:	Cognitive Strategy Use		LPK:	Linking with Prior Knowledge
AI:	Analyzing Inductively		PN:	Practicing Naturalistically
APR:	Applying Rules		REP:	Repeating/Rehearsing
ASSOC:	Associating		SUMM:	Summarizing
CLAR:	Clarifying/Verifying		TRF:	Transferring from L1 to L2
INF:	Inferencing		TRL:	Translating

Table 5.2 presents the internal consistency reliability estimates for the cognitive strategy use variables. The reliabilities for the 11 strategy-type variables ranged from 0.45 for the clarifying/verifying strategy scale to 0.75 for the repeating/rehearsing scale. The reliability estimates for these newly-formed composite variables were mixed: some were relatively high (AI, TRL, REP, PN, TRF) and others moderate (CLAR, INF, ASSOC, LPK, SUMM, APR).

Table 5.2
Reliability Estimates for the Cognitive Strategy Use Variables

	No.	Items used	Reliability estimates
1. Comprehending Processes (COMP)			
• Analyzing Inductively (AI)	3	36, 39, 40	0.73
• Clarifying/Verifying (CLAR)	4	20, 38	0.45
• Inferencing (INF)	2	34, 37	0.59
• Translating (TRL)	2	9, 14	0.71
2. Storing/Memory Processes (MEM)			
• Associating (ASSOC)	4	10, 11, 12, 13	0.49
• Linking with Prior Knowledge (LPK)	3	1, 2, 6, 22	0.55
• Repeating/Rehearsing (REP)	4	4, 27, 28, 29, 30	0.75
• Summarizing (SUMM)	2	7, 33	0.55
3. Using/Retrieval Processes (RET)			
• Applying Rules (APR)	5	8, 18, 32	0.53
• Practicing Naturalistically (PN)	5	21, 23, 25, 27, 35	0.70
• Transferring from L1 to L2 (TRF)	3	15, 16, 19, 24	0.70

5. Findings and discussion

Testing the Factorial Validity of Cognitive Strategy Use

The hypothesized model: Model 1.1

Based on the results of the reliability analysis, the Cognitive Strategies Questionnaire was represented schematically as a three-factor model of cognitive strategy use. This initially-hypothesized model is presented in Figure 5.1. It contains three intercorrelated factors (COMP, MEM and RET) with 11 observed variables (AI, CLAR, INF, TRL, ASSOC, LPK, REP, SUMM, APR, PN, TRF) and each observed variable is hypothesized to load on only one factor. The error associated with each observed variable (E2 through E12) is postulated to be uncorrelated. These errors or uniquenesses include both measurement errors and specificity.

Figure 5.1

Initially-Hypothesized 3-Factor Model of Cognitive Strategy Use: Model 1.1

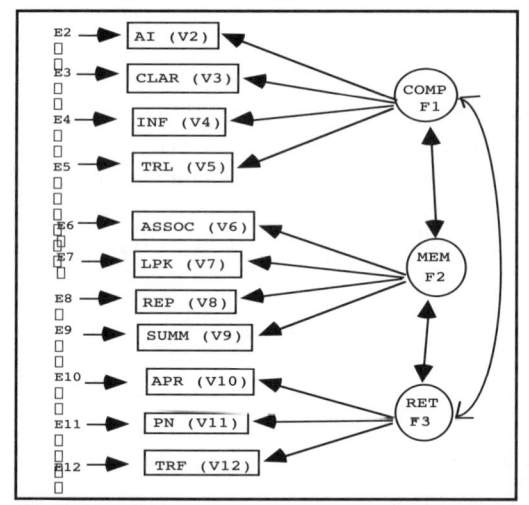

CSU:	Cognitive Strategy Use		
AI:	Analyzing Inductively	REP:	Repeating/Rehearsing
APR:	Applying Rules	SUMM:	Summarizing
ASSOC:	Associating	TRF:	Transferring from L1 to L2
CLAR:	Clarifying/Verifying	TRL:	Translating
INF:	Inferencing	COMP:	Comprehending Processes
LPK:	Linking with Prior Knowledge	MEM:	Storing/Memory Processes
PN:	Practicing Naturalistically	RET:	Retrieval/Using Processes

Model 1.1 is a first-order confirmatory factor analysis designed to test the multidimensionality of cognitive strategy use. More specifically, it tests the hypothesis that cognitive strategy use is a multidimensional construct

5. Findings and discussion

composed of comprehending (COMP), memory (MEM) and retrieval (RET) processes. However, given the exploratory nature of this study, I did not limit the current investigation to a simple confirmation or rejection of this particular model. Rather, I explored the relationships among the variables with the goal of generating the best fitting and most substantively meaningful model. To date, a number of descriptive studies have supported the multidimensionality of cognitive strategy use in which a large number of specific strategies were grouped under broad categories (e.g., O'Malley & Chamot, 1990; Oxford, 1990; Wenden, 1991), but no study has modeled and tested this statistically.

Model 1.1 addresses the following research question:

> *Q1: What is the trait structure of cognitive strategy use as measured by the Cognitive Strategies Questionnaire? In other words, what is the relationship between the cognitive strategy use item types (e.g., the "clarifying/verifying" strategy type) and the cognitive processes (e.g., comprehending, memory and retrieval). Also, what is the relationship among these processes?*

The results for Model 1.1

To explore the trait structure of cognitive strategy use, I first examined the statistical assumptions underlying the estimation procedure used in these analyses and then assessed model-data fit.

With respect to the statistical assumptions, I examined the univariate and multivariate sample statistics for sample normality. This was done given the strong underlying assumption of multivariate normality associated with the maximum likelihood estimation procedures utilized in SEM[2]. As seen previously in Table 5.1, the skewness and kurtosis values for the individual cognitive strategy use variables were within the limits, indicating that these variables were univariately normally distributed. However, with regard to multivariate kurtosis, these data produced a Mardia's coefficient of 5.5703, with an associated z statistic (i.e., the normalized estimate) that was relatively high (6.1223), as seen in Table 5.3. This finding suggests that these variables might, in fact, be multivariately nonnormal (peaked)[3].

To explore this possibility further, I reanalyzed these data using robust statistics[4] and found that (1) the S-Bχ^2 statistic was approximately the same value as the ordinary χ^2 statistic under the normality assumption, and (2) the ordinary maximum likelihood and robust standard errors yielded very similar values. These results indicated that the degree of nonnormality shown in the data does not affect key statistical conclusions regarding model adequacy and significance of parameter estimates. Following this, I inspected the data for individual cases which might have been contributing excessively to normalized multivariate kurtosis[5]. Six cases (244, 251, 933, 1040, 1175 and 1337) were flagged as

5. Findings and discussion

possible outliers, and these cases were earmarked for deletion in subsequent analyses (see the results for Model 1.2). Deletion of these cases produced a lower Mardia's coefficient.

Next, I examined all other statistical assumptions of the estimation procedure (e.g., identification and number of iterations for conversion) and found no significant violations in the data.

Finally, I assessed the hypothesized model to determine to what extent the model fit the sample data. First, with respect to model adequacy as a whole, the data produced an average off-diagonal value for the standardized residuals of 0.0674, indicating a degree of global misfit. Also, the goodness-of-fit index for the initially-hypothesized three-factor model of cognitive strategy use produced a chi-square value of 705.740 with 41 degrees of freedom (df) ($p < 0.001$). This chi-square/df ratio was well beyond the recommended value of 2, again suggesting a poorly fitting model. However, since the chi-square likelihood ratio test is notoriously sensitive to sample size, the comparative fit index (CFI), as the index of choice (Bentler, 1990), was examined. Model 1.1 produced a CFI of 0.717, thereby providing confirmation of a poorly fitting model. These results are presented in Table 5.3.

Table 5.3

Results for the Initially-Hypothesized 3-Factor Model of Cognitive Strategy Use: Model 1.1

Multivariate kurtosis	
Mardia's coefficient (G2,P)	5.5703
Normalized estimate	6.1223
Standardized residuals	
Average absolute standardize Residuals	0.0562
Average off-diagonal absolute Standard residuals	0.0674
Goodness of fit summary	
Independance model chi-square (on 55 degrees of freedom)	2402.251
Bentler-bonett normed fit index	0.706
Bentler-bonett nonnormed fit index	0.620
Comparitive fit index	0.717

Chi-square = 705.740 based on 41 degrees of freedom
Probability value for the chi-square statistic is less then 0.001
The normal theory RLS chi-square for this ML solution is 819.025.

5. Findings and discussion

Once I assessed the model as a whole, I evaluated the individual parameters. The loadings of the 11 variables on their respective factors were highly significant, as were the variances of the independent variables (both the factors and the errors) and the covariances among the factors. However, as the overall model was misfitting, I did not interpret these parameters.

The hypothesized model: Model 1.2

Based on the results of Model 1.1, I performed a series of post hoc fitting procedures, which included the use of the LM and Wald tests along with substantive rationale in the respecification of models. In this process, I made a number of changes to the cognitive strategy use model generated from the EFAs. One change involved the recoding of variables. To explain, several strategy types showed strong loadings on factors other than the ones they had originally been hypothesized to measure. For example, "inferencing" was originally thought to measure the COMP processes, but subsequent analyses showed that it loaded more strongly on the RET processes. Another change involved the number of variables in the model. I found that one variable, the translating strategies (V5), consistently produced statistically unreasonable and substantively uninterpretable standardized parameter estimates. Byrne (1994) warns that estimates falling outside the "admissible" range indicate that either the model is wrong or the input matrix lacks sufficient information. Therefore, as all attempts at substantively-sound respecification of the models produced the same results with relation to "translating" and since "translating" represented only two items in the questionnaire, I dropped it from the analyses, leaving ten strategy-type variables to represent cognitive strategy use instead of 11. In sum, the model which represented the data well from both a substantive and statistical point of view was Model 1.2, presented in Figure 5.2. Appendix K provides the correlation matrix generated from the raw data by EQS for the observed and latent variables.

Model 1.2 is summarized as follows. Cognitive strategy use involves three intercorrelated factors (COMP, MEM and RET) with ten observed variables. AI and CLAR are hypothesized to represent the COMP processes factor; ASSOC, REP, SUMM, TRF and APR to measure the MEM processes factor; and AI, TRF, INF, LPK, APR and PN to represent the RET processes factor. Three variables (AI, TRF and APR) are hypothesized to cross-load. Finally, the error terms associated with CLAR-TRF, ASSOC-TRF, and REP-PN are hypothesized to be correlated.

5. Findings and discussion

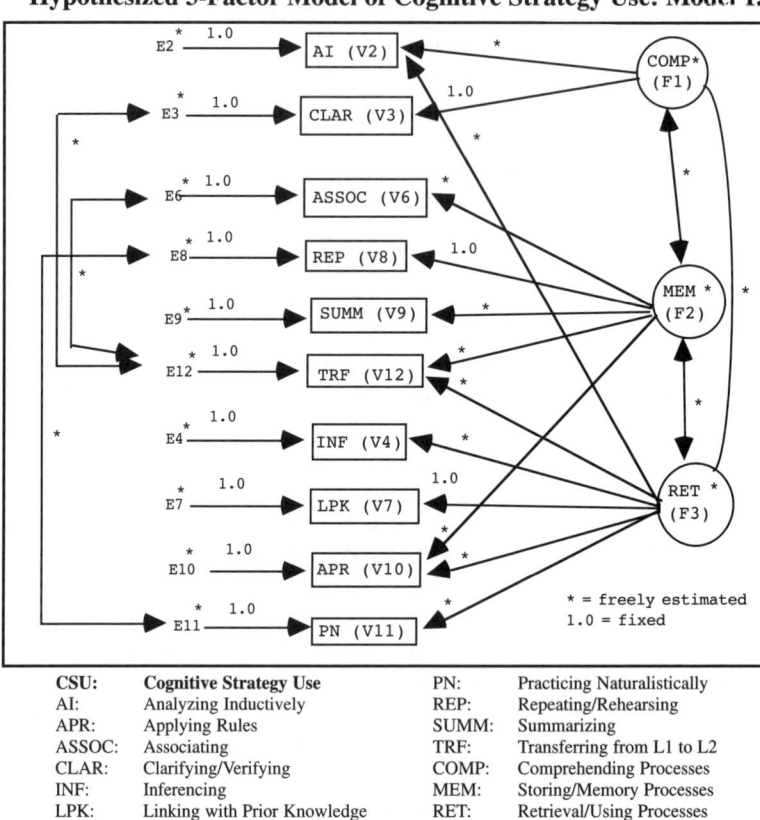

Figure 5.2
Hypothesized 3-Factor Model of Cognitive Strategy Use: Model 1.2

CSU:	Cognitive Strategy Use	PN:	Practicing Naturalistically
AI:	Analyzing Inductively	REP:	Repeating/Rehearsing
APR:	Applying Rules	SUMM:	Summarizing
ASSOC:	Associating	TRF:	Transferring from L1 to L2
CLAR:	Clarifying/Verifying	COMP:	Comprehending Processes
INF:	Inferencing	MEM:	Storing/Memory Processes
LPK:	Linking with Prior Knowledge	RET:	Retrieval/Using Processes

The results for Model 1.2

Based on the sample statistics, all ten variables again showed satisfactory skewness and kurtosis values, and six cases (244, 551, 933, 1040, 1175 and 1337) were dropped this time for contributing excessively to multivariate kurtosis. The data produced a Mardia's coefficient of 3.6755 with an associated z statistic of 4.4004, again suggesting multivariate normality, as seen in Table 5.4.

With respect to goodness of fit, Model 1.2 produced an average off-diagonal value for the standardized residuals of 0.0262, indicating an insignificant degree of misfit. It also produced a χ^2 statistic of 102.301 with 26df, representing an enormous drop in overall chi-square ($\Delta\chi^2(15) = 603.439$) from the initially-hypothesized model[6]. This decrease in χ^2 exhibited a highly significant improvement in goodness of fit. Consistent with this statistical

5. Findings and discussion

assessment, the CFI (0.963) also reflected a substantial improvement in model–data fit ($\Delta = 0.246$).

Table 5.4
Results for the 3-Factor Model of Cognitive Strategy Use: Model 1.2

Multivariate kurtosis	
Mardia's coefficient (G2,P)	3.6755
Normalized estimate	4.4004
Standardized residual matrix:	
Average absolute coveriance residuals	0.0217
Average off-diagonal absolute covariance Residuals	0.0262
Goodness of fit summary	
Independance model chi-square (on 45 degrees of freedom)	2113.372
Bentler-bonett normed fit index	0.952
Bentler-bonett nonnormed fit index	0.936
Comparitive fit index	0.963

Chi-square = 102.301 based on 261 degrees of freedom
Probability value for the chi-square statistic is less then 0.001
The normal theory RLS chi-square for this ML solution is 101.619

These statistics provided strong evidence for acceptance of Model 1.2. Moreover, in examining the measurement equations of the individual parameter estimates, I found all the unstandardized estimates to be reasonable and statistically significant at the 0.05 level.[7] even though some of the loadings appeared to be low and the uniquenesses high, a common characteristic of instruments trying to measure learners' behaviors, attitudes, feelings or motivations (Jöreskog & Sörbom, 1993). The variances and covariances of all the independent variables were also statistically significant at the 0.05 level.

Turning to the standardized solution presented in Table 5.5, we see that Model 1.2 is presented in the form of substantive relationships represented by mathematical equations. For example, the equation for "analyzing inductively" shows that the AI (V2) items depend on two latent variables, the COMP processes (F1) and the RET processes (F3), and one error term (E2), which accounts for any measurement error in this variable as well as any specific systematic component of the variable not captured in the latent variables. Similarly, the equation for the "clarifying/verifying" strategy items states that CLAR (V3) depends only on the COMP factor (F1) and its associated uniqueness (E3). The loadings in the standardized solution ranged

5. Findings and discussion

from a low 0.236 for "applying rules" to a moderately high 0.641 for "repeating/rehearsing." Nonetheless, all factor loadings were found to be statistically significant at the 0.05 level.

Table 5.5
Parameter Estimates for Cognitive Strategy Use: Model 1.2

Standardized Solution:					
AI	=V2	= 0.416*F1	+ 0.377 F3	+ 0.737 E2	
CLAR	=V3	= 0.555*F1	+ 0.832 E3		
INF	=V4	= 0.398*F3	+ 0.917 E4		
ASSOC	=V6	= 0.459*F2	+ 0.889 E6		
LPK	=V7	= 0.579*F3	+ 0.815 E7		
REP	=V8	= 0.641*F2	+ 0.768 E8		
SUMM	=V9	= 0.530*F2	+ 0.848 E9		
APR	=V10	= 0.300*F2	+ 0.236 F3	+ 0.875 E10	
PN	=V11	= 0.605*F3	+ 0.796 E11		
TRF	=V12	= 0.514*F2	+ -0.386 F3	+ 0.914 E12	

CSU:	Cognitive Strategy Use	PN:	Practicing Naturalistically
AI:	Analyzing Inductively	REP:	Repeating/Rehearsing
APR:	Applying Rules	SUMM:	Summarizing
ASSOC:	Associating	TRF:	Transferring from L1 to L2
CLAR:	Clarifying/Verifying	F1 (COMP):	Comprehending Processes
INF:	Inferencing	F2 (MEM):	Storing/Memory Processes
LPK:	Linking with Prior Knowledge	F3 (RET):	Retrieval/Using Processes

Figure 5.3 provides a diagrammatic representation of Model 1.2 in which the standardized parameter estimates are indicated. An inspection of Model 1.2 shows that cognitive strategy use is represented by three highly-related underlying factors measured by ten observed variables. The relatively high (0.45 to 0.73) interfactor correlations suggest that the shared variance of these three factors might be indicative of a higher order cognitive strategy use factor, a possibility that was examined and rejected.[8]

Model 1.2 also presents a solution in which three of the ten strategy variables measure more than one underlying factor. These include AI, TRF and APR. These cross-loadings indicate that the variables are not uniquely related to one strategy use factor, but represent more than one. This finding provides some interesting information regarding the substantive nature of these strategies.

For example, "applying rules" performed as an indicator of both the MEM and the RET processes, suggesting that it operated both in learning (to store input) and in retrieval (to generate output). In other words, when test-takers are "applying rules" to a test item, they engage in storing test input (a MEM process) and in retrieving information from long-term memory for output (a RET process). However, "applying rules" apparently played a larger role in

5. Findings and discussion

storing or remembering information (0.30) than it did in retrieving it (0.24). These results made sense given the processing time constraints inherent in retrieval. These findings seem to refute Westney's (1994) claim that explicit rules (and by extension, formal grammar instruction) simply constitute "a manifestation both of a general problem-solving strategy in situations demanding the imposition of some order and of a psychological need for security" (p. 93). Rather, these findings support two notions: (1) APR during both storing and retrieval is an essential part of the learning process, contributing to both acquisition and use; and (2) student cravings for explicit rules and formal grammar instruction constitute one of several essential strategies related to effective learning and use. The latter finding ultimately supports the work of DeKeyser (1995, 1998), Ellis (1993,1994), Long (1988), Van Patten (1996) and many others in their claims that formal instruction of grammar promotes higher levels of second language performance.

Similarly, the strategy "analyzing inductively" performs as a marker of both the COMP and the RET processes when a test-taker endeavors to understand or use linguistic information to formulate hypotheses and make generalizations. In this case, "analyzing inductively" seems to be equally important to both processes, with loadings of 0.42 on the COMP process and 0.38 on the RET process, a finding that highlights the importance of inductive analysis in understanding input and producing output.

Finally, Model 1.2 provides some interesting insights on the "transferring" strategies. In this solution, "transferring" differs from the other strategy types in that it shows a relatively strong positive relationship with the MEM process (0.52), but a negative one with the RET process (-0.39). These results suggest that when test-takers use prior linguistic knowledge from their L1 to store or remember input, there is a positive relationship between transferring and remembering, but when they use these same strategies to retrieve or use prior linguistic knowledge from their L1 for output, there is a negative relationship. This difference could be taken to mean that the "transferring" strategies might be effective behaviors to invoke in learning (positive transfer), but might be counterproductive during the retrieval stage of language use (negative transfer or interference). Therefore, the results in Model 1.2 seem to suggest that the "transferring" strategy items are more "complex" than the other strategy types in that (1) they are related to more than one underlying factor and this relationship is both negative and positive, and (2) the uniqueness associated with the "transferring" strategies is statistically related to the uniqueness associated with two other strategy types (i.e., CLAR, ASSOC). Clearly, the role of L1–L2 transferring strategies in learning and use merits further investigation.

Finally, Model 1.2 produced three error terms that were significantly related to each other. The correlations ranged from 0.09 to 0.28, indicating that there was some redundant content being measured across strategy types.

5. Findings and discussion

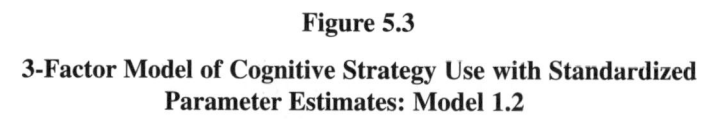

Figure 5.3

3-Factor Model of Cognitive Strategy Use with Standardized Parameter Estimates: Model 1.2

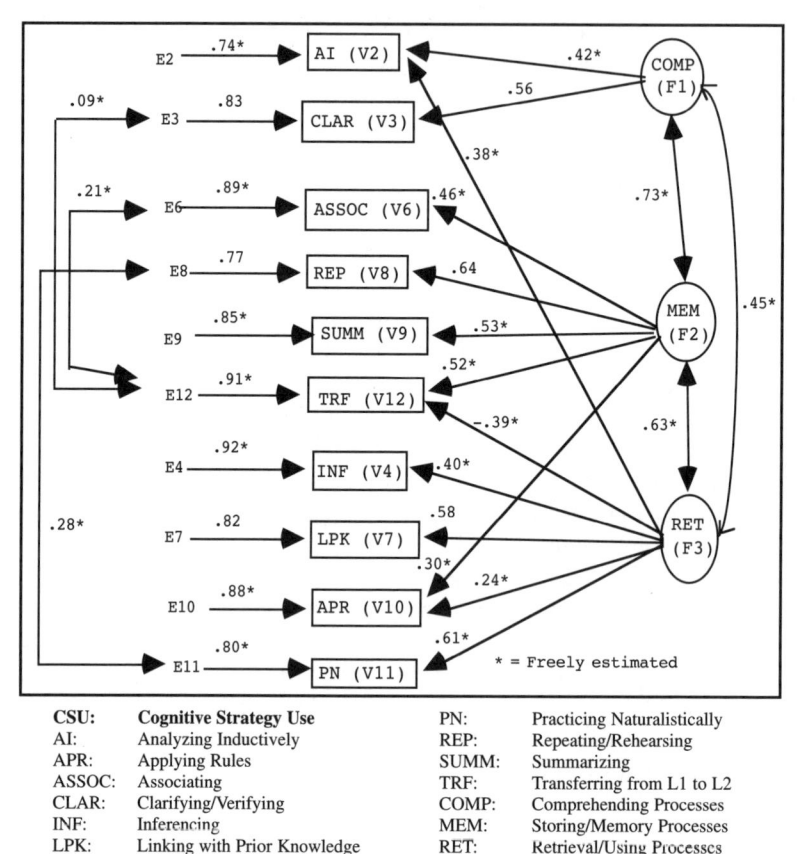

CSU:	**Cognitive Strategy Use**	PN:	Practicing Naturalistically
AI:	Analyzing Inductively	REP:	Repeating/Rehearsing
APR:	Applying Rules	SUMM:	Summarizing
ASSOC:	Associating	TRF:	Transferring from L1 to L2
CLAR:	Clarifying/Verifying	COMP:	Comprehending Processes
INF:	Inferencing	MEM:	Storing/Memory Processes
LPK:	Linking with Prior Knowledge	RET:	Retrieval/Using Processes

In summary, Model 1.2 provides a reasonable explanation of cognitive strategy use in this study. With its three intercorrelated factors, ten measured variables and three correlated errors, this model generally supports the hypothesis that cognitive strategy use is a multidimensional construct consisting of the COMP, MEM and RET processes, thereby supporting the Gagné *et al.* (1993) notion of information processing. Factor 1, the COMP process, is represented by those questionnaire items relating to analyzing inductively and clarifying/verifying; factor 2, the MEM or storing process, measures those items relating to associating, repeating/rehearsing, summarizing, transferring and applying rules; and factor 3, the RET process, is represented by those items relating to transferring, analyzing inductively,

5. Findings and discussion

inferencing, linking with prior knowledge, applying rules and practicing naturalistically. However, given the relatively high inter-factor correlations, the cross-loadings and the correlated errors, many of the cognitive strategy use variables cannot be seen as purely independent measures, but should be treated more as complex cognitive behaviors that are related to one another, a notion supported by Wesche (1987).

In the following section, I will examine the factorial validity of metacognitive strategy use.

The metacognitive processes

Distributions and reliabilities

Based on the results of the EFAs in Chapter 4, I created four composite metacognitive strategy use variables, as seen in Table 4.10. Table 5.4 presents the summary descriptive statistics for the four variables. The means ranged from 3.09 for "assessing the situation" to 3.79 for the "self-evaluating" strategies. Compared with the cognitive strategy use variables, these means were relatively high since the cognitive strategy use variable means ranged from 1.92 to 3.57, indicating that on average the participants reported using the metacognitive strategies more than the cognitive strategies. Also, less variance was observed with the metacognitive strategy use variables than with the cognitive strategy use variables, as the standard deviations ranged from 0.63 to 0.83 for the metacognitive strategy use variables compared with a range of 0.81 to 1.36 for the cognitive strategy use variables. All values for skewness and kurtosis were within the acceptable limits, indicating that the metacognitive strategy use variables appeared to be normally distributed.

Table 5.4

Distributions for the Metacognitive Strategy Use Variables

Variable	Mean	Std Dev	Kurtosis	Skewness	Minimum	Maximum
ASSIT	3.09	0.83	0.18	-0.49	0.00	5.00
MON	3.43	0.81	-0.27	-0.27	0.75	5.00
ST	3.45	0.75	-0.20	-0.41	0.88	5.00
SE	3.79	0.63	0.13	-0.62	1.20	5.00

MSU: **Metacognitive Strategy Use**
ASSIT: Assessing the Situation ST: Self-Testing
MON: Monitoring SE: Self-Evaluating

Table 5.5 presents the internal consistency reliability estimates for the metacognitive strategy use variables. The reliabilities for the four strategy-

5. Findings and discussion

type variables ranged from 0.60 for the monitoring strategy scale to 0.79 for the self-testing scale. The reliability estimates for these newly-formed composite variables were all relatively high.

Table 5.5

Reliability Estimates for the Metacognitive Strategy Use

	No.	Items used	Reliability estimates
1. On-Line Assessment Processes (OL-ASSESS)			
• Assessing the Situation (ASSIT)	8	41, 42, 58, 63, 65, 66, 67, 72	0.72
• Monitoring (MON)	4	52, 57, 60, 68	0.60
2. Post-Assessment Processes (P-ASSESS)			
• Self-Evaluating (SE)	10	47, 49, 59, 62, 64, 69, 71, 73, 78, 79	0.73
• Self-Testing (ST)	8	45, 46, 50, 51, 61, 70, 74, 76	0.79

Testing the factorial validity of metacognitive strategy use

The hypothesized model: Model 2.1

Generated from results of the reliability analysis, the Metacognitive Strategies Questionnaire was represented as a two-factor model of metacognitive strategy use. This initially-hypothesized model is presented in Figure 5.4 and contains two intercorrelated factors: the on-line assessment processes and the post-assessment processes with four observed variables--assessing the situation, monitoring, self-evaluating and self-testing. Each observed variable is postulated to load on only one factor. The uniquenesses associated with the observed variables are postulated to be uncorrelated.

Model 2.1 is a first-order confirmatory factor analysis designed to test the multidimensionality of metacognitive strategy use. It tests the hypothesis that metacognitive strategy use is a multidimensional construct consisting of "on-line assessment" processes and "post-assessment" processes. This hypothesis derives from Wenden (1991), who characterized metacognitive strategy use in terms of time (before, during and after the act). In addition to Wenden, a number of other researchers (e.g., Faerch & Kasper, 1983; O'Malley & Chamot, 1990; Oxford, 1990) have supported the notion that metacognitive strategy use is a multidimensional construct, but again, none of these models has been put to statistical tests.

5. Findings and discussion

Figure 5.4

Initially-Hypothesized 2-Factor Model of Metacognitive Strategy Use: Model 2.1

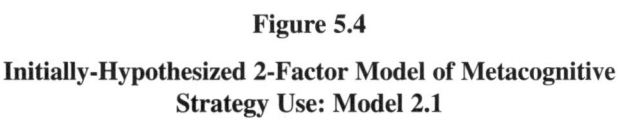

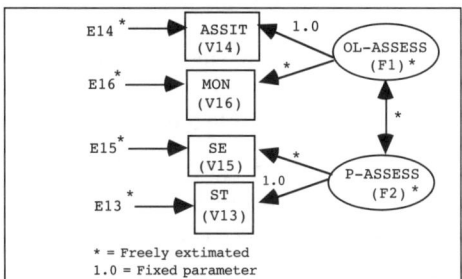

```
E14* → ASSIT (V14)  1.0  ↘
                              OL-ASSESS (F1)*
E16* → MON (V16)      ↗
                              ↕
E15* → SE (V15)       ↘
                              P-ASSESS (F2)*
E13* → ST (V13)   1.0 ↗

* = Freely extimated
1.0 = Fixed parameter
```

MSU:	**Metacognitive Strategy Use**		
ASSIT:	Assessing the Situation	ST:	Self-Testing
MON:	Monitoring	OL-ASSESS:	On-Line Assessment
SE:	Self-Evaluating	P-ASSESS:	Post-Assessment

Model 2.1 addresses the following research question:

Q2: What is the trait structure of metacognitive strategy use as measured by the Metacognitive Strategies Questionnaire? In other words, what is the relationship between the metacognitive strategy item types (e.g., the "monitoring" strategy type) and the metacognitive processes (e.g., goal-setting, planning and assessment). Also, what is the relationship among these processes?

The results for Model 2.1

Prior to exploring the trait structure of metacognitive strategy use, I examined the statistical assumptions underlying the maximum likelihood estimation procedures. The univariate values for skewness and kurtosis for the individual metacognitive strategy use variables, as presented in Table 5.4, showed that these variables were univariately normally distributed. However, this sample produced a Mardia's coefficient of 2.4021 with an associated normalized estimate that was again relatively high (6.447). As a result, I identified four cases[9] (80, 666, 940 and 948) as contributing excessively to multivariate kurtosis and dropped them from the study. This produced a Mardia's coefficient at an acceptable 1.7468 with an associated z statistic of 4.6696, as seen in Table 5.6.

I then examined all other statistical assumptions of the estimation procedure (e.g., identification and number of iterations for conversion) and found no significant violations.

5. Findings and discussion

Finally, the results produced an average off-diagonal value for the standardized residuals of 0.0068, indicating an insignificant degree of misfit. Similarly, the goodness-of-fit index for the initially-hypothesized two-factor model of metacognitive strategy use produced a chi-square value of 1.750 with 1df (p > 0.05) and a CFI of 0.999, as seen in Table 5.6. These results suggested that Model 2.1 might be an excellent representation of the data.

Table 5.6

Results for the Initially-Hypothesized 2-Factor Model of Metacognitive Strategy Use: Model 2.1

Multivariate kurtosis:	
Mardia's coefficient (G2,P)	1.7468
Normalized estimate	4.6696
Standardized residual matrix:	
Average absolute coveriance residuals	0.0041
Average off-diagonal absolute covariance	
Standardized residuals	0.0068
Goodness of fit summary	
Independance model chi-square	1112.260
(on 6 degrees of freedom)	
Bentler-bonett normed fit index	0.998
Bentler-bonett nonnormed fit index	0.996
Comparitive fit index	0.999

Chi-square = 1.750 based on 1 degrees of freedom;
Probability value for the chi-square statistic is less then 0.18584;
The normal theory RLS chi-square for this ML solution is 1.749

However, inspecting the standardized parameter estimates, I found that this model produced an inter-factor correlation estimate greater than 1.0 (r = 1.019), suggesting that metacognitive strategy use, as operationalized in this questionnaire, was perhaps, not a multi-dimensional construct, but rather, on-line assessment strategies and post-assessment strategies were actually one in the same. As a result, I respecified Model 2.1 as a one-factor model of metacognitive strategy use, and reanalyzed the model.

The hypothesized model: Model 2.2

Model 2.2 represents a one-factor model of metacognitive strategy use with four observed variables (ASSIT, MON, SE and ST). Again the uniquenesses associated with the observed variables were assumed to be uncorrelated. In this model, metacognitive strategy use is seen as a set of assessment processes

5. Findings and discussion

with no distinction between "on-line assessment" and "post-assessment." Figure 5.5 provides a schematic representation of the one-factor model of metacognitive strategy use. Appendix L provides the correlation matrix generated from the raw data by EQS for the metacognitive strategy use variables.

Figure 5.5
1-Factor Model of Metacognitive Strategy Use: Model 2.2

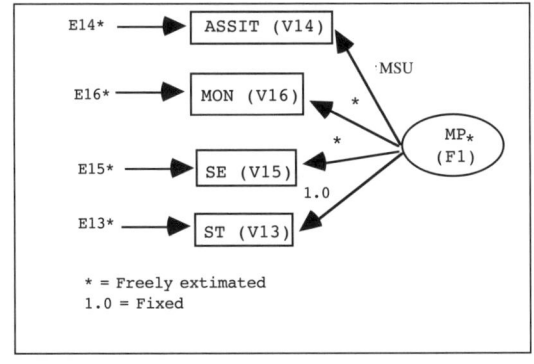

```
E14* ──▶ ASSIT (V14)
                         ·MSU
E16* ──▶ MON (V16)
                    *
                        *       MP*
E15* ──▶ SE (V15)              (F1)
                    1.0
E13* ──▶ ST (V13)

* = Freely extimated
1.0 = Fixed
```

MSU: Metacognitive Strategy Use
ASSIT: Assessing the Situation   SE: Self-Evaluating
MON: Monitoring   ST: Self-Testing

The results of Model 2.2

Model 2.2 produced a chi-square statistic of 1.968 with 2df and a CFI of 1.000, as seen in Table 5.7. These results show that this model is an excellent representation of the model, provided the individual parameter estimates are viable and statistically significant.

Table 5.7

Results for the 1-Factor Model of Metacognitive Strategy Use: Model 2.2

Goodness of fit summary	
Independance model chi-square	1112.260
(on 6 degrees of freedom)	
Bentler-bonett normed fit index	0.998
Bentler-bonett nonnormed fit index	1.000
Comparitive fit index	1.000

Chi-square = 1.968 based on 2 degrees of freedom;
Probability value for the chi-square statistic is less then 0.37380;
The normal theory RLS chi-square for this ML solution is 1.991.

5. Findings and discussion

Examining the feasibility of the individual parameter estimates, I found that with respect to the unstandardized solution, the estimates of the measurement equations with standard errors and test statistics were all reasonable and statistically significant at the 0.05 level. The variances of the error terms were also found to be statistically significant.

Turning to the standardized solution presented in Table 5.8, the factor loadings for Model 2.2 were all within the expected limits and ranged from a moderate 0.506 for assessing the situation to a relatively high 0.774 for self-evaluating.

Table 5.8
Parameter Estimates for Metacognitive Strategy Use: Model 2.2

Standardized Solution:

ST   = V13 = 0.684 F1 + 0.730 E13
ASSIT = V14 = 0.506 F1 + 0.863 E14
SE   = V15 = 0.774 F1 + 0.633 E15
MON = V16 = 0.581 F1 + 0.814 E16

Model 2.2 along with the standardized parameter estimates is presented in Figure 5.6.

Figure 5.6
1-Factor Model of Metacognitive Strategy Use with Standardized Parameter Estimates: Model 2.2

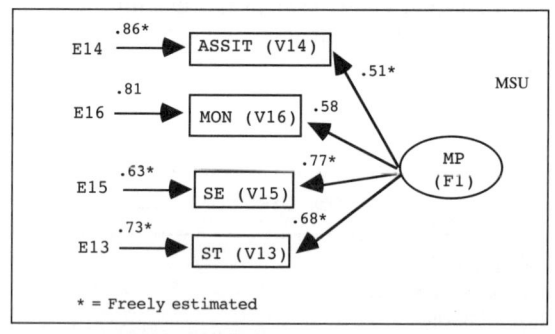

MSU: Metacognitive Strategy Use
ASSIT: Assessing the Situation   SE: Self-Evaluating
MON: Monitoring   ST: Self-Testing

To summarize, Model 2.2 provided strong evidence for acceptance of the one-factor model of metacognitive strategy use as a reasonable explanation of the correlations among the observed variables. This model rejects the hypothesis that metacognitive strategy use is a multidimensional construct consisting of "on-line assessment" and "post-assessment" strategies proposed

5. Findings and discussion

by Wenden (1991) and supports the notion that metacognitive strategy use consists of only one underlying factor represented by general assessment processes. This finding does not preclude the fact that metacognitive strategy use might, in fact, include other strategies (i.e., goal-setting or planning) as discussed in the literature; however, the data in the current study support only the unidimensional notion of metacognitive strategy use, where the assessment processes are represented by those questionnaire items relating to assessing the situation, monitoring, self-evaluating and self-testing. This finding, therefore, questions the mulidimentional depiction of metacognitive strategy use proposed by Faerch and Kasper (1983), O'Malley and Chamot (1990), Oxford (1990) and others.

The *FCE Anchor Test*

Distributions and reliabilities

Based on the results of the EFAs in Chapter 4, I created six composite variables to measure SLTP. They include: (1) grammar (GR); (2) vocabulary (VOC);[10] (3) passage comprehension (PC); (4) word formation (WF); (5) cloze (CLZ) and (6) sentence formation (SF). Table 5.9 presents the summary descriptive statistics for these six variables, as they appear in each test section. It also presents the descriptive statistics for the entire *Anchor Test*.

Table 5.9
Distributions of the *FCE Anchor Test* (61 items)

Variable	Mean	Std Dev	Kurtosis	Skewness	Min	Max	# Poss.
Section 1: Grammar/Vocabulary							
GR	3.71	2.79	0.11	0.96	0.00	11.00	11
VOC	3.17	1.67	-0.89	-0.07	0.00	6.00	6
Section 2: Passage Comprehension							
PC	4.38	2.15	-0.67	0.21	0.00	9.00	9
Section 3: Word Formation							
WF	3.22	2.72	-0.47	0.77	0.00	10.00	10
Section 4: Cloze							
CLZ	3.59	2.85	1.43	1.32	0.00	14.00	15
Section 5: Sentence Formation							
SF	2.65	2.34	0.20	1.00	0.00	10.00	10
The Entire Exam							
TOT	20.72	12.24	0.15	1.02	2.00	60.00	61

5. Findings and discussion

Based on these results, the test-takers found the cloze section to be the most challenging, as the mean score of 3.59 (out of 15 possible points) represents a mere 24% correct, while the vocabulary section posed the least problems with a mean score of 3.17 (out of 6), representing 53% correct. The standard deviation for all six tests ranged from 1.67 for the vocabulary section to 2.85 for the cloze. All values for skewness and kurtosis were within the limits, indicating that the SLTP variables were univariately normally distributed.

Table 5.10 displays the reliability estimates for internal consistency (Cronbach's alpha) for all test sections but the cloze. Reliability estimates for the cloze are again based on the Guttman's split-half reliability procedure. The reliability estimates for the subtests were all reasonably high ranging from 0.61 to 0.83.

Table 5.10

Reliability Estimates for the *FCE Anchor Test* (61 items)

	N	Reliability Estimates
• **Section A: The Reading Comprehension Section**		
Part 1: Grammar composite (GR)	11 items	0.77
Vocabulary composite (VOC)	6 items	0.61
Part 2: Passage Comprehension composite (PC)	9 items	0.63
• **Section B: The Use of English Section**		
Part 1: Word Formation composite	10 items	0.83
Part 2: Cloze composite	15 items	0.81
Part 3: Sentence Formation composite	10 items	0.76
Total Test	61 items	0.94

Testing the factorial validity of the *FCE Anchor Test*

The hypothesized model: Model 3.1

Based on the results of the reliability analysis, the *FCE Anchor Test* was represented as a two-factor model of SLTP and contains two intercorrelated factors, reading ability and lexico-grammatical ability (L-G), and six observed variables (PC, RDG, CLZ, GR, VOC, WF and SF), with each variable hypothesized to load on only one factor. The uniqueness terms are postulated to be uncorrelated. This initially-hypothesized model is presented in Figure 5.7. This is a first-order confirmatory factor analysis designed to test the multidimensionality of the SLTP as measured by the *FCE Anchor Test*. The model tests the hypothesis that SLTP consists of two underlying factors: reading ability and lexico-grammatical ability.

5. Findings and discussion

Model 3.1 addresses the following research question:

Q3: What is the trait structure of second or foreign language test performance as measured by the FCE Anchor Test?

Figure 5.7

Initially-Hypothesized 2-Factor Model of Second Language Test Performance: Model 3.1

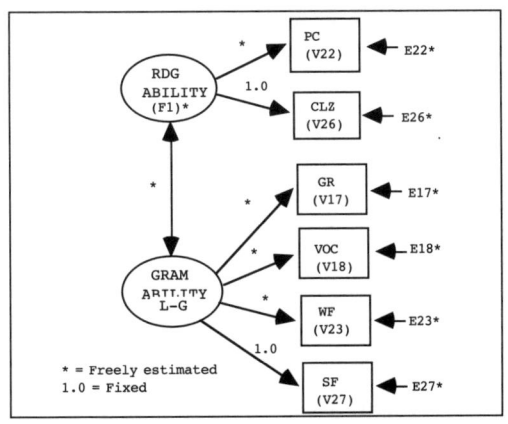

```
                          *        PC
                       ┌──────→  (V22)  ←── E22*
              RDG      │
            ABILITY ───┤ 1.0
             (F1)*     │        CLZ
                       └──────→ (V26)  ←── E26*
               ↑
               │ *
               ↓              *   GR
                       ┌──────→ (V17)  ←── E17*
                       │
                       │    *    VOC
              GRAM     ├──────→ (V18)  ←── E18*
            ABILITY ───┤
              L-G      │    *    WF
                       ├──────→ (V23)  ←── E23*
                       │
                       │ 1.0    SF
                       └──────→ (V27)  ←── E27*

* = Freely estimated
1.0 = Fixed
```

SLTP: Second Language Test Performance
RDG Ability (F1): Reading Ability   **L-G Ability (F2)**: Lexico-Grammatical Ability
        PC: Passage Comprehension   GR: Grammar
        CLZ: Cloze Passage   VOC: Vocabulary
                                                          WF: Word Formation
                                                           SF: Sentence Formation

The results for Model 3.1

Prior to exploring the trait structure of SLTP, I again examined the statistical assumptions underlying the maximum likelihood estimation procedures. The univariate values for skewness and kurtosis for the individual SLTP variables, as seen in Table 5.9, were univariately normally distributed. Then, to avoid multivariate kurtosis, I removed 14 cases (80, 241, 277, 326, 403, 551, 666, 933, 940, 945, 948, 1040, 1175 and 1337) from these analyses as recommended by EQS. In the reanalysis of this model, the sample produced a Mardia's coefficient of 0.0429 with an associated normalized estimate that was low (0.8737), as seen in Table 5.11. Appendix M provides the correlation matrix generated from the raw data by EQS for the observed and latent variables for this model. All other statistical assumptions of the estimation procedure were examined, and no significant violations were found.

I then evaluated the model for overall model–data fit, as seen in Table 5.11.

5. Findings and discussion

The results produced an average off-diagonal value for the standardized residuals of 0.0171, indicating an insignificant degree of misfit. Similarly, the goodness-of-fit index for the initially-hypothesized two-factor model of SLTP produced a chi-square value of 73.593 with 8df, and a CFI of 0.988. Such a high CFI suggested that Model 3.1 might be an excellent representation of the data.

Table 5.11

Results for the Initially-Hypothesized 2-Factor Model of SLTP: Model 3.1

Multivariate kurtosis:	
Mardia's coefficient (G2,P)	0.4629
Normalized estimate	0.8737
Standardized residual matrix:	
Average absolute coveriance residuals	0.0122
Average off-diagonal absolute Standardized residuals	0.0171
Goodness of fit summary	
Independance model chi-square (on 15 degrees of freedom)	5343.707
Bentler-bonett normed fit index	0.986
Bentler-bonett nonnormed fit index	0.977
Comparitive fit index	0.988

Chi-square = 73.593 based on 8 degrees of freedom;
Probability value for the chi-square statistic is less then 0.001;
The normal theory RLS chi-square for this ML solution is 78.469.

I then examined the feasibility of the individual parameter estimates and found all to be reasonable and statistically significant at the 0.05 level. This implies that the underlying factors are well measured by the observed variables and that these variables are measuring extant reading or lexico-grammatical ability. The variances of the error terms were also found to be statistically significant.

Turning to the standardized solution in Table 5.12, we see that the factor loadings for Model 3.1 were all within the expected limits and ranged from a moderate 0.676 to a high 0.883.

5. Findings and discussion

Table 5.12

Parameter Estimates for Model 3.1

Standardized Solution:					
GR	= V17 =	0.845 F2	+	0.535 E17	
VOC	= V18 =	0.676 F2	+	0.737 E18	
PC	= V22 =	0.728 F1	+	0.686 E22	
WF	= V23 =	0.883 F2	+	0.469 E23	
CLZ	= V26 =	0.835 F1	+	0.550 E26	
SF	= V27 =	0.844 F2	+	0.536 E27	

SLTP: Second Language Test Performance

RDG Ability (F1):	Reading Ability	**L-G Ability (F2):**	Lexico-Grammatical Ability
PC:	Passage Comprehension	GR:	Grammar
CLZ:	Cloze Passage	VOC:	Vocabulary
		WF:	Word Formation
		SF:	Sentence Formation

Model 3.1 along with the standardized parameter estimates is presented in Figure 5.8.

Figure 5.8
2-Factor Model of SLTP with Standardized Parameter Estimates: Model 3.1

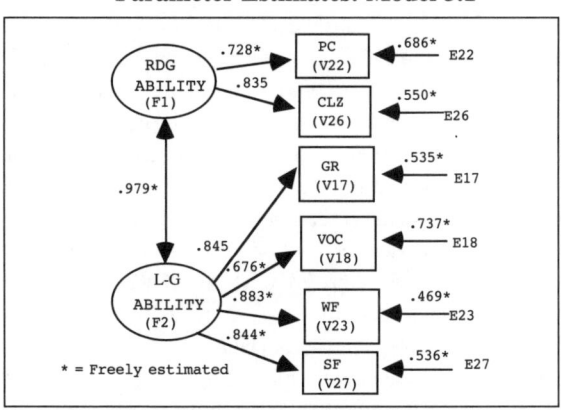

SLTP: Second Language Test Performance

RDG Ability (F1):	Reading Ability	**L-G Ability (F2):**	Lexico-Grammatical Ability
PC:	Passage Comprehension	GR:	Grammar
CLZ:	Cloze Passage	VOC:	Vocabulary
		WF:	Word Formation
		SF:	Sentence Formation

In sum, Model 3.1 provided strong evidence for acceptance of the two-factor solution of SLTP as a reasonable explanation of the correlations among the observed variables. This solution affirms the notion that SLTP, as measured by the *FCE Anchor Test*, consists of two underlying factors: reading ability and

5. Findings and discussion

lexico-grammatical ability. According to this model, the variance in reading ability is explained by the test items in the passage comprehension and the cloze sections of the *FCE Anchor Test*, while the variance in lexico-grammatical ability is represented by items in the grammar and vocabulary section, the word formation and the sentence formation sections of the test. However, this solution produced an extremely high inter-factor correlation (r = .979) between reading ability and lexico-grammatical ability, suggesting that the SLTP variables measured by the *FCE Anchor Test* cannot be seen as purely independent measures of these abilities. Rather, reading ability and the variables that measure it seem to be inextricably related to lexico-grammatical ability and vice versa. This high inter-factor correlation suggests that the shared variance of these two factors might be indicative of a higher order SLTP factor, a possibility that was subsequently examined and rejected.[11]

Testing the validity of the Full Latent Variable Model: the relationships between test-takers' reported strategy use and SLTP

The hypothesized model: Model 4.1

Based on the results of the previous analyses, I formulated a full latent variable model of the relationships between test-takers' reported strategy use and their SLTP. This model, presented in Figure 5.9, involved a combination of the three measurement models already discussed. In this conceptualization, cognitive strategy use (CSU) is represented by Model 1.2, the three-factor model of CSU with ten observed variables and three inter-correlated underlying factors, representing the COMP, MEM and RET processes; metacognitive strategy use (MSU) is characterized by Model 2.2, the one-factor model of MSU with four observed variables and only one underlying factor relating to the assessment processes; and SLTP is depicted by Model 3.1, the two-factor model of SLTP with six observed variables and two inter-correlated underlying SLTP factors, representing reading and lexico-grammatical ability.

With regard to the structural models, metacognitive strategy use is hypothesized to have a direct impact on reading and lexico-grammatical ability, but to have no impact on cognitive strategy use. Similarly, cognitive strategy use is hypothesized to have a direct impact on both reading and lexico-grammatical ability, but no impact on metacognitive strategy use. The underlying cognitive process factors (COMP, MEM and RET) are all hypothesized to be correlated with each other.

Model 4.1 addresses the following research question:

> *Q4: What is the relationship between the test-takers' reported use of cognitive and metacognitive strategy use and their performance on second or foreign language tests?*

5. Findings and discussion

Model 4.1, the initially-hypothesized full latent variable model, is presented in Figure 5.9. The legend will be used with all subsequent models presented in this chapter.

Figure 5.9

Initially-Hypothesized Model of Strategy Use and SLTP: Model 4.1

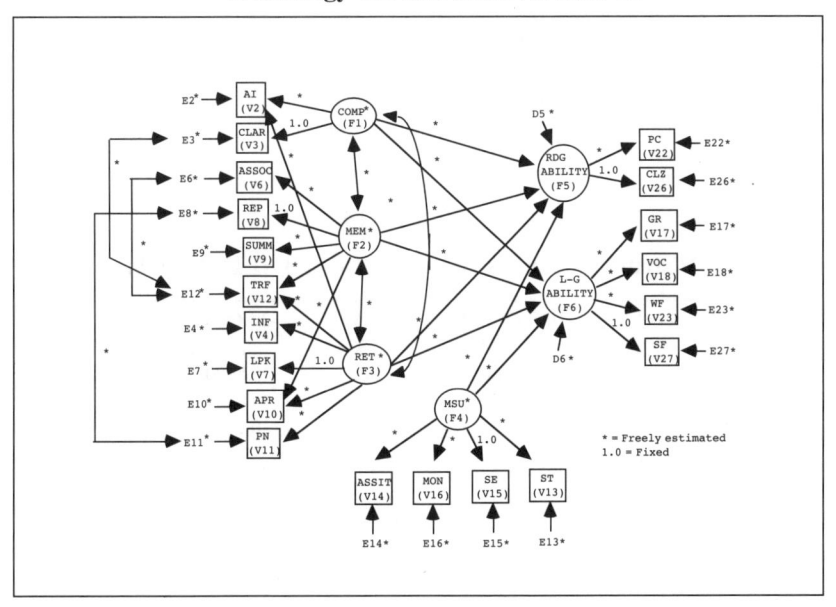

LEGEND

CSU - Cognitive Strategy Use

AI	(V2):	Analyzing Inductively	APR	(V10):	Applying Rules
CLAR	(V3):	Clarifying/Verifying	PN	(V11):	Practicing Naturalistically
INF	(V4):	Inferencing	TRF	(V12):	Transferring from L1 to L2
ASSOC	(V6):	Associating	COMP	(F1):	Comprehending Process
LPK	(V7):	Linking with Prior Knowledge	MEM	(F2):	Storing/Memory Process
REP	(V8):	Repeating/Rehearsing	RET	(F3):	Retrieval/Using Process
SUMM	(V9):	Summarizing			

(F4) MSU - Metacognitive Process

ST	V13:	Self-Testing	SE	V15:	Self-Evaluating
ASSIT	V14:	Assessing the Situation	MON	V16:	Monitoring

SLTP - Second Language Test Performance

GR	(V17):	Grammar	PC	(V22):	Passage Comprehension
VOC	(V18):	Vocabulary	CLZ	(V26):	Cloze
WF	(V23):	Word Formation	RDG	(F5):	Reading Ability
SF	(V27):	Sentence Formation	L-G	(F6):	Lexico-Grammatical Ability

5. Findings and discussion

The results for Model 4.1

Before investigating the inter-relationships between strategy use and SLTP, I examined the statistical assumptions underlying the maximum likelihood estimation procedures. The univariate values for skewness and kurtosis for the observed variables indicated that these variables were univariately normally distributed. However, Model 4.1 produced an initial Mardia's coefficient of 19.0586 with a normalized estimate (11.9419) that was very high. Therefore, to avoid multivariate kurtosis, I removed the 15 cases which contributed most to multivariate kurtosis (80, 244, 258, 289, 295, 354, 551, 666, 750, 831, 923, 1040, 1242, 1346) from the analysis and reanalyzed the model.

The summary descriptive statistics for the 1,367 cases are presented in Table 5.13.

Table 5.13

Distributions of the Strategy Use and SLTP Variables

VARIABLE	AI (V2)	CLAR (V3)	INF (V4)	ASSOC (V6)	LPK (V7)
MEAN	2.6131	2.5724	3.5768	2.3950	3.2394
STD DEV	1.0480	1.1840	1.0060	0.8990	0.8040
SKEWNESS	-0.1126	-0.0232	-0.4772	0.0181	-0.2700
KURTOSIS	-0.3666	-0.6116	-0.4003	-0.3060	-0.0584
VARIABLE	REP (V8)	SUMM (V9)	APR (V10)	PN (V11)	TRF (V12)
MEAN	3.1627	2.3705	3.5208	3.0556	1.9250
STD DEV	0.9650	1.1780	0.9060	0.9610	1.0690
SKEWNESS	-0.3161	0.1061	-0.5388	-0.1074	0.2761
KURTOSIS	-0.4343	-0.5909	-0.0122	-0.6157	-0.6295
VARIABLE	ST (V13)	ASSIT (V14)	SE (V15)	MON (V16)	GR (V17)
MEAN	3.4548	3.0975	3.7891	3.4265	3.6818
STD DEV	0.7460	0.8200	0.6250	0.7990	2.7740
SKEWNESS	-0.3886	-0.4691	-0.5802	-0.2618	0.9617
KURTOSIS	-0.2600	0.1561	-0.0194	-0.2968	0.1309
VARIABLE	VOC (V18)	PC (V22)	WF (V23)	CLZ (V26)	SF (V27)
MEAN	3.1595	4.3702	3.1997	3.5655	2.6255
STD DEV	1.6630	2.1430	2.7000	2.8150	2.3150
SKEWNESS	-0.0582	0.2050	0.7709	1.2993	0.9940
KURTOSIS	-0.8911	-0.6519	-0.4593	1.3779	0.1657

After the cases were dropped, the sample for Model 4.1 produced a Mardia's coefficient of 12.959 with an associated normalized estimate that was much lower (8.0758), as seen in Table 5.14.

I then examined other statistical assumptions of the estimation procedure and noticed a number of problems. First, the disturbance associated with reading ability (D5) was flagged as being constrained "at the lower bounds" (0.0) by EQS for computational and theoretical reasons (Bentler, 1992), suggesting that reading ability was perfectly predicted from the model. Although this condition might raise suspicion about the interpretability of the final results, Bentler (personal communication, July 1995) maintained that disturbances which are constrained at zero can be acceptable and not necessarily indicative of model misidentification if they do not produce linear dependencies or convergence difficulties. Upon inspection, I observed no linear dependencies in the model; however, in examining the number of iterations required for convergence, I noticed that this particular model required more than the recommended 30, thereby suggesting that the originally-hypothesized model with inter-correlated factors might, in fact, be unacceptable. To explore this possibility further, I inspected the overall model–data fit statistics and saw that Model 4.1 produced a chi-square value of 2,059.832 with 154df and a low CFI of 0.818, as seen in Table 5.14. Therefore, I made several adjustments to the model before embarking on further analyses.

Table 5.14

Results for the Initially-Hypothesized Model of Strategy Use and SLTP: Model 4.1

Multivariate kurtosis:	
Mardia's coefficient (G2,P)	12.9590
Normalized estimate	8.0758
Standardized residual matrix:	
Average absolute coveriance residuals	0.0963
Average off-diagonal absolute Standardized residuals	0.1054
Goodness of fit summary	
Independance model chi-square (on 190 degrees of freedom)	10661.070
Bentler-bonett normed fit index	0.807
Bentler-bonett nonnormed fit index	0.775
Comparitive fit index	0.818

Chi-square = 2059.832 based on 154 degrees of freedom;
Probability value for the chi-square statistic is less then 0.001;
The normal theory RLS chi-square for this ML solution is 1808.095.

As Model 4.1 was misfitting, I made no interpretation of the individual parameter estimates. Instead, I used these results to respecify a model that might better represent the sample data.

5. Findings and discussion

The hypothesized model: Model 4.2

Based on the results of Model 4.1, I reconceptualized the full latent variable model of the relationships between strategy use and SLTP by means of a series of post hoc fitting procedures which included the use of the LM and Wald tests along with substantive rationale in the iterative respecification of models. I examined numerous models and most were misfitting or substantively meaningless. However, the one model which appeared to represent the sample data well from both a substantive and statistical point of view was Model 4.2, displayed in Figure 5.10.

Model 4.2 represents the relationships between test-taker strategy use and SLTP. This full latent variable model combines the CSU, MSU and SLTP models into a network of relationships, where the cognitive strategy use model consists of three underlying process factors with ten observed variables, and the metacognitive strategy use model is comprised of one underlying process factor with four observed variables. The uniqueness of seven variables within the CSU and MSU models are hypothesized to be correlated. Also, the SLTP model consists of two underlying factors and six observed variables within which lexico-grammatical ability is hypothesized to influence reading ability. Finally, the uniquenesses associated with two SLTP variables are hypothesized to be correlated.

With regard to the structural model, metacognitive strategy use is hypothesized to have a direct impact on each of the cognitive strategy use factors, but no direct impact on SLTP. Similarly, the three cognitive strategy use factors are hypothesized to influence lexico-grammatical ability, but to have no direct influence on reading ability. Finally, two observed metacognitive strategy use variables (MON and SE) and two observed cognitive strategy use variables (INF and LPK) are hypothesized to have a direct effect on lexico-grammatical ability.

Figure 5.10 provides a schematic representation of Model 4.2.

5. Findings and discussion

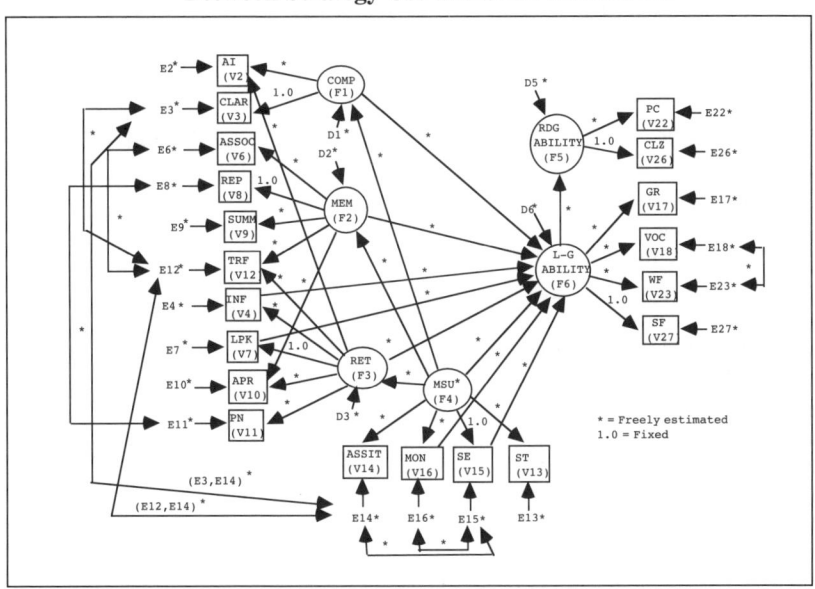

Figure 5.10

The Hypothesized Model of the Relationships Between Strategy Use and SLTP: Model 4.2

The results for Model 4.2

I examined the statistical assumptions underlying the maximum likelihood estimation procedures and found that the univariate values for skewness and kurtosis for the individual variables, as presented in Table 5.13, appeared to be univariately normally distributed. Also, the sample produced a Mardia's coefficient of 12.9590 with an associated normalized estimate of 8.0758, as seen in Table 5.15. To ensure that this sample was not multivariately nonnormal (peaked), I analyzed these data using robust statistics and found (1) that the S-Bχ^2 statistic was approximately the same value as the ordinary χ^2 statistic under the normality assumption and (2) that the ordinary maximum likelihood and robust standard errors yielded very similar values. As a result, the degree of nonnormality shown in the data again does not seem to affect key statistical conclusions regarding model adequacy and significance of parameter estimates.

I then examined all other statistical assumptions of the estimation procedure and saw no indication of data convergence problems. On the contrary, the program converged after only 11 iterations. Finally, I found no evidence of linear dependencies.

Next, I examined Model 4.2 for overall model–data fit. As seen in Table 5.15, this model produced an average off-diagonal value for the standardized residuals of 0.0487, indicating a small degree of misfit, and the distribution of standardized

5. Findings and discussion

residuals was symmetrical and appropriately centered around zero (i.e., within the range of -0.1 to 0.1). Finally, this model produced a chi-square value of 776.051 with 148df and a CFI of 0.940. Such a high CFI indicated that Model 4.2, the full latent variable model of the relationships between strategy use and SLTP, was a fairly good representation of the sample data.

Table 5.15
Results for the Model of Strategy Use and SLTP: Model 4.2

Multivariate kurtosis:	
Mardia's coefficient (G2,P)	12.9590
Normalized estimate	8.0758
Standardized residual matrix:	
Average absolute coveriance residuals	0.0460
Average off-diagonal absolute	
Standardized residuals	0.0487
Goodness of fit summary	
Independance model chi-square	10661.070
(on 190 degrees of freedom)	
Bentler-bonett normed fit index	0.927
Bentler-bonett nonnormed fit index	0.923
Comparitive fit index	0.940

Chi-square = 776.051 based on 148 degrees of freedom;
Probability value for the chi-square statistic is less then 0.001;
The normal theory RLS chi-square for this ML solution is 787.032

These statistics provided strong evidence for acceptance of Model 4.2. Examining the individual parameter estimates for statistical significance, I found all values to be reasonable and within the expected limits, and all but two estimates to be statistically significant at the 0.05 level. These two exceptions included (1) the path from the COMP processes factor to the lexico-grammatical ability factor and (2) the variance of the disturbance related to reading ability. I will discuss these parameters in more depth in the next section. To summarize, Model 4.2 seemed to represent the sample data well and was utilized as the baseline model for the relationships between test-takers' reported strategy use and SLTP.

Further information on the standardized parameter estimates is provided in Table 5.16, where each variable in Model 4.2 is presented in equation form. The squared multiple correlation for each variable is also included in this table as this statistic was used as an index for determining the amount of variance accounted for in each dependent variable by the predictor variables. I calculated this statistic by subtracting 1.0 from the square of the standardized residual (Bentler, 1990). To illustrate, the self-testing variable had a standardized residual of 0.499. Therefore, $1.0 - (.499)^2 = 0.7510$. Further discussion and interpretation of these results will also be taken up in the next section.

Table 5.16

Parameter Estimates for Model 4.2

Standardized Solutions:										R^2
AI	= V2	=	0.421* F1	+	0.350*F3	+	0.744 E2			0.45
CLAR	= V3	=	0.551 F1	+	0.834 E3					0.30
INF	= V4	=	0.389* F3	+	0.921 E4					0.15
ASSOC	= V6	=	0.424* F2	+	0.906 E6					0.18
LPK	= V7	=	0.584 F3	+	0.812 E7					0.34
REP	= V8	=	0.643 F2	+	0.766 E8					0.41
SUMM	= V9	=	0.486* F2	+	0.874 E9					0.24
APR	= V10	=	0.327* F2	+	0.250*F3	+	0.844 E10			0.29
PN	= V11	=	0.591* F3	+	0.807 E11					0.35
TRF	= V12	=	0.441* F2	−	0.353*F3	+	0.952 E12			0.09
ST	= V13	=	0.867* F4	+	0.499 E13					0.75
ASSIT	= V14	=	0.423* F4	+	0.906 E14					0.18
SE	= V15	=	0.605* F4	+	0.796 E15					0.37
MON	= V16	=	0.484* F4	+	0.875 E16					0.13
GR	= V17	=	0.834* F6	+	0.551 E17					0.70
VOC	= V18	=	0.631* F6	+	0.775 E18					0.40
PC	= V22	=	0.712* F5	+	0.703 E22					0.51
WF	= V23	=	0.854 F6	+	0.521 E23					0.73
CLZ	= V26	=	0.824 F5	+	0.566 E26					0.68
SF	= V27	=	0.831* F6	+	0.556 E27					0.69
COMP	= F1	=	0.595* F4	+	0.804 D1					0.35
MEM	= F2	=	0.863* F4	+	0.505 D2					0.75
RET	= F3	=	0.837* F4	+	0.548 D3					0.70
RDG	= F5	=	0.985* F4	+	0.172 D5					0.97
L-G	= F6	=	0.191* V4	+	0.212*V7	+	0.465*V15	+		
			0.095*	V16 −	0.023*F1	−	0.932*F2	+		
			0.228*	F3 +	0.700 D6					0.51

Model 4.2 along with the standardized parameter estimates is presented in Figure 5.11.

5. Findings and discussion

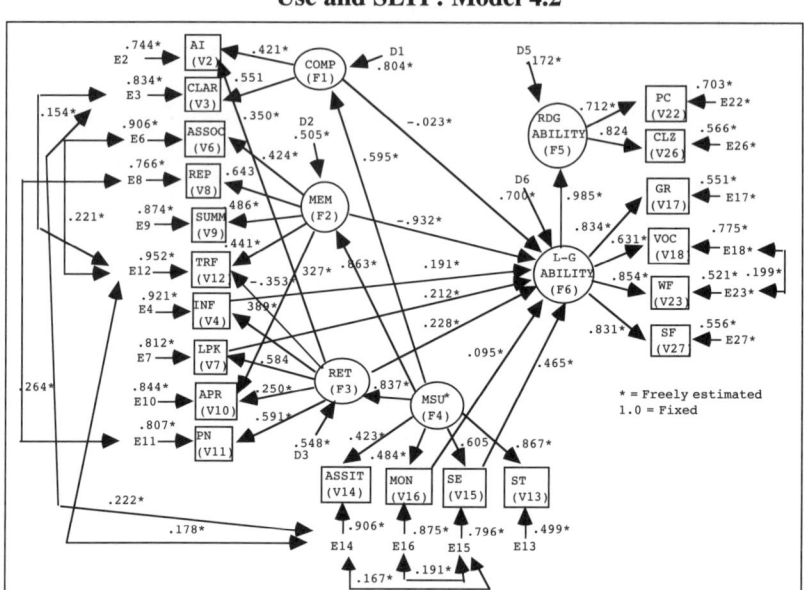

Figure 5.11

The Model of the Relationships Between TTs' Strategy Use and SLTP: Model 4.2

Discussion of Model 4.2

As seen in Figure 5.11, the relationship between strategy use and SLTP is indeed a complex one. In combining the three measurement models with the structural models using all variables in the study, I noticed several changes to the individual measurement models. Such changes are to be expected since the more variables one adds to a model, the greater the chances are that they will affect its final shape. In other words, the more information we include in our models, the more comprehensive they will be and the better they will serve to explain the complex of relationships resulting from multiple sources of data.

In this section, I describe the final full latent variable model of strategy use and performance. First, I will discuss the individual measurement models and will then focus on the relationships observed within the structural model.

The SLTP model

UCLES originally designed the *FCE Anchor Test* to measure SLTP as a function of two factors: reading comprehension and use of English. However, a series of confirmatory factor analyses revealed that this test did indeed measure reading comprehension (i.e., passage comprehension), but "use of

5. Findings and discussion

English" was defined somewhat narrowly as the ability to use grammar and vocabulary in multiple choice or limited production contexts. Therefore, the *FCE Anchor Test* measures SLTP through two highly-related factors: reading ability and lexico-grammatical ability, as seen in Figure 5.12, and all references to SLTP reflect this definition.

This model also showed that the underlying lexico-grammatical ability factor was measured by variables designed to measure both grammatical knowledge (GR and SF) and vocabulary knowledge (VOC and WF). In short, the *Anchor Test* does not measure grammar and vocabulary knowledge discretely, but captures instead an apparent symbiotic relationship between the two. The notion of a lexico-grammatical continuum is not new in the literature. However, these results provide empirical evidence for, as Lyons (1968) states, an indeterminate distinction between lexical and grammatical categories.

In sum, SLTP was explained by reading ability and lexico-grammatical ability. Reading ability was well-measured by the test-takers' performance on the passage comprehension and the cloze sections of the test, since both variables displayed a relatively strong, significant (at 0.05 level) association with reading ability. More specifically, the passage comprehension section had an R^2 of 0.51 and the cloze an R^2 of 0.68. Similarly, the lexico-grammatical ability factor was well-measured by the grammar, vocabulary, word formation and sentence formation sections of the test. These sections produced R squares ranging from 0.40 for the vocabulary section to 0.73 for the word formation section, as seen in Table 5.16.

Model 4.2 also showed that unsurprisingly, the uniquenesses associated with the vocabulary and the word formation variables were significantly related to one another, producing a correlation coefficient of 0.199. Finally, SLTP in this model showed that reading and lexico-grammatical ability were not only correlated with each other, but lexico-grammatical ability had a very strong impact on reading ability in this test, given the large standardized loading (0.985) of the path from lexico-grammatical to reading ability and the nonsignificant disturbance (D5) observed in reading ability (0.172).

These results might be explained by inspecting the two tasks used to measure reading ability. The first, passage comprehension, measured (according to the EFAs in Chapter 4) two distinct abilities: (1) "reading for explicit information" (REI), where test-takers needed to answer questions about specific information in the text and to understand synonymous words or sentences, and (2) "reading for inferential information" (RII), where they needed to infer information not explicitly stated in the text, such as the author's attitude. REI (7 items) triggers bottom-up processing of reading, requiring test-takers to decode input at the lexical and syntactic levels, while RII (2 items) triggers top-down or interactive processing of reading, requiring

5. Findings and discussion

test-takers both to process input at the semantic and discourse levels (e.g. to process endophoric and exophoric references) and to relate it to prior knowledge schemata.

The second reading-type task, the cloze, measured (according to the EFAs in Chapter 4) the test-takers' ability (1) to use contextual cues in the passage to supply missing content words (11 items) and (2) to use syntactic cues to supply missing function words (4 items). Similar to the passage comprehension task, the cloze seems to trigger (1) bottom-up processing of reading by requiring students to supply function words by decoding input at the lexical and syntactic levels and (2) top-down processing of reading by requiring test-takers to supply content words by decoding input at the semantic and discourse levels and by relating it to prior knowledge schemata.

From these results, we can draw several conclusions. First, as witnessed in both tasks, reading comprehension, by its very nature, involves varying degrees of both top-down and bottom-up processing of reading, a finding supported by most SL reading researchers (Grabe, 1997), and the *FCE Anchor Test*, as a test of reading ability, is no different. Second, given the fact that the items in these subtests depended more heavily on the test-takers' ability to decode text at the lexical and syntactic levels, rather than at an inferential level, it is no wonder that lexico-grammatical ability was highly related to reading ability in this test; indeed, could this be the case in all standardized tests of reading ability? Clearly, this finding has serious implications for the validity of the *FCE Anchor Test* as a measure of both lexico-grammatical and reading ability and warrants further examination.

Finally, these results also suggest that second language reading ability at the intermediate level of proficiency (i.e., 75% of the test-takers) rests more on the ability to decode grammar and vocabulary than on the ability to do top-down, interactive reading at higher levels of processing. This comes as no surprise to most second language educators who see their intermediate students struggling with the lexico-grammatical features of text rather than concentrating on the inferential features. Similar findings have been made by a number of SL reading researchers (Barnett, 1989; Carrell, 1988; Clarke, 1980; Coady, 1979) over the years. Nonetheless, the notion that models of second language reading ability should be different for different proficiency levels merits further empirical investigation. The use of SEM in a multi-group design would provide a useful analytic tool for establishing baseline models of second language reading ability for ability-level groups and for testing their equivalence across these different levels, a notion I will examine in the following chapter.

Figure 5.12 presents the SLTP portion of the full latent variable model (4.2).

5. Findings and discussion

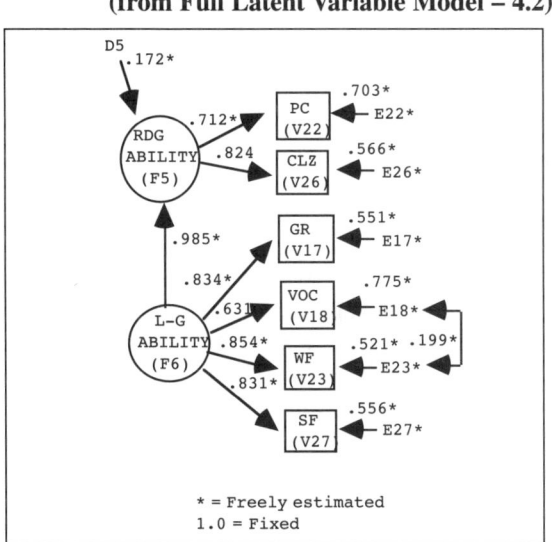

Figure 5.12

**Model of SLTP as Measured by the *FCE Anchor Test*
(from Full Latent Variable Model – 4.2)**

```
D5
 .172*
                        .703*
              PC    ←── E22*
     .712* ↘ (V22)
 RDG          .566*
 ABILITY .824 CLZ   ←── E26*
  (F5)         (V26)
                        .551*
              GR    ←── E17*
     .985*    (V17)
                        .775*
     .834*    VOC   ←── E18* ←┐
       .631   (V18)             │
 L-G                    .521* .199*
 ABILITY .854* WF   ←── E23* ←┘
  (F6)   .831* (V23)
                        .556*
              SF    ←── E27*
              (V27)
```

* = Freely estimated
1.0 = Fixed

The Cognitive Strategy Use model

Based on the information-processing models proposed by Hunt (1982) and Gagné *et al.* (1993), the Cognitive Strategies Questionnaire was originally designed to measure three underlying factors: comprehending processes, memory or storing processes, and retrieval or using processes, each represented by a cluster of strategy types. A series of confirmatory factor analyses showed that the items grouped into ten strategy types, which, in turn, measured one or more of the three underlying factors of cognitive strategy use.

When included in a full latent variable model, cognitive strategy use was, indeed, explained by the COMP, MEM and RET processes, as seen in Figure 5.13. The COMP processes were moderately well-explained by the "analyzing inductively" strategies with a loading of 0.421 ($R^2 = 0.45$) and by the "clarifying/verifying" strategies with a loading of 0.551 ($R^2 = 0.30$). Each path was statistically significant at the 0.05 level. Also, the MEM strategies were explained by the "associating" strategies with a loading of 0.424 ($R^2 = 0.18$), the "repeating/rehearsing" strategies with a loading of 0.643 ($R^2 = 0.41$), the "summarizing" strategies with a loading of 0.486 ($R^2 = 0.24$), the "applying rules" strategies with a loading of 0.327 ($R^2 = 0.29$), and the "transferring" strategies with a loading of 0.441 ($R^2 = 0.09$). Again, all paths were significant.

5. Findings and discussion

Finally, the RET strategies were moderately well explained by the strategies for "analyzing inductively" with a loading of 0.350 ($R^2 = 0.45$), "inferencing" with a loading of 0.389 ($R^2 = 0.15$), "linking with prior knowledge" with a loading of 0.584 ($R^2 = 0.34$), "applying rules" with a loading of 0.250 ($R^2 = 0.29$), and "transferring" with a loading of -.353 ($R^2 = 0.09$). Again, all paths were significant.

The cognitive strategy use model also produced three strategy-type cross-loadings. The "analyzing inductively" strategy type was significantly related to both the COMP and the RET processes, producing a loading of 0.421 on the COMP processes and 0.350 on the RET processes. Similarly, the "applying rules" strategy type was significantly related to the MEM and RET processes, with loadings of 0.347 and 0.250 respectively. Finally, the "transferring from L1 to L2" strategy type loaded significantly on both the MEM and RET strategies. This third cross-loading, however, was intriguing in that the "transferring" strategies, as an indicator of storing input, yielded a significant, positive loading (0.441), while as a marker of the RET processes, it produced a significant, negative loading (-0.353). These results suggest that L1–L2 transfer might be beneficial in remembering or storing input (i.e., learning), but may be detrimental when invoked during retrieval or use (i.e., performance). This finding controverts Corder's (1983) notion that learners primarily invoke transfer as a communication strategy in performance. Rather, it shows that transfer does, in fact, play a role in learning. It also gives empirical support to Schachter's (1983) "new account of transfer" in which she conceptualized transfer in a cognitive framework as one strategy (of many) functioning within a general process of hypothesis construction and testing.

Finally, the cognitive strategy use model captured the substantively meaningful relationships that existed among the error terms of four variables (CLAR, TRF, ASSOC and PN), as these error terms were found to be significantly correlated with one another. To illustrate, the uniqueness associated with both the "clarifying/verifying" strategies and the "associating" strategies were significantly correlated with the error term of the "transferring" strategies. From a substantive point of view, it is not surprising that "clarifying," "verifying" and "associating" behaviors should be related to the behavior of transferring knowledge and skills from the L1 to the L2. Also, the uniqueness associated with the "repeating/rehearsing" strategies were significantly related to the uniqueness of the "practicing naturalistically" strategies. Again, this relationship makes sense, as one can easily imagine a second language learner rehearsing a linguistic script mentally in order to prepare to use it in naturalistic interaction. In short, as one might expect, the cognitive strategy use measure, like all measures, appears to be fallible to some degree; nonetheless, SEM was able to account

5. Findings and discussion

for these obviously systematic sources of error in the overall model.

Figure 5.13 presents the model of self-reported cognitive strategy use based on the full latent variable model.

Figure 5.13

**Model of Self-Reported Cognitive Strategy Use
(from Full Latent Variable model – 4.2)**

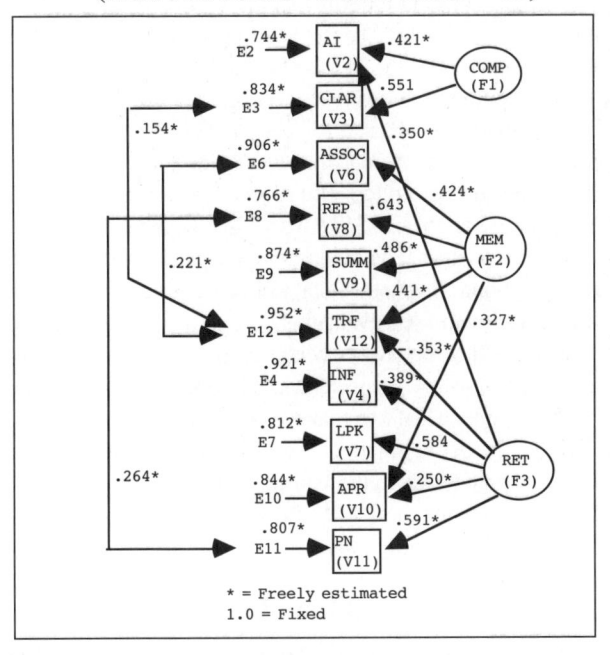

The metacognative strategy use model

Based on Wenden's (1991) research in which metacognitive behaviors were characterized as occurring before, during and after the act, the Metacognitive Strategies Questionnaire (Items 41 through 80) was originally designed to measure two factors: on-line metacognitive processes and post-assessment processes, each represented by a cluster of strategy types. However, a series of confirmatory factor analyses showed that the items grouped into four strategy types, all of which related to assessment, and no grouping based on time was observed in the data. These strategy types, in turn, seemed to measure, not two, but one underlying factor. Hence, metacognitive strategy use in this study can be defined in terms of assessment behaviors. This finding supports the Gagné et al. (1993) depiction of metacognitive strategy use as only one set of overarching control processes with no individual distinction between goal-setting, planning or evaluating factors. These results also support the notion that

5. Findings and discussion

metacognitive strategy use predominantly involves assessment with goal-setting and planning strategies as special cases of assessment.

When included in a full latent variable model, metacognitive strategy use was explained by the following assessment-related strategy types: "assessing the situation," "monitoring," "self-evaluating" and "self-testing," as seen in Figure 5.14. These strategy types varied considerably as to the degree to which they explained metacognitive strategy use in the model. The "self-testing" strategies were highly related to metacognitive strategy use with a loading of 0.867 ($R^2 = 0.75$), while the "self-evaluating" strategies produced a more moderate loading of 0.605 ($R^2 = 0.37$). The "assessing the situation" and "monitoring" strategy types showed the weakest relationships with loadings of 0.423 ($R^2 = 0.18$) and 0.484 ($R^2 = 0.13$) respectively. In spite of the strength of these relationships, all paths were significant at the 0.05 level.

Finally, the metacognitive strategy use model captured the relationships among the error terms of three variables (ASSIT, MON and SE) which produced significant correlations with one another. The uniqueness associated with both the "assessing the situation" and "monitoring" strategies yielded significant correlations with the uniqueness associated with "self-evaluating." From a substantive perspective, this came as no surprise since behaviors which involve "assessing the situation" or "monitoring" might also be characterized as being closely related to "self-evaluating." For example, when a test-taker assesses what needs to be done to write an essay in English, he or she might also evaluate the potential for meeting those needs or even the degree to which those needs can be met.

Figure 5.14 presents the model of self-reported metacognitive strategy use based on the full latent variable model.

Figure 5.14

**Model of Self-Reported Metacognitive Strategy Use
(from Full Latent Variable Model – 4.2)**

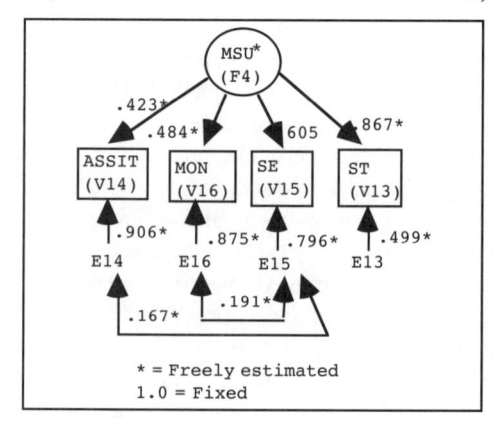

5. Findings and discussion

The relationships between cognitive strategy use and metacognitive strategy use

Following an analysis of the measurement models, I tested several models to explore the relationships between cognitive strategy use and metacognitive strategy use and all produced highly inter-related factors. In the full latent variable model presented in Figure 5.15, metacognitive strategy use had a direct, positive impact on all three of the cognitive strategy use variables. More specifically, metacognitive strategy use had a moderate, direct influence on the COMP processes (0.595) and a strong direct impact on both the MEM (0.863) and the RET processes (0.837). All three relationships were significant at the 0.05 level. These results are interesting since they provide empirical evidence in support of the notion put forth by a number of researchers (e.g., Bachman & Palmer, 1996; Brown *et al.*, 1983; Faerch & Kasper, 1983; O'Malley & Chamot, 1990; Wenden, 1991) that the metacognitive strategies perform an executive function in the higher order thinking processes. In other words, these strategies constitute self-management behaviors that oversee and manage the cognitive behaviors in SL acquisition, use and testing, just as Gagné *et al.* (1993) had posited.

In addition to the direct influences of metacognitive strategy use on cognitive use, the model presented in Figure 5.15 shows that the uniqueness of several variables (CLAR-TRF, ASSOC-TRF, REP-PN, ASSIT-SE, MON-SE, TRF-ASSIT and CLAR-ASSIT) were significantly correlated. For example, the error term associated with the "clarifying/verifying" strategies was related to the uniqueness associated with the "assessing the situation" strategies. Again, the model pointed to a relationship that made substantive sense since clarifying or verifying input are most likely behaviors that are also invoked when a second language learner is "assessing the situation" during SL acquisition, use or testing. Similarly, the uniqueness associated with "transferring" and "assessing the situation" were found to be significantly correlated. Again, this relationship is logical in the context of a learner who would utilize prior knowledge or skills in the L1 to "assess the situation" during SL acquisition, use or testing.

In sum, these results show that metacognitive strategy use and cognitive strategy use are highly related. Similarly, given the number of cross-loadings, some strategic behaviors represent one stage of the information process, while others represent more than one, thereby demonstrating that strategies may serve multiple purposes in the learning process, and not just one, as is often depicted in the taxonomies in the literature (e.g., O'Malley & Chamot, 1990; Oxford, 1990). Finally, given the relatedness between the error terms, the questionnaires themselves, as fallible measures of strategic behaviors, are highly related in apparently systematic ways. These findings clearly demonstrate the complex nature of metacognitive and cognitive strategy use

5. Findings and discussion

and the need to assume that questionnaires, like all measures, contain non-random error. At least, a SEM approach to the analysis of these data allows for this error to be incorporated in the models along with the other relationships.

Figure 5.15 presents the model of self-reported cognitive and metacognitive strategy use based on the full latent variable model.

Figure 5.15

Model of Self-Reported Cognitive and Metacognitive Strategy Use (from Full Latent Variable Model – 4.2)

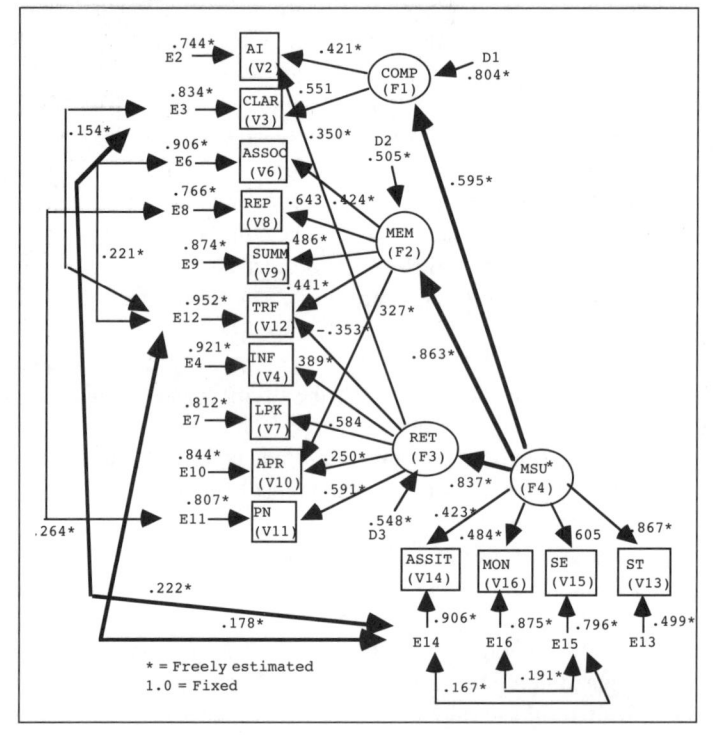

The relationships between self-reported cognitive and metacognitive strategy use and SLTP

The full latent variable model showing the relationships between self-reported cognitive and metacognitive strategy use and SLTP produced some unexpected findings. This model is presented in Figure 5.16.

5. Findings and discussion

Figure 5.16
**Model of the Relationships Between Strategy Use and SLTP:
(from the Full Latent Variable Model – 4.2)**

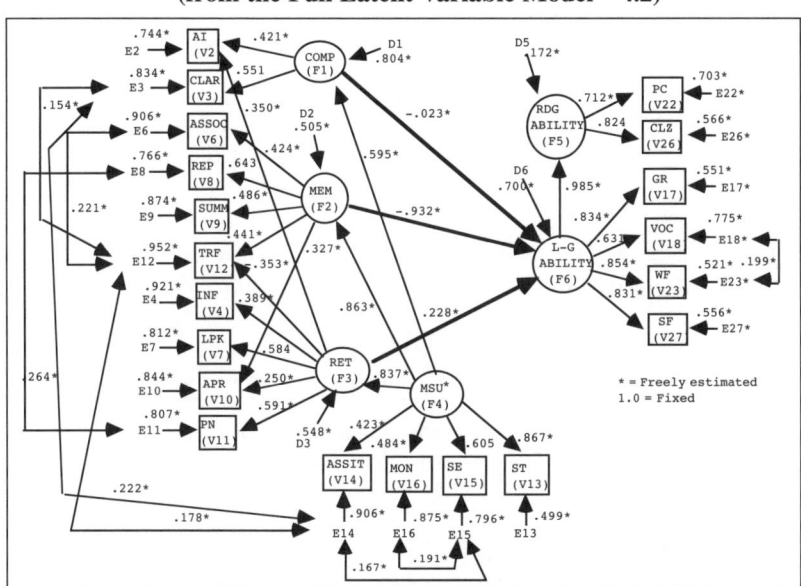

[Figure 5.16: Path diagram showing latent variables COMP (F1), MEM (F2), RET (F3), MSU (F4), RDG ABILITY (F5), L-G ABILITY (F6) with observed indicators AI (V2), CLAR (V3), ASSOC (V6), REP (V8), SUMM (V9), TRF (V12), INF (V4), LPK (V7), APR (V10), PN (V11), ASSIT (V14), MON (V16), SE (V15), ST (V13), PC (V22), CLZ (V26), GR (V17), VOC (V18), WF (V23), SF (V27), with error terms E2–E27 and disturbances D1–D6, and path coefficients. * = Freely estimated; 1.0 = Fixed]

I had originally hypothesized that both cognitive strategy use and metacognitive strategy use would exert a direct, positive impact on SLTP; however, contrary to expectation, these effects did not appear in the data. In fact, surprising as it might be, metacognitive strategy use as a latent trait showed no direct impact on SLTP, but did have a significant, indirect effect (-.135) on SLTP by means of the cognitive strategy use. The standardized and non-standardized values for the indirect effects are presented in Table 5.17.

These results are important for two reasons. First, an examination of the non-standardized effects showed that, for example, "assessing the situation" or "monitoring" alone did not significantly affect performance, but that using metacognitive strategies to invoke one or more of the RET-type strategies did. Also, given the strong relationships between metacognitive strategy use and cognitive strategy use, it would be misleading to say that cognitive strategy use works alone to affect performance. In other words, even though a repertoire of cognitive strategies is important in the learning and use processes, cognitive strategy use seems to function in concert with metacognitive strategy use, which functions in an executive capacity. In short, a student needs to use metacognitive and cognitive strategies together to maximize learning or performance.

These findings have significant implications for the modeling of strategic knowledge in Bachman's (1990) and Bachman and Palmer's (1996) model of communicative language ability. In fact, they show that one can no longer

5. Findings and discussion

operationalize strategic competence solely in terms of a metacognitive component; rather, strategic competence should minimally include cognitive strategy use and metacognitive strategy use. Finally, this model clarifies the nature of Bachman and Palmer's (1996) interaction between strategic competence and language ability, because here strategic competence clearly exerts an effect on performance.

Second, the fact that metacognitive strategy use had no direct impact on performance seemed somewhat curious, as this finding suggests that perhaps "too much thinking" on what might be perceived by many test-takers to be a speeded language test[12] could have a deleterious effect on performance. It would be interesting to examine if this relationship is, indeed, observed when performance is measured within the context of language learning, rather than language use or testing, where students would be less pressured to perform in the act.

Table 5.17
Decomposition of Indirect Effects of SLTP

Decomposition of effects with standardized values
Parameter indirect effects

SLTP = F6 = 0.000*V4 (INF) +   0.000*V7 (LPK) + 0.000*V15 (SE) + 0.000*V16 (MON)
             -0.000*F1 (COMP)   - 0.000*F2 (MEM) + 0.198*F3 (RET) -   0.135 F4 (MSU)
              0.176 E4 (INF) +   0.172 E7 (LPK) + 0.370 E15 (SE) + 0.083 E16 (MON)
             -0.018 D1 (COMP) - 0.471 D2 (MEM) + 0.233 D3 (RET)

Decomposition of effects with nonstandardized values
Parameter indirect effects

SLTP = F6 = 0.000*V4 (INF) + 0.000*V7 (LPK) + 0.000*V15 (SE) + 0.000*V16 (MON)
             0.000   0.000   0.000   0.000
            16.500   68.956   37.158   23.662

            -0.000*F1 (COMP) - 0.000*F2 (MEM) + 0.937*F3 (RET) - 0.300 F4 (MSU)
             0.000   0.000   0.130   0.071
           -28.511   -45.446   7.182   -4.252

             0.421 E4 (INF)   + 0.585 E7 (LPK)   + 1.657 E15 (SE) + 0.265 E16 (MON)
             0.066   0.105   0.136   0.081
             6.413   5.550   12.158   3.286

            -0.078 D1 (COMP) - 3.327 D2 (LPK) + 2.016 D3 (LPK)
             0.186   0.367   0.435
            -0.419   -9.065   4.631

F1 = COMP processes; F2 = MEM processes; F3 = RET processes; F4 = MSU

N.B.
Line 1 presents the amount of indirect impact in nonstandardized values; line 2 presents the standard error and line 3 shows the significance of the path (≥1.96 = significance at the 0.05 level).

5. Findings and discussion

The effect of cognitive strategy use on SLTP also presented some unexpected results. First, I had originally hypothesized that the COMP, MEM and RET processes would each have a direct impact on both reading and lexico-grammatical ability. This seemed to make sense since one would presume that in taking a set of reading and grammar tests, the test-taker would have to use the COMP strategies to decode input, the MEM strategies to remember it (especially in reading) and the RET strategies to get information from long-term memory, and that this process would be invoked in both the reading and grammar subtests. However, such a relationship was not observed in the data. Rather, Model 4.2 showed that the COMP, MEM and RET processes had a direct impact on lexico-grammatical ability, but no direct influence on reading ability. This finding is, perhaps, not so surprising when considering the fact that grammar ability had such a strong influence on reading ability in the *FCE Anchor Test*, as previously observed, and the fact that the *Anchor Test* is essentially a test of lexico-grammatical ability.

Further examination of these relationships revealed that the COMP processes produced an extremely low, direct, negative influence (-.023) on lexico-grammatical ability, an effect which was not statistically significant, but one which did significantly improve model–data fit. This seems to suggest that the test-takers' use of the COMP processes had no noticeable effect on how well they performed on the grammar or reading sections of the *Anchor Test*. Further examination of the indirect effects of the COMP processes on reading and lexico-grammatical ability, as seen in Figure 5.17, also showed no significant impact. Finally, in an effort to explore the relationships between the COMP processes and reading ability, models were tested in which the individual analyzing inductively and clarifying strategy-types were hypothesized to have a direct impact on reading, apart from the shared effects of the general COMP factor. However, these paths were also found to be statistically nonsignificant.

Inspecting these relationships further, I found that the MEM processes produced a very large, direct, *negative* effect on lexico-grammatical ability (-.932), a statistical effect that was significant. This finding appeared surprising at first until the relationship between the strategies that explain the MEM processes was related to the kinds of behaviors that might be invoked during language use or test-taking. From a substantive point of view, the MEM processes, characterized by strategies such as associating (new words with sounds or places), repeating (new words), rehearsing (scripts to practice oral communication), summarizing (new information), transferring (grammar or vocabulary from L1 to L2) and applying rules, are, for all practical purposes, behaviors that might be more closely associated with "learning" than with language use or test-taking. For that reason, it does not appear surprising to see that the more the students reported their use of the MEM processes in a language use or testing situation, the worse they would perform. This situation might even be exacerbated if the test-taker perceived the

5. Findings and discussion

test to be speeded, in which case the use of MEM strategies might deter from retrieval of information from long-term memory, resulting in poor performance. Conversely, the less students used the MEM (or COMP) strategies in language use or test-taking situations, the better the students might perform, provided they spend their time on the metacognitive behaviors and on retrieval. In sum, these findings suggest that "good test-taking strategies" might be empirically defined as the ability to retrieve information from long-term memory without spending time trying to "learn" or "remember" during a test. After all, to utilize both types of strategies on a test takes more time, which would most definitely have an impact on rate of recall, a common measure in language aptitude and intelligence tests. Similarly, "good language use strategies" might involve the same process if taken in the context of a face-to-face interaction.

Finally, the RET processes represented the only factor that had a direct, *positive* impact on lexico-grammatical ability, and although the magnitude of that impact was modest (0.228), it was still statistically significant. In other words, behaviors such as "analyzing inductively," "inferencing," "linking with prior knowledge," "applying rules" and "practicing naturalistically" seemed to have a positive effect on lexico-grammatical ability.

These findings raise two important issues about test-taking style or the characteristic ways in which individuals orient to the test-taking process. The first relates to a description of the nature of an individual's cognitive, test-taking style. The results in this study suggest that cognitive test-taking style might be characterized along a continuum ranging from process or learning-oriented to product or testing-oriented. Thus, a product-oriented test-taker might be characterized as one who views test input simply as the context from which to provide the expected response (i.e., to retrieve information), and a process-oriented test-taker as one who views test input as the opportunity to remember (i.e., learn) as well as to retrieve. In this characterization, the latter would invoke both MEM and RET processes, while the former would simply engage the RET processes.

A second issue relates to the impact that an individual's test-taking style might have on performance, a question already investigated by Hansen and Stansfield (1981) and Stansfield and Hansen (1983). The above finding suggests that we can define cognitive test-taking style according to the type of cognitive processes a test-taker invokes during testing and the degree to which the test-takers use the cognitive processes. From this, we might postulate that product-oriented test-takers would perform better on tests than process-oriented test-takers. Clearly, the notion of test-taking style as it relates to the MEM and RET processes is intriguing and merits further investigation.

The "specific" effects of self-reported cognitive and metacognitive strategy variables on SLTP

The standard structural equation models seen in the previous sections allowed for the exploration of the consequences of general constructs on each other. These

5. Findings and discussion

standard models, however, ignore the potentially important, "specific" effects that V-variables might have on F-factors (V->F) or the effects that a uniqueness might have on another component in the model (Bentler, 1992). In the current study, I examined numerous relationships between the observed variables and the lexico-grammatical and reading ability factors for any potential "specific" effects; however, as seen in Figure 5.17, only four strategy-type variables exhibited significant, special effects on lexico-grammatical ability, apart from the shared effect that they had on it by their underlying factors.

The two most interesting of these "special effects" involve "inferencing" (V4) and "linking with prior knowledge" (V7), both of which produced a positive, direct influence on lexico-grammatical ability with significant loadings of 0.191 and 0.212 respectively. More precisely, these "specific" effects are associated with both the direct effect that each strategy had on lexico-grammatical ability[13] as well as the indirect effect the underlying factor and its associated uniqueness had on lexico-grammatical ability. For example, this model shows a specific effect of linking with prior knowledge (V7) on lexico-grammatical ability (F6). This represents the direct impact of "linking with prior knowledge" (V7) on lexico-grammatical ability (F6). However, since "linking with prior knowledge" consists of $0.584F3 + E3$, we note that F3 and E7 also have an indirect effect on lexico-grammatical ability (F6) via "linking with prior knowledge." Therefore, aside from the effect that these variables had on lexico-grammatical ability as RET processes, "inferencing" and "linking with prior knowledge" also impacted lexico-grammatical ability specifically. Similarly, the RET strategies showed both a direct and an indirect impact on lexico-grammatical ability via the "inferencing" and "linking with prior knowledge" strategies.

Substantively, the special effect of "inferencing" on lexico-grammatical ability seems to explain some of the variability in lexico-grammatical ability that relates to vocabulary knowledge, since both the "inferencing" items (34 and 37) refer to the test-takers' strategies in relating words with meaning. Similarly, the special effect of "linking with prior knowledge" on lexico-grammatical ability seemed to explain some of the variability in the model stemming from the test-takers' reported use of prior topical knowledge (items 1, 2, 6, 22). These findings seem to suggest a special role that "meaning" or prior knowledge structures contribute to test score variation. In short, strategies relating to "inferencing" and "linking with prior knowledge" seem to play an important role in SLTP, a role that certainly merits further examination.

Similarly, two metacognitive strategy use variables, "self-evaluating" and "monitoring." produced a direct, positive effect on lexico-grammatical ability, with significant loadings of 0.465 and 0.095 respectively. In this case, the shared variance of the metacognitive strategy use showed no direct effect on SLTP other than through their indirect influence on the cognitive strategy use factors and through their indirect influence on the "monitoring" and "self-evaluating" variables. Nonetheless, the specific effects of "monitoring" and especially "self-evaluating"

5. Findings and discussion

did yield a significant, direct, positive impact on lexico-grammatical ability.

These results are interesting in that they enabled us to identify the "specific" effect that an observed variable (e.g., inferencing) had on an SLTP factor (e.g., lexico-grammatical ability), regardless of whether the underlying processing factor associated with that observed variable (e.g., RET processes) had a direct effect on an SLTP factor (e.g., lexico-grammatical ability) or not. As all strategy variables in the model were tested in this manner and only four produced significant effects on lexico-grammatical ability, these relationships, as Bentler (1992) suggested, do have a potentially important effect and deserve examination.

Figure 5.17 highlights these special effects in the schematic representation of the full latent variable model.

Figure 5.17

Model of the Cognitive and Metacognitive Strategy Use and SLTP: the Specific Effects of Individual Variables on SLTP

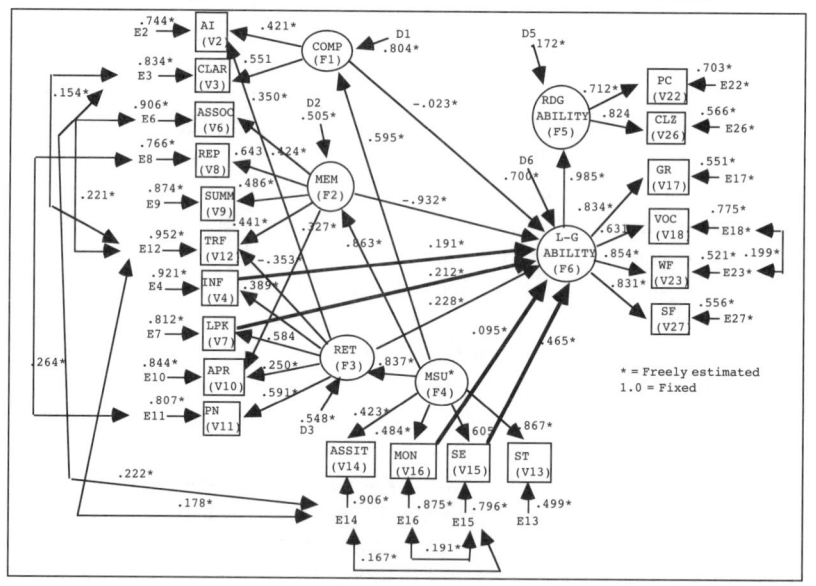

Summary

This chapter used the composite variables generated in Chapter 4 to postulate and test models of the inter-relationships between strategy use and SLTP. Separate CFAs were performed on each of the three measurement models and the initially-hypothesized models were all rejected. Following this, a series of post hoc analyses were performed until substantively-sound models which fit the sample data were found. These analyses confirmed the multidimensionality of cognitive strategy use and SLTP, but rejected the multidimensionality of metacognitive strategy use. Then, the full latent variable model of the inter-relationships between strategy use and SLTP was formulated. The results showed that SLTP was explained by a lexico-grammatical ability and a reading ability factor, with lexico-grammatical ability showing a strong relationship with reading ability. Metacognitive strategy use showed a highly significant, direct impact on cognitive strategy use, but no direct influence on SLTP, while cognitive strategy use had a mixed effect on SLTP, where the COMP processes had no impact on SLTP at all, the MEM processes had a direct, negative impact on lexico-grammatical ability, and the RET processes had a direct, positive one. Finally, four observed variables were found to have a significant, specific, direct effect on lexico-grammatical ability.

In the next chapter, I will use this baseline model of strategy use and performance to determine if this model holds across high and low-ability groups.

Endnotes

1. An earlier and an abbreviated version of this chapter was presented at the 1996 American Association for Applied Linguistics Conference in Chicago and subsequently published in 1997 in *Language Learning*, 47, 2, 289–294.
2. If one or more variables had been multivariately non-normally distributed, interpretations based on the chi-square statistic and on the CFI might have been problematic.
3. If this is so, the ML method of estimation would seriously invalidate hypothesis testing (Hu et al., 1992). In this event, Bentler (1992) recommends using an estimation method that assumes an underlying normal distribution (e.g., ML), and then using a test statistic that accounts for the nonnormality such as the Satorra-Bentler Scaled Statistic (S-Bχ^2) in the assessment of model fit.
4. "Robust" refers to the fact that the S-Bχ^2 statistics and the standard errors associated with these errors are valid in spite of the fact that the normality assumption may have been violated.
5. EQS provides diagnostics to identify the five cases in the sample that contribute most to normalized multivariate kurtosis. This is not in the form of an absolute value for identifying outliers, but rather those five cases and their corresponding estimates are assessed relative to each other. In this analysis, it was difficult to determine which cases were outside the range relative to each other; therefore, a series of analyses were performed in which cases were eliminated one by one and the effect examined.
6. $\chi^2(41)$ (for Model 1.1) = 705.740   CFI = 0.717
   $\chi^2(26)$ (for Model 1.2) = 102.301   CFI = 0.963
   $\Delta\chi^2(15)$ = 603.439 Δ = 0.246

5. Findings and discussion

7. Based on $\partial = 0.05$, the test statistic must be greater than ± 1.96.
8. The possibility of a higher-order was examined and both the correlated factors model (Model 1.2) and the higher-order factor model provided reasonable representations of CP. For the purposes of the current study, however, Model 1.2 was utilized because the treatment of separate, but intercorrelated, cognitive use factors allowed for a more direct investigation of the relationship (1) between these factors and the metacognitive strategies on the one hand and (2) between these factors and the SLTP factors on the other.
9. This makes a total of ten cases so far that have been dropped from the analyses. Six cases were deleted from the CSU analyses and four from the MSU analyses.
10. The GR and the VOC composites come from the discrete-point grammar and vocabulary section of the test, Section 1. Since the EFAs in Chapter 4 produced two discrete factors, a grammar factor and a vocabulary factor, these two composites were treated as separate subtests.
11. In examining for a higher-order factor, I posited a model with a fixed path (at 1.0) from SLTP to reading ability, a necessary imposition in order to allow the model to be identified. However, EQS produced a warning message that the variance of D2 was constrained at the lower bound. Furthermore, this model produced a chi-square statistic of 582.461 with 8df and a CFI of 0.892, values that clearly indicated a significant degree of model–data misfit.

    To address the warning message, I could have imposed an equality constraint (as suggested by Bentler, 1992; Rindkoff & Rose, 1988) between the variances of the disturbances, leaving the path from SLTP to RDG ability free to be estimated and the model to be identified; however, given these results and the notion of an artificial constraint to the model, I decided to use the two-factor model of SLTP.

    Furthermore, with factors correlated at 0.979, the question is whether the correlation could be considered 1.0 or whether a one-factor model would fit significantly worse. To determine this, I performed a chi-square difference test with the results seen below.

    $\chi^2(9)$ (for a 2F Model) = 77.600   CFI = 0.988
    $\chi^2(8)$ (for a 1F Model) = 73.593   CFI = 0.987
    $\Delta\chi^2(1)$ = 4.007 $\Delta = 0.001$

    These results show that the models are significantly different at .01 level ($\chi^2(1) < 6.638$); however, they show no significant difference at the .05 level ($\chi^2(1) > 3.841$). Given this ambiguity, I used the 2-factor model in the analyses based on substantive rationale.
12. Some test-takers might have considered the *Anchor Test* to be "speeded" since they were only given an hour and a half to complete it. Further support for this notion stems from the relatively high number of test-takers who did not finish at least one section of the test (approximately 280) and who were subsequently dropped from the analyses. (For more information, see the section in Chapter 3 regarding missing data.)
13. Bentler (1990) states that if analyzed simultaneously with other strategies which have a common effect stemming from a group of actions, the unique consequence of a strategy can be determined.

6 Multiple-group analyses[1]

Introduction

In Chapter 5, a baseline model for examining the relationships between strategy use and second language test performance was proposed. This entire-group model showed that the strategic behaviors of test-takers influenced how they performed on second language tests, thereby providing empirical support for what Wesche (1987) and Chamot, Küpper and Impink-Hernandez (1988) had alluded to—that the relationships between strategy use and second language proficiency are extremely complex and at times very subtle given the multidimensional nature of the constructs involved and the number of possible interactions among the variables. The findings in Chapter 5 suggested that (1) high and low-ability learners utilize strategies differently and that (2) these differences relate to the differential performance of successful and unsuccessful language learners. However, before claims about group-specific models based on ability level can be made, we first need to model the relationships between strategy use and performance for each ability-level group separately; then, the web of relationships needs to be examined for both groups together to determine the degree to which these models are indeed similar. In other words, if we wish to determine whether the final model of strategy use and performance in Chapter 5 held for each ability-level group (high and low) and across each group, we need to test the invariance of the factorial structure of each group by estimating the parameters for the two groups simultaneously. To do this, we would have had to impose cross-group equality constraints and test statistically for invariance across the parameters of interest.

Given that these cross-group assumptions have not been tested for thus far, the goal of Chapter 6 is to investigate the degree to which the whole-model of strategy use and performance holds for the individual ability-level groups and the degree to which these two models are invariant when modeled separately and simultaneously. A simultaneous comparison of the two ability-group models could provide invaluable information on how successful and unsuccessful learners process tests.

135

The high and low ability groups

To perform the multi-group analyses, I divided the 1,382 study participants into a high-ability group (N = 234) and a low-ability group (N = 941). Ability level was defined by the student's total score on the *FCE Anchor Test* and by the UCLES cut-off scores for the different levels. Test-takers who had total scores between 34 and 60 were placed in the high-ability group and those with scores between 2 and 22 were included in the low-ability group. The 15 percent in the middle were not included in the study.

Multi-group procedures and analyses

Although multi-group structural equation modeling procedures were mentioned in Chapter 3, a more complete and detailed description of these procedures is warranted here.

Preliminary statistical studies

Similar to the single-group analyses seen in Chapter 5, I routinely performed a number of statistical procedures with the different group-related data sets. I first calculated descriptive statistics and inspected the assumptions regarding univariate and multivariate normality. I then examined the assumptions relating to the maximum likelihood estimation procedures (i.e. multivariate normality with Mardia's coefficient, identification and the number of iterations for data convergence). All estimation procedures relating to the multi-sample modeling were again based on covariance matrices generated from raw data (see Appendices O and P). Maximum likelihood was used as the method of estimation throughout the multi-group analyses.

Multi-group SEM procedures

In this chapter multi-group analysis was used to determine if the relationships in the model of strategy use and performance posited in Chapter 5 were invariant when they were examined across the high and low ability-level groups. However, prior to testing the hypotheses related to cross-group invariance, I performed a series of preliminary single-group analyses (1) to establish a baseline model for each ability-level group and (2) to examine the degree to which these two models were different. In comparing these models, one may observe that the individual baseline models for each group are different for certain parameters: a strong possibility when dealing with high and low-ability groups. Such cases do not preclude subsequent simultaneous tests for invariance (Byrne, Shavelson & Muthén, 1989); however, it is natural that this divergent information would be included in the models and the variant parameters modeled as "unconstrained" across groups. In the context of multi-sample structural equation modeling, Byrne (1989) refers to this as *partial measurement invariance*.

Once these baseline models were identified, I examined cross-group equivalence by imposing between-group equality constraints on the parameters to be tested for invariance. The null hypothesis tests for between-group invariance on specific parameters in the model. In other words, it tests to see if parameter x in group one is equal to parameter x in group two. If the null hypothesis is rejected ($p<0.05$), we say the parameters in question are variant across the groups; if the null hypothesis cannot be rejected ($p\geq0.05$), the parameters are said to be invariant across groups, or the parameter functions in the same way for both groups. In EQS, the Lagrange Multiplier (LM) Test serves as a means of assessing the univariate and multivariate tenability of these cross-group equality constraints.

In the current study, I performed the following analyses for each ability-level group. I first analyzed the three measurement models for the high and low ability-level group. This involved separate, single-group analyses of the cognitive strategy use, metacognitive strategy use and SLTP models for the high and low-ability groups. This was followed by separate analyses of the full latent variable model of relationships between strategy use and SLTP again for the high and low-ability groups. These models represented the best fit to the data based on substantive meaningfulness, model parsimony and adequate model–data fit (CFI$\geq$0.90).[2]

Once the individual baseline (full latent variable) models had been established, I formulated a multi-group model including both groups so that these models could be estimated *simultaneously* as outlined in Bentler (1992) and Byrne (1994). To do this, I imposed a series of cross-group equality constraints on all parameters of interest. These parameters included the cross-group invariance of the factor loadings (F–>V) in the measurement models, the cross-group equivalence of the regression paths (F–>V) in the structural models, and the cross-group equivalence of the factor variances. Other parameter equivalences (i.e. the factor disturbances and the observed variable error variances and covariances) were not examined. Also eliminated from these cross-group constraints were the parameters that existed in one model, but not in the other, as well as the fixed parameters. Once the equality constraints were imposed, the models were estimated, and at the same time, simultaneous, univariate, multivariate tests of cross-group equivalence were performed. I was then able to assess the tenability of the constraints by inspecting the results of the LM Test. This procedure allowed me to identify the source of univariate and multivariate non-invariance in the model, since the LM test produces a univariate and multivariate LM Chi-square statistic along with a probability value for each constraint. If the probability value is greater than 0.05, the hypothesized equality constraint is said to hold across the two groups. In other words, the two groups are invariant on that parameter. If, however, the parameters are observed to be variant ($p \le 0.05$) across groups, the multi-sample model is respecified to reflect the cross-group non-equivalence and the model is reestimated. This procedure was performed iteratively until a model with only tenable cross-group constraints was identified.

I might note at this point that this explanatory use of SEM in which models are iteratively modified in order to "establish" a model with a significantly good fit, also known as specification search, is a somewhat controversial topic in the SEM literature (MacCallum, 1995; MacCallum, Roznoswki & Necowitz, 1992). In this regard, I should add that the criteria for model respecification were not limited to statistical fit. Rather, model respecification decisions were first based on substantive meaningfulness of the model and model parsimony. In this way, SEM was used in a more heuristic, model-generating fashion proposed by Jöreskog (1993).

Results and discussion of the multi-group analyses

Descriptive statistics of the high and low-ability groups

Table 6.1 presents the descriptive statistics for each variable in the high and low-ability groups. A comparison of the strategy means across group showed that the high-ability group reported using only five strategies more frequently than the low-ability group did. These included three cognitive strategy use strategies (inferencing, linking with prior knowledge and practicing naturalistically) and two metacognitive strategy use strategies (self-evaluating and monitoring). All other strategies were reportedly used more by the low-ability group. The means for the test performance variables were obviously higher for the high group. The standard deviations for each variable showed an acceptable range of variation. Finally, all values for univariate skewness and kurtosis were within the acceptable range with regard to univariate normality. Also, as seen in Table 6.1, the values for the Mardia's coefficient adequately satisfied the assumptions of multivariate normality. Based on these statistics, no significant violation in univariate or multivariate normality was observed.

Table 6.1

Descriptive Statistics for High and Low-Ability Groups

	Mean		SD		Skewness		Kurtosis	
	Low*	High*	Low*	High	Low*	High*	Low*	High*
Cognitive Strategy Use (CSU)								
Analyzing Inductively (AI)	2.66	2.60	1.02	1.15	-.13	.02	-.31	-.53
Clarifying/Verifying (CLAR)	2.65	2.44	1.20	1.12	-.03	-.16	-.63	-.68
Inferencing (INF)	3.44	4.04	.99	.96	-.40	-1.03	-.48	.51
Associating (ASSOC)	2.50	1.96	.88	.81	-.02	.11	-.28	-.21
Linking w/Prior Knowledge (LPK)	3.14	3.47	.79	.80	-.24	-.47	.05	-.02
Repeating/Rehearsing (REP)	3.29	2.73	.91	1.04	-.38	.03	-.29	-.63
Summarizing (SUMM)	2.51	1.94	1.14	1.22	-.00	.51	-.52	-.39
Applying Rules (APR)	3.53	3.34	.88	1.02	-.48	-.73	-.11	.33
Practicing Naturalistically (PN)	3.03	3.13	.99	.86	-.12	-.10	-.66	-.55
Transferring from L1 to L2 (TRF)	2.05	1.55	1.08	.98	.20	.50	-.66	.03
Metacognitive Strategy Use (MSU)								
Self-Testing (ST)	3.52	3.18	.72	.79	-.45	-.27	-.13	-.51
Assessing the Situation (ASSIT)	3.13	2.90	.78	.92	-.44	-.51	.26	-.02
Self-Evaluating (SE)	3.68	4.07	.64	.54	-.54	-.73	-.13	.33
Monitoring (MON)	3.35	3.61	.80	.75	-.22	0.29	0.28	0.20
Second Language Test Performance (SLTP)								
Grammar (GR)	2.27	8.53	1.42	1.71	-.57	-.48	.19	-.16
Vocabulary (VOC)	2.48	5.02	1.43	.91	.17	-.83	-.58	1.08
Passage Comprehension (PC)	3.41	7.22	1.60	1.35	.11	-.76	-.39	.57
Word Formation (WF)	1.73	7.67	1.40	1.51	.79	-.64	.14	.24
Cloze (CLZ)	2.22	8.44	1.35	2.59	.37	-.06	-.17	-.64
Sentence Formation (SF)	1.46	6.43	1.22	1.74	.92	-.32	.78	-.42

*Low Group: N = 941; High Group: N = 234

High group
Multivariate kurtosis
Mardia's coefficient (G2,P) = 10.5129   Normalised estimate = 2.7106

Low group
Multivariate kurtosis
Mardia's coefficient(G2,P) = 11.6586   Normalised estimate = 5.9958

6. Multiple-group analyses

Separate baseline models of strategy use and SLTP

Each model in the subsequent analyses was compared to the whole-group, baseline model of the relationships between strategy use and SLTP seen in Figure 5.17. This whole-group model presented a one-factor model of metacognitive strategy use, a three-factor model of cognitive strategy use, and a two-factor model of SLTP. Metacognitive strategy use was represented by one general assessment factor; cognitive strategy use by the comprehending, memory and retrieval factors; and SLTP by lexico-grammatical and reading ability factors.

As for the strucural model, metacognitive strategy use had a significant, direct, positive effect on cognitive strategy use, but surprisingly, no significant, direct impact on SLTP. Then, cognitive strategy use produced both a direct, positive and a direct, negative impact on lexico-grammatical ability, but had no significant, direct influence on reading ability. Finally, lexico-grammatical ability had a strong direct influence on reading ability.

At issue then is the equivalence of this model across the two ability-level groups. If the models are not found to be equivalent, how do they differ and how might this impact our understanding of how test-takers process language tests?

The separate high ability-level model

Of the numerous models tested, the baseline model of strategy use and SLTP for the high-ability group, presented in Figure 6.1 appeared to fit the data well both statistically and substantively. This model produced a CFI of 0.910, indicating an acceptable representation of the sample data. All parameter estimates in the model were substantively credible and statistically significant at the 0.05 level.

In examining the assumptions underlying the statistical procedures, I first inspected the sample statistics for univariate and multivariate normality and found the variables to be univariately and multivariately normal. I also examined the other statistical assumptions of the ML estimation procedure (e.g. identification and number of iterations) and no significant violations in the data were found.

An examination of the measurement model for the separate, high-ability group revealed a number of similarities to the model presented in Figure 5.17. Metacognitive strategy use was well-measured by one general assessment factor represented by the self-testing (0.907), assessing the situation (0.317), self-evaluating (0.471) and monitoring (0.371).

6. Multiple-group analyses

Figure 6.1
Separate Group Analysis for Strategy Use and SLTP: Model of High-Ability Learners

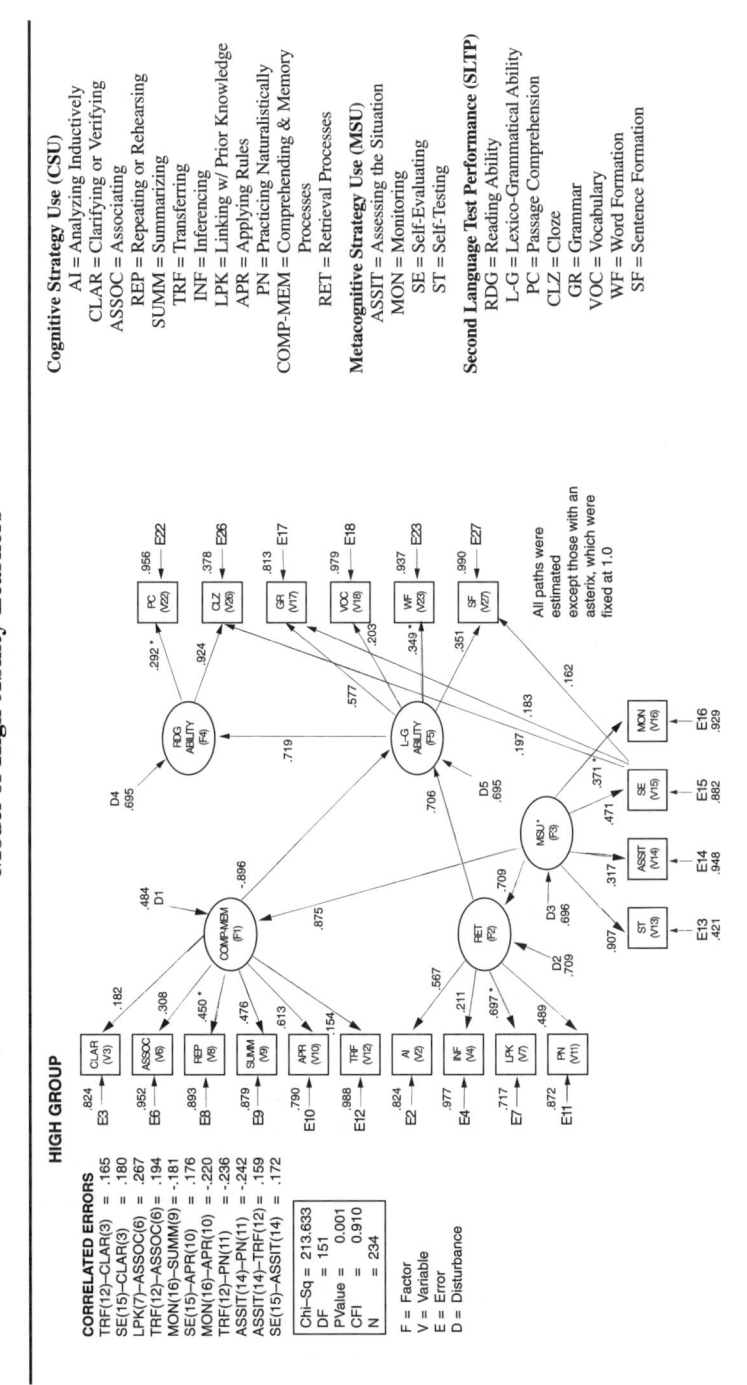

6. Multiple-group analyses

Then, with regard to cognitive strategy use, the separate high-ability data produced a somewhat different model from the one presented in figure 5.17. First, this model presented a two rather than a three-factor model of cognitive strategy use in which cognitive strategy use consisted of a combined comprehending-memory factor (COMP-MEM) and a retrieval (RET) factor. Interpreted in the context of information processing, cognitive strategy use in this model might be viewed uniquely as a set of intake and retrieval processes, where the COMP-MEM factor was explained by clarifying/verifying (0.182), associating (0.308), repeating/rehearsing (0.450), summarizing (0.476), applying rules (0.613), and the L1–L2 transfer strategies (0.154), while the RET factor was represented by analyzing inductively (0.567), inferencing (0.211), linking with prior knowledge (0.697) and practicing naturalistically (0.489). Also, unlike the whole-group model, the high-ability group produced no cross-factor loadings, but did produce a number of correlated errors between the strategy types of the same measuring instruments, an expected finding with learner background characteristic scales measured by questionnaires. The error correlations ranged from 0.159 to 0.267 and suggest that redundant content is being measured across the scales. For example, a relatively high error correlation (0.267) was observed between the linking with prior knowledge and associating error terms. Given these two strategy types, one could easily imagine these strategies tapping into similar content.

Finally, similar to the whole-group model, the multidimensional construct of SLTP was well-measured by two highly-related factors: lexico-grammatical (L-G) and reading (RDG) ability. L-G ability was represented by the grammar (0.577), vocabulary (0.203), word formation (0.349) and sentence formation (0.351) subtests, and the RDG ability by the passage comprehension (0.292) and cloze (0.924) subtests. Although in Figure 5.17, L-G ability had an extremely strong, direct effect on the RDG ability (0.985) for the entire group, L-G ability had a lesser effect on RDG ability (0.719) for the separate, high-ability group. Nonetheless, this influence was still fairly large and statistically significant.

With regard to the structural model, we see in Figure 6.1 that metacognitive strategy use displayed no significant, direct effect on lexico-grammatical ability, but similar to the entire-group model, did have a strong, direct impact on cognitive strategy use. More precisely, metacognitive strategy use produced a significant, positive effect on both the COMP-MEM (0.875) and RET (0.709) factors, thereby confirming for the high-ability group the executive role that metacognitive strategy use seemed to exert over cognitive strategy use.

This relationship might be further examined by looking beyond the direct effects of metacognitive strategy use on cognitive strategy use toward the indirect and total effects. To explain further, the direct effect of one variable (latent or observed) on another is indicated by the path between the two

6. Multiple-group analyses

variables, the indirect effect of one variable on another is the product of the paths that connect them, and the total effect of one variable on another is the sum of the direct and indirect effects (Bentler, 1995). In Figure 6.1, for example, we see that the direct effect of MSU on RET was 0.709, and the direct effect of RET on AI was 0.567; the indirect effect of MSU on AI is 0.402 (.567 x .709), and the total effect of MSU on AI is 0.402 (0 + .402). In this case, the total effect is the same as the indirect effect, since there is no path between MSU and AI, and hence no direct effect.

With this in mind, further evidence of the influence of metacognitive strategy use on cognitive strategy use is seen by examining the parameter total effects (which includes both the direct and indirect effects in the model) produced by EQS. A decomposition of the total effects is seen in Table 6.2. The results relating to COMP-MEM and RET show that aside from the *direct* effects of metacognitive strategy use on these factors, metacognitive strategy use also had a significant, *total* effect on all the variables measuring COMP-MEM and RET. These total effects ranged from 0.134 for L1–L2 transferring to 0.537 for applying rules.

Table 6.2

**Parameter Total Effects for the Separate
High-Ability Group with Standardized Values**

The Effect of MSU on Observed CSU Variables		**The Effect of MSU on Observed SLTP Variables**		**The Effect of MSU on Latent SLTP Variables**	
AI (V2)	0.402*	GR (V17)	-.078	RDG (F4)	-.204
CLAR (V3)	0.159*	VOC (V18)	-.058	L-G (F5)	-.284
INF (V4)	0.150*	PC (V22)	-.060*		
ASSOC (V6)	0.269*	WF (V23)	-.099*		
LPK (V7)	0.494*	CLZ (V26)	-.096		
REP (V8)	0.393*	SF (V27)	-.024		
SUMM (V9)	0.417*				
APR (V10)	0.537*				
PN (V11)	0.346*				
TRF (V12)	0.134*				

The Effect of COMP-MEM on Observed SLTP Variables		**The Effect of RET on Observed SLTP Variables**		**The Effect of COMP-MEM and RET on RDG**	
GR (V17)	-.518*	GR (V17)	0.408*	COMP-MEM (F1)	-.645*
VOC (V18)	-.182*	VOC (V18)	0.143*	RET (F2)	0.508*
PC (V22)	-.188*	PC (V22)	0.148*		
WF (V23)	-.312*	WF (V23)	0.246*		
CLZ (V26)	-.596*	CLZ (V26)	0.469*		
SF (V27)	-.315*	SF (V27)	0.248*		

The Effect of L-G on Observed RDG Variables					
PC (V22)	0.210*				
CLZ (V26)	0.664*			* = significant at the 0.05 level	

143

6. Multiple-group analyses

Table 6.2 highlights the role that metacognitive strategy use played in how the high-ability test-takers deployed the cognitive strategies. This finding clearly supports the notion of metacognition proposed by Bachman and Palmer (1996) and many other researchers. It also provides strong evidence against Krashen's (1985) Monitor Theory, which characterizes the monitor as a device used specifically for inspecting and altering output of an acquired language system. Rather, as the data show, monitoring, along with the other metacognitive strategies, is invoked in all stages of information processing, from comprehending to retrieval in contexts related to language acquisition, use and test-taking.

With regard to the total effect of metacognitive strategy use on SLTP, it is interesting to note in Table 6.2 that aside from having no significant, *direct* effect on reading or lexico-grammatical ability, metacognitive strategy use (F3) also showed no significant, total effect on RDG ability (-.204), L-G ability (-.284), or on how students performed on the cloze, grammar, vocabulary, and sentence formation subtests. Nonetheless, metacognitive strategy use did have a trivial, but significant, *negative* effect on performance with the passage comprehension (-.060) and word formation (-.099) subtests.

Although metacognitive strategy use displayed no *direct* effect on second language test performance except through cognitive strategy use, and produced only a minor, *indirect* effect on SLTP, there was one observed metacognitive strategy use variable, self-evaluating, which showed a small, but significant, *direct* effect on three observed performance variables.[3] The self-evaluating strategy had a significant, *direct* effect on the grammar (0.183), sentence formation (0.162) and the cloze (0.197) subtests. These effects may be attributed, in part, to the constant reminders the students received to check their work. What is interesting in these findings is that self-evaluating in this model had a dual function. As an indicator of metacognitive strategy use, it played a general role in how high-ability test-takers understood, remembered and retrieved information, but it also played a more specific role in performance by showing a significant, direct effect on the more grammatically-oriented sections of the test, including the cloze. These results suggest that the high-ability test-takers seemed to invoke self-evaluating specifically to focus on the formal properties of the language and in so doing, achieved better performance. In this instance, these results supported Krashen's (1985) Monitor Theory, where the monitor is ascribed an editing function—when conditions permit (i.e. test-taking). These results also appear to support current research on self-assessment that depicts metacognitive strategy use as fundamental to second language acquisition and performance. Clearly, the role of self-evaluating in language learning, use and testing merits further investigation.

With regard to the overall effect of cognitive strategy use on SLTP, the

COMP-MEM factor again showed no significant, *direct* effect on reading ability, but as seen in Table 6.2, it did have a considerable, significant, *total* effect on reading ability (-.645) through the lexico-grammatical factor. More precisely, the COMP-MEM factor exerted a significant, *negative*, total effect on how test-takers performed on the passage comprehension test (-.188) and the cloze subtest (-.596), suggesting that the more the test-takers reported using the COMP-MEM strategies, strategies geared toward decoding and remembering information, the worse they performed.

Similar to the entire-group model, the COMP-MEM factor here displayed a very strong, statistically significant, direct, *negative* impact on the L-G ability (-.896) factor, as seen in Figure 6.1. This effect again demonstrated that the use of the COMP-MEM strategies during a perceived, speeded test on L-G ability seemed to adversely affect performance. In fact, as seen in Table 6.2, the use of the COMP-MEM processes negatively impacted performance on the individual L-G subtests, with significant, total effects ranging from -.182 for vocabulary to -.518 for grammar.

On the other hand, the RET factor produced a statistically significant and a relatively strong, positive, *direct* effect on lexico-grammatical ability (0.706), along with a significant, positive, total effect on the L-G subtests. The values for these effects ranged from 0.143 for vocabulary to 0.408 for grammar.

Finally, the RET factor again showed no *direct* effect on RDG ability, as seen in Figure 6.1, but as seen in Table 6.2, did show a strong, significant, *total* effect (0.508) on reading through the lexico-grammatical ability factor and a significant, *total* effect on the passage comprehension (0.148) and the cloze (0.469) subtests. In other words, the use of the retrieval processes appeared to impact the high-ability test-takers' L-G ability, which, in turn, affected how well they performed on the reading tests. Further evidence of this is observed in Table 6.2 with the significant, total effect the L-G ability had on the passage comprehension (0.210) and cloze (0.664) subtests. These results provide clear evidence that the retrieval strategies worked together with the test-takers' lexico-grammatical ability to enhance test performance on the reading test.

The separate low ability-level model

Following several modifications, the baseline model of strategy use and SLTP for the low-ability group, presented in Figure 6.2, also fit the data well statistically and substantively. It produced a CFI of 0.931, again indicating a relatively modest degree of misfit. The model parameter estimates were substantively viable and statistically significant at the 0.05 level.

6. Multiple-group analyses

Figure 6.2
Separate Group Analysis of Strategy Use and SLTP: Model for Low-Ability Learners

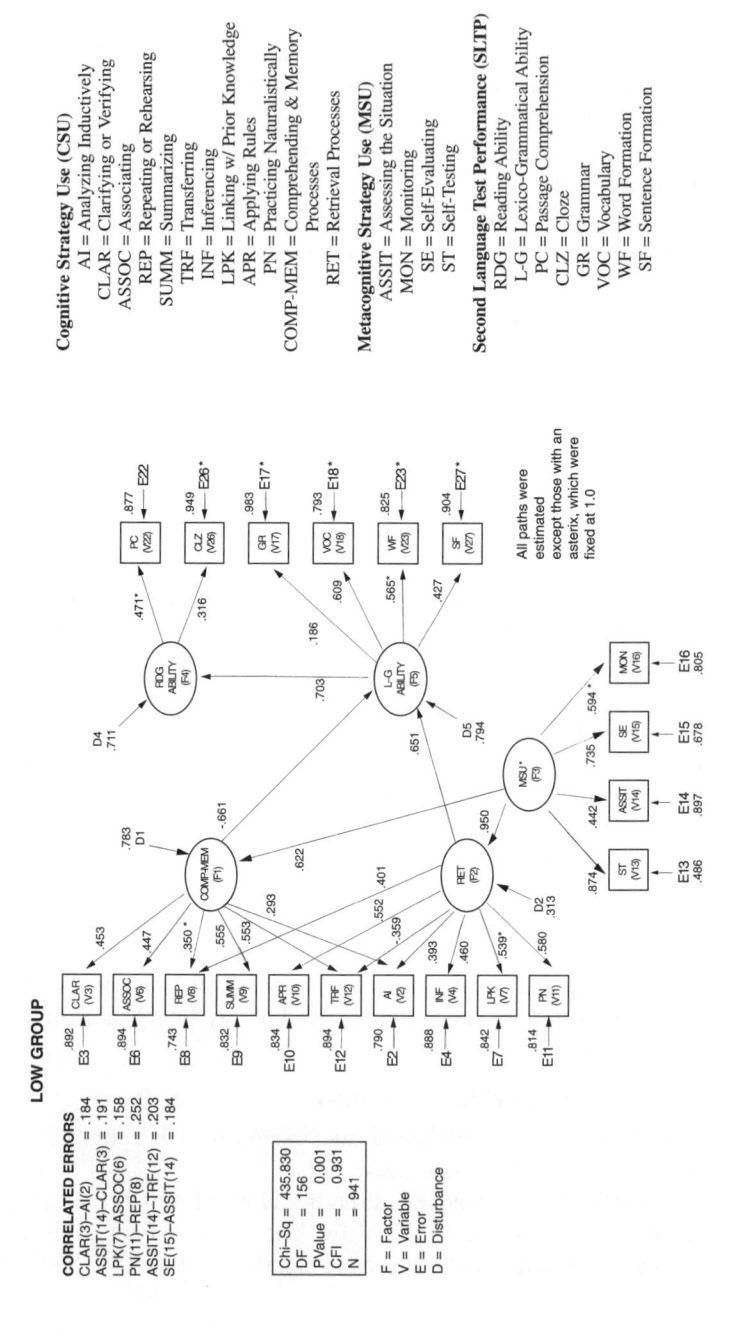

Cognitive Strategy Use (CSU)
- AI = Analyzing Inductively
- CLAR = Clarifying or Verifying
- ASSOC = Associating
- REP = Repeating or Rehearsing
- SUMM = Summarizing
- TRF = Transferring
- INF = Inferencing
- LPK = Linking w/ Prior Knowledge
- APR = Applying Rules
- PN = Practicing Naturalistically
- COMP-MEM = Comprehending & Memory Processes
- RET = Retrieval Processes

Metacognitive Strategy Use (MSU)
- ASSIT = Assessing the Situation
- MON = Monitoring
- SE = Self-Evaluating
- ST = Self-Testing

Second Language Test Performance (SLTP)
- RDG = Reading Ability
- L-G = Lexico-Grammatical Ability
- PC = Passage Comprehension
- CLZ = Cloze
- GR = Grammar
- VOC = Vocabulary
- WF = Word Formation
- SF = Sentence Formation

All paths were estimated except those with an asterix, which were fixed at 1.0

LOW GROUP

CORRELATED ERRORS
CLAR(3)–AI(2)   = .184
ASSIT(14)–CLAR(3) = .191
LPK(7)–ASSOC(6)   = .158
PN(11)–REP(8)   = .252
ASSIT(14)–TRF(12) = .203
SE(15)–ASSIT(14) = .184

Chi-Sq = 435.830
DF   = 156
PValue = 0.001
CFI   = 0.931
N   = 941

F = Factor
V = Variable
E = Error
D = Disturbance

146

6. *Multiple-group analyses*

Again, I found the sample to be univariately and multivariately normal with no significant violations in the data with regard to the statistical assumptions underlying the ML estimation procedure.

Separate low-ability group analyses: the measurement models

With regard to metacognitive strategy use, the separate, low-ability model was again very similar to the ones presented in Figures 5.17 and 6.1. Metacognitive strategy use was explained by self-testing (0.874), assessing the situation (0.442), self-evaluating (0.735) and monitoring (0.594), as seen in Figure 6.2.

As for cognitive strategy use, the low-ability group model was again somewhat different from the one presented in Figure 5.17, as it supported a two rather than a three-factor model of cognitive strategy use. It was, however, similar to the high-ability model in that cognitive strategy use was comprised of the COMP-MEM and RET factors, with COMP-MEM being measured by clarifying/verifying (0.453), associating (0.447), repeating/rehearsing (0.350), summarizing (0.555), L1–L2 transferring (.553), and analyzing inductively (0.293), while RET was explained by repeating/rehearsing (0.401), applying rules (0.552), L1–L2 transferring (-.359), analyzing inductively (0.393), inferencing (0.460), linking with prior knowledge (0.539) and practicing naturalistically (0.580).

Unlike the high-ability model, however, the low-ability group model produced three cross-factor loadings, as seen in model 6.2. These loadings (involving repeating/rehearsing, transferring and analyzing inductively) suggest that learners used these strategies both while trying to understand or remember a second language, and while trying to retrieve second language information from long-term memory for use.

The first cross-factor loading involved repeating/rehearsing. In this case, repeating and rehearsing in the low-ability model captured the dual nature of the variable by loading on both the COMP-MEM (0.350) and RET factors (0.401), whereas in the high-ability model, it was uniquely a measure of COMP-MEM (0.450). This cross-loading suggests that by being exposed to new linguistic input in the test, the low-ability group used this strategy to understand or remember information during the test (i.e. repeating) as well as retrieve it to prepare to answer the questions (i.e. rehearsing). The high-ability group, on the other hand, used this strategy uniquely to understand or remember test input.

The second cross-factor loading involved transferring from L1 to L2, a pattern also observed in the entire-group model. In the low-ability group model, interestingly, the L1–L2 transferring strategies provided a strong *positive* measure of COMP-MEM (0.553), but a *negative* measure of RET (-.359). In other words, the L1–L2 transferring strategies seemed to aid lower-ability learners in comprehending and remembering a second language, but when invoked during retrieval, they interferred with performance. Conversely, the L1–L2 transferring

6. Multiple-group analyses

strategies for the high-ability group, as seen in Figure 6.1, were uniquely a measure of COMP-MEM (0.154), to be used in understanding and remembering, but not necessarily during retrieval.

Finally, analyzing inductively loaded on both the COMP-MEM (0.293) and RET (0.393) factors for the low-ability group, while with the high-ability group, analyzing inductively appeared to be a strong measure of RET (0.567)

In sum, these cross-factor loadings added to the factorial complexity of the low-ability model, suggesting that perhaps cognitive strategy use for the low-ability group might involve a more complex and by extension, a less automatic and less discrete depiction of information-processing than what was seen with the high-ability group.

Aside from the cross-factor loadings, the low and high-ability group models differed in one other way that warrants mention. For the high-ability group, applying rules provided a strong measure of the COMP-MEM strategies (0.631), while for the low-ability group, it only provided a strong measure of retrieval (0.552). In other words, the high performers seemed to be using APR strategies to understand and remember, but not to retrieve information during use, whereas the low-ability group appeared to be using "applying rules" as a measure of retrieval during language use. These results are interesting since they suggest that the explicit application of rules appears to be a fundamental strategy for both groups. As indicated by the strong significant loadings in each model, "applying rules" does not, as Westney (1994) claimed, simply constitute "a manifestation both of a general problem-solving strategy in situations demanding the imposition of some order and of a psychological need for security" (p. 93). Even more interesting is the fact that the application of rules is a very strong indicator of how high-ability students understand and remember a second language, but not a strategy to be invoked during language use. The importance of applying rules in both ability-level models seems to support DeKeyser's (1998) assertion that grammar rules are an important component in how second language learners process grammar and how they contribute to the development of language ability.

The low-ability group model also produced a number of correlated errors between the strategy types of the same measuring instrument. These error correlations ranged from 0.158 to 0.252 and are again suggestive of redundant content across the strategy types. In each case, the correlations again seemed to represent substantively plausible relationships.

Finally, like in both the entire-group model and the high-ability group models, second language test performance was measured by the lexico-grammatical and the reading ability factors for the low-ability group. L-G ability was represented by the grammar (0.186), vocabulary (0.609), word formation (0.565) and sentence formation (0.427) subtests, and RDG ability by the passage comprehension (0.471) and cloze (0.361) tasks. Again, L-G ability showed a very strong, statistically significant, direct effect on RDG ability (0.703) for the low-ability group.

Separate low-ability group analyses: Strategy use and performance

As we have seen with the entire-group and high-ability group models, the metacognitive strategy use factor for the low-group model yielded no significant, direct impact on L-G ability, but did have a strong, direct impact on the cognitive strategy use factors. More precisely, metacognitive strategy use produced a significant, direct, *positive* effect on both COMP-MEM (0.622) and RET (0.950), as seen in Figure 6.2. Again these results further reaffirm the executive role of metacognitive strategy use over cognitive strategy use.

Also, an inspection of the parameter total effects for the low-ability group model, presented in Table 6.3, showed that aside from the *direct* effects of metacognitive strategy use on COMP-MEM and RET, metacognitive strategy use also produced a significant, *total* effect on all the cognitive strategy use variables for the high-ability group except transferring from L1 to L2. These total effects ranged from 0.278 for "associating" to 0.598 for "repeating/rehearsing," effects that appear stronger on average with the low than with the high-ability group.

Table 6.3

Parameter Total Effects for the Separate Low-Ability Group with Standardized Values

The Effect of MSU on Observed CSU Variables		The Effect of MSU on Observed SLTP Variables		The Effect of MSU on Latent SLTP Variables	
AI (V2)	0.556*	GR (V17)	0.035*	RDG (F4)	0.132*
CLAR (V3)	0.282*	VOC (V18)	0.114*	L-G (F5)	0.188*
INF (V4)	0.437*	PC (V22)	0.064*		
ASSOC (V6)	0.278*	WF (V23)	0.106*		
LPK (V7)	0.512*	CLZ (V26)	0.042*		
REP (V8)	0.598*	SF (V27)	0.080*		
SUMM (V9)	0.345*				
APR (V10)	0.524*				
PN (V11)	0.551*				
TRF (V12)	0.003				
The Effect of COMP-MEM on Observed SLTP Variables		**The Effect of RET on Observed SLTP Variables**		**The Effect of COMP-MEM and RET on RDG**	
GR (V17)	-.128*	GR (V17)	0.121*	COMP-MEM (F1)	-.486*
VOC (V18)	-.421*	VOC (V18)	0.396*	RET (F2)	0.458*
PC (V22)	-.234*	PC (V22)	0.220*		
WF (V23)	-.390*	WF (V23)	0.367*		
CLZ (V26)	-.154*	CLZ (V26)	0.145*		
SF (V27)	-.296*	SF (V27)	0.278*		
The Effect of L-G on Observed on RDG Variables					
PC (V22)	0.339*				
CLZ (V26)	0.222*			* = significant at the 0.05 level	

6. Multiple-group analyses

These results again emphasize the important role that metacognitive strategy use played in how the low-ability test-takers used the cognitive strategies—a finding that also held for the high-ability group.

Then, an examination of the *total* effects of metacognitive strategy use on the L-G and RDG ability factors revealed that unlike the high-ability group, metacognitive strategy use for the low-ability group produced a small, but significant, *total* effect on both RDG (0.132) and L-G (0.188) ability. However, although MSU had no significant, total effect on how the high-ability test-takers performed on the cloze, grammar, vocabulary, and sentence formation subtests, it did yield a small, but significant, *total* effect on all the SLTP subtests with the low-ability group. The effects ranged from a negligible 0.035 for the grammar subtest to 0.114 for the vocabulary subtest. These results show that metacognitive strategy use made a statistically significant, indirect contribution to SLTP with the low-ability group in all cases, whereas metacognitive strategy use made almost no statistically significant contribution to SLTP with the high-ability group; however, given the size of the effects in these models, it is difficult to ascertain if metacognitive strategy use actually had anything more than a trivial effect on how the two groups performed on the test.

One further difference between the high and low-ability groups is seen with the self-evaluating strategies. Interestingly, in the high-ability group model, self-evaluating showed a significant, *direct* effect on the grammar, sentence formation and cloze subtests, whereas with the low-ability group, it produced no such effects, even though these students had also been reminded to check their work during the test. This result again seems to highlight the importance that self-evaluating appeared to play in SLTP with the high-ability performers.

With regard to the overall effect of cognitive strategy use on SLTP, the COMP-MEM factor again showed no *direct* effect on reading ability, but did show a relatively strong, statistically significant, *negative*, total effect on RDG (-.486) through the L-G factor. More specifically, the COMP-MEM factor had a significant, negative, total effect on the passage comprehension (-.234) and the cloze (-.154) subtests, suggesting again that the more the test-takers invoked the COMP-MEM strategies—strategies for decoding and remembering information—during a perceived speeded language test, the worse they performed.

Similar to the high-ability group model, the COMP-MEM factor for the low-ability group model had a relatively strong, statistically significant, direct, *negative* impact on lexico-grammatical ability (-.691). Furthermore, it produced a negative, *total* effect on all the individual L-G subtests, with values ranging from -.128 for grammar to -.421 for vocabulary. In short, in both the high and low-ability models, the reported use of these "learning" strategies seemed to negatively impact performance on the *FCE Anchor Test*.

Then, similar to the high-ability group model, the RET factor in the low-ability group model showed a statistically significant and relatively strong, positive, *direct* influence on L-G ability (0.651) and significant, positive, *total* effects on all the L-G subtests, again with values ranging from 0.121 for grammar to 0.367 for word formation.

Finally, RET showed no direct effect on RDG ability, but did have a strong, significant, *indirect* effect on RDG (0.458) through the L-G factor. It also showed a significant, *total* effect on the passage comprehension (0.220) and cloze (0.145) subtests. Furthermore, as seen with the high-ability group, lexico-grammatical ability had a significant, total impact on the passage comprehension (0.339) and cloze (0.222) subtests, again highlighting the role of retrieval and lexico-grammatical ability in reading performance.

In summary, when analyzed separately, the high and low-ability models of the relationships between strategy use and performance were very similar. Each contained five components of the measurement models with MSU, RDG ability and L-G ability yielding the exact same underlying structure for both groups. The COMP-MEM and RET factors produced slightly different structures. Also, cognitive strategy use for the high-ability group appeared more discrete and less complex than with the low-ability group, given the number of cross-loadings in the latter. These findings allude to how the high and low-ability groups might differ in their use of the cognitive strategies. Also, both groups had identical structural models with differences observed in the strengths of the relationships. Finally, the effects that the self-evaluating strategies had on performance with the grammar, vocabulary and close sections of the test were emphasized in the high-ability model.

Although these models appeared similar in many ways, it is impossible to determine from these analyses whether the components of the measurement and structural models actually displayed invariance across both the high and low-ability groups. To claim cross-group equivalence, we would need to estimate the parameters for both groups *simultaneously* and then test each parameter of interest for multi-group invariance.

In the next section, I will test these models for cross-group invariance. The parameters to be tested include the factor loadings in the measurement models (F->V), the path coefficients in the structural models (F->F) and the factor variances. I will then discuss the results of these simultaneously-analyzed, multi-group models and report the results of the cross-group tests of invariance.

6. Multiple-group analyses

Simultaneously-estimated models of strategy use and SLTP

Testing for invariance across ability level

As mentioned earlier, the establishment of separate baseline models of strategy use and SLTP for both groups is a pre-requisite for testing hypotheses related to cross-group invariance (Byrne, 1994). As a result, two separate models of strategy use and SLTP were established in the previous section. However, even though these models produced similar underlying structures, this does not necessarily mean that their measurement and structural models demonstrate equivalence across groups when estimated simultaneously—a much more stringent hypothesis. In other words, even though the high and low-ability groups produced acceptably similar models, the equivalence of the factor loadings might still not hold once the models are analyzed simultaneously with cross-group equality constraints imposed. In this section, I will discuss the cross-group tests of equivalence as well as a multi-group model of strategy use and SLTP, where both groups are analyzed simultaneously and where equality constraints are imposed.

The models in Figures 6.2 and 6.3, considered optimal representations of strategy use and SLTP for both high and low-ability groups, were estimated simultaneously with all the factor loadings in the measurement models, the path coefficients in the structural models and the factor variances constrained to be equal across groups. The paths without equality constraints included those that were fixed to 1.0 for identification purposes and those that existed in one model, but not in the other. To illustrate, the high group model contained no path between applying rules and retrieval, and obviously, a hypothesis of cross-group equivalence would make no sense in this situation. In other words, the simultaneous estimation of two slightly different models invoked the use of partial measurement invariance in testing for the equality of parameters, as explained by Byrne, Shavelson and Muthén (1989). Furthermore, the errors for the observed variables were not constrained to be equal, since they were generally uncorrelated with other variables, and the focus of the investigation was mainly on the invariance of factor loadings, the path coefficients and the factor invariances.

When estimated simultaneously, the fully-constrained, multi-group model of strategy use and performance produced a CFI of 0.895, which was an unacceptable degree of model–data misfit. Therefore, the multivariate tests of equivalence for each parameter were examined and seven of the twenty multivariate equality constraints were found to display probability values associated with the LM Chi-Square statistic of greater than 0.05, suggesting that the hypothesized cross-group equality for those parameters did not hold. In other words, several parameters in the models were different across the two groups. Consequently, these models were re-estimated with the parameters in question specified as unconstrained across the groups and the models reanalyzed. In subsequent analyses, equality constraints were iteratively released and the models retested until all the imposed constraints were statistically tenable.

Among the models examined, a model of strategy use and SLTP for the high and low-ability groups with seven cross-group equality constraints provided a statistically significant and substantively plausible representation of the sample data. It produced a CFI of 0.925, suggesting a reasonably good model–data fit with all parameter estimates significant at the 0.05 level. This simultaneous, multi-group model is presented in Figures 6.3 and 6.4.

6. Multiple-group analyses

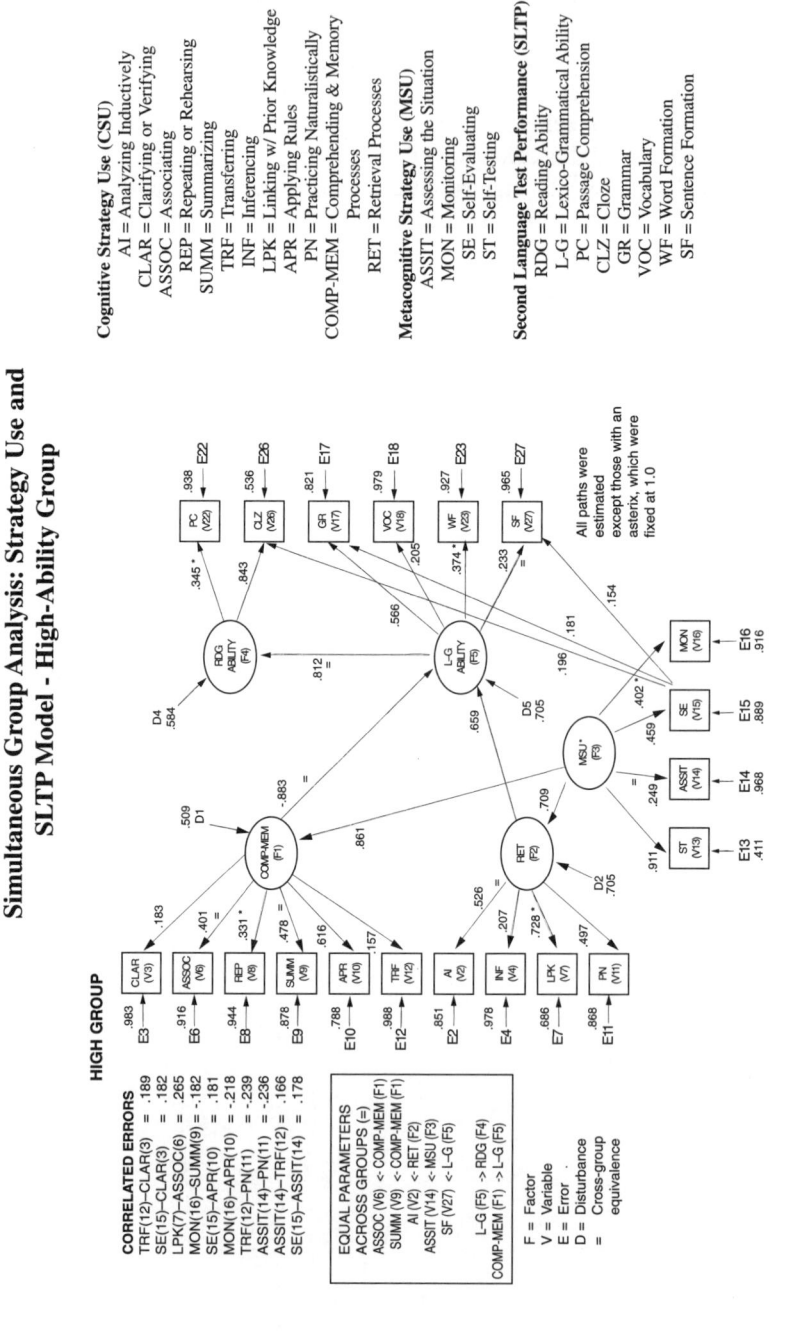

Figure 6.3
Simultaneous Group Analysis: Strategy Use and SLTP Model - High-Ability Group

Figure 6.4
Simultaneous Group Analysis: Strategy Use and SLTP Model - Low-Ability Group

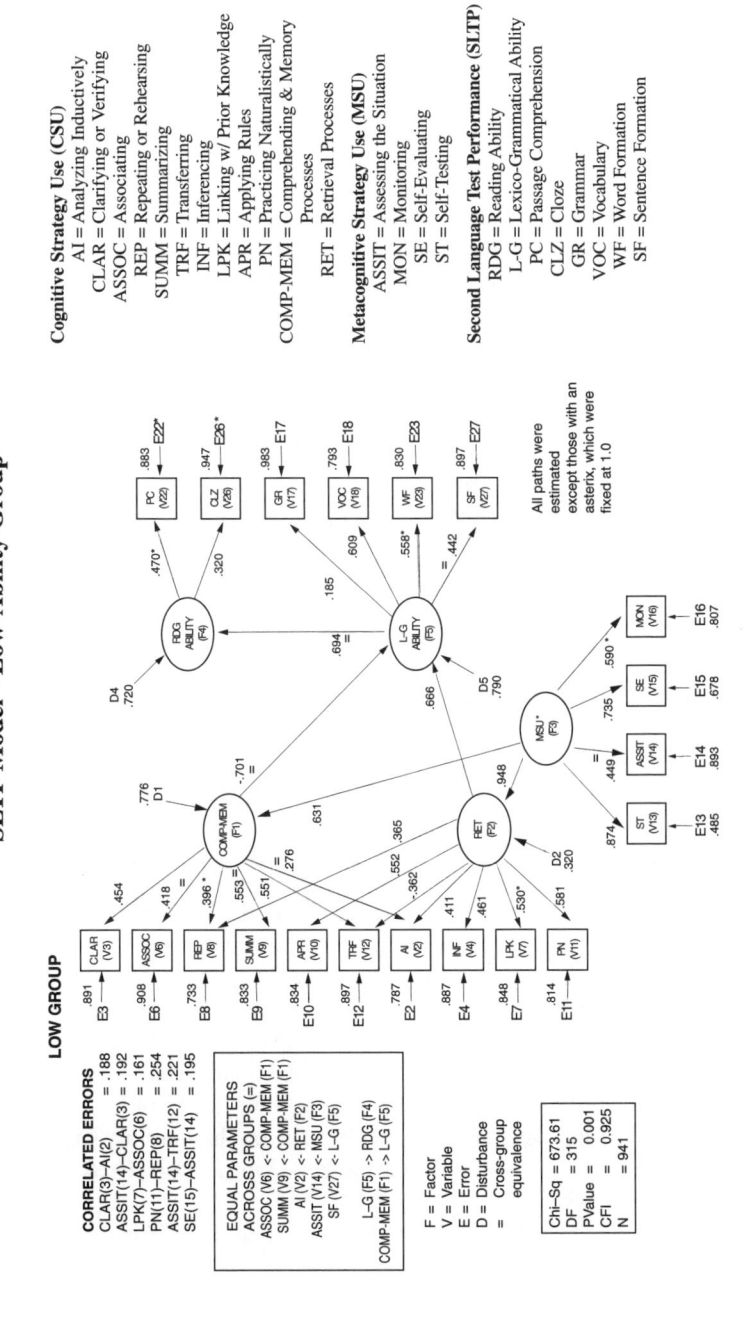

Cognitive Strategy Use (CSU)
AI = Analyzing Inductively
CLAR = Clarifying or Verifying
ASSOC = Associating
REP = Repeating or Rehearsing
SUMM = Summarizing
TRF = Transferring
INF = Inferencing
LPK = Linking w/ Prior Knowledge
APR = Applying Rules
PN = Practicing Naturalistically
COMP-MEM = Comprehending & Memory Processes
RET = Retrieval Processes

Metacognitive Strategy Use (MSU)
ASSIT = Assessing the Situation
MON = Monitoring
SE = Self-Evaluating
ST = Self-Testing

Second Language Test Performance (SLTP)
RDG = Reading Ability
L-G = Lexico-Grammatical Ability
PC = Passage Comprehension
CLZ = Cloze
GR = Grammar
VOC = Vocabulary
WF = Word Formation
SF = Sentence Formation

All paths were estimated except those with an asterix, which were fixed at 1.0

LOW GROUP

CORRELATED ERRORS
CLAR(3)–AI(2)   = .188
ASSIT(14)–CLAR(3)   = .192
LPK(7)–ASSOC(6)   = .161
PN(11)–REP(8)   = .254
ASSIT(14)–TRF(12)   = .221
SE(15)–ASSIT(14)   = .195

EQUAL PARAMETERS ACROSS GROUPS (=)
ASSOC (V6) < COMP-MEM (F1)
SUMM (V9) < COMP-MEM (F1)
AI (V2) < RET (F2)
ASSIT (V14) < MSU (F3)
SF (V27) < L-G (F5)

L-G (F5) -> RDG (F4)
COMP-MEM (F1) -> L-G (F5)

F = Factor
V = Variable
E = Error
D = Disturbance
= = Cross-group equivalence

Chi-Sq = 673.61
DF   = 315
PValue = 0.001
CFI   = 0.925
N   = 941

6. Multiple-group analyses

Simultaneous analyses: The measurement models

In modeling both groups simultaneously, a number of cross-group patterns were observed. In this section, I will first discuss the results of these analyses and then examine the results of the tests of cross-group equivalence.

With regard to metacognitive strategy use, the high and low-ability models produced identical factorial structures. In both cases, MSU was represented by self-testing, assessing the situation, self-evaluating and monitoring, as seen in Figure 6.3 and 6.4. However, a comparison of MSU for both groups, presented in Table 6.4, showed that the factor loadings for assessing the situation, self-evaluating and monitoring were higher with the low-ability group, whereas the loading for self-testing was higher with the high-ability group. In other words, the metacognitive strategy variables on average seemed to be stronger measures of MSU for the low-ability group than for the high-ability one.

Table 6.4

Simultaneous Group Analysis: MSU for the High and Low-Ability Groups

High-Ability Group	Low-Ability Group
ST = V13 = .911 MSU + .411 E13	ST = V13 = .874 MSU + .485 E13
ASSIT = V14 = .249 MSU + .968 E14	ASSIT = V14 = .449 MSU + .893 E14
SE = V15 = .459 MSU + .889 E15	SE = V15 = .735 MSU + .678 E15
MON = V16 = .402 MSU + .916 E16	MON = V16 = .590 MSU + .807 E16

MSU = Metacognitive Strategy Use
ST = Self-testing   SE = Self-evaluating
ASSIT = Assessing the situation   MON = Monitoring

With regard to cognitive strategy use, the high-ability model was also similar to the low-ability model as they both supported a two-factor structure of CSU that included an underlying COMP-MEM factor and retrieval factor. Also, COMP-MEM in both groups was measured by clarifying/verifying, associating, repeating/rehearsing, summarizing, and transferring from L1 to L2, and in all cases, these strategies loaded more heavily on COMP-MEM for the low-ability group than they did for the high-ability group. APR was uniquely a measure of COMP-MEM for the high-ability group, whereas it was only a measure of RET for the low-ability group. These results are seen in Table 6.5.

Table 6.5

Simultaneous Group Analysis: CSU for the High and Low-Ability Groups

High-Ability Group	Low-Ability Group
AI = V2 = .526 RET + .851 E2	AI = V2 = .276 C-M + .411 RET + .787 E2
CLAR = V3 = .183 C-M + .983 E3	CLAR = V3 = .454 C-M + .891 E3
INF = V4 = .207 RET + .978 E4	INF = V4 = .461 RET + .887 E4
ASSOC = V6 = .401 C-M + .916 E6	ASSOC = V6 = .418 C-M + .908 E6
LPK = V7 = .728 RET + .686 E7	LPK = V7 = .530 RET + .848 E7
REP = V8 = .331 C-M + .944 E8	REP = V8 = .396 C-M + .365 RET + .733 E8
SUMM = V9 = .478 C-M + .878 E9	SUMM = V9 = .553 C-M + .833 E9
APR = V10 = .616 C-M + .788 E10	APR = V10 = .552 RET + .834 E10
PN = V11 = .497 RET + .868 E11	PN = V11 = .581 RET + .814 E11
TRF = V12 = .157 C-M + .988 E12	TRF = V12 = .551 C-M − .362 RET + .897 E1

CSU = Cognitive Strategy Use
AI   = Analyzing Inductively   TRF = Transferring
CLAR = Clarifying or Verifying   INF = Inferencing
ASSOC = Associating   LPK = Linking with Prior Knowledge
REP = Repeating or Rehearsing   APR = Applying Rules
SUMM = Summarizing   PN   = Practicing Naturalistically
C-M = Comprehending & Memory Processes RET = Retrieval Processes

---

Then, RET with both groups was represented by analyzing inductively, inferencing, linking with prior knowledge and practicing naturalistically. As seen in Table 6.5, analyzing inductively and linking with prior knowledge were stronger measures of RET for the low-ability group, whereas inferencing and practicing naturalistically were stronger measures of RET for the low-ability group. RET was also measured by repeating/rehearsing, applying rules, and transferring from L1 to L2 in the low-ability group model, but not in the high-ability model. In short, the low-ability model again appeared much more complex than the high-ability one.

As seen in Figures 6.3 and 6.4, the cognitive strategy use model differed across ability-group in other ways. For instance, the high-ability model contained no cross-factor loadings; the low-ability model contained three. More precisely, analyzing inductively, repeating/rehearsing and transferring from L1 to L2 loaded on both the COMP-MEM and the RET factors with the low-ability group, but not with the high-ability group. These results provide further support that CSU for the low-ability group involved a more complex cognitive process.

As seen in Table 6.5, further examination of these cross-factor loadings showed that with the low-ability group, analyzing inductively was both a weak indicator of COMP-MEM (0.276) and a moderate indicator of RET

6. Multiple-group analyses

(0.411), whereas with the high-ability group, it served uniquely as a relatively strong measure of RET (0.526). In other words, for the high-ability group, the use of analyzing inductively seemed to contribute to language retrieval or use, but for the low-ability group, it also contributed to understanding and remembering.

Another difference can be seen with the repeating/rehearsing cross-factor loading. For the high-ability group, this strategy measured COMP-MEM (0.396) and RET (0.365). Finally, the L1–L2 transferring strategies produced cross-factor loadings which presented more interesting information on how the high and low-ability groups seemed to differ. With the high-ability group, transferring was a statistically significant, but very weak measure (0.157) of COMP-MEM; it did not measure RET at all. However, with the low-ability group, transferring from L1 to L2 provided a relatively strong, *positive* indicator of COMP-MEM (0.551) and a moderate, *negative* measure of RET (-.362). In other words, the high performers used L1–L2 transfer strategies only to decode or remember information, and given its weak loading on COMP-MEM, this strategy did not appear to play an important role in the process. For the low-ability group, however, transferring was an integral part of how test-takers understood or remembered information, and to a lesser degree, how they retrieved information from long-term memory. Furthermore, given the negative loading, the use of transfer seemed to inhibit retrieval.

To summarize thus far, the results show that when compared, 11 out of 14 metacognitive and cognitive strategy use variables loaded more heavily on the processing factors for the low-ability test-takers. In fact, the only strategies loading more heavily for the high-ability test-takers were self-testing, analyzing inductively and linking with prior knowledge. In spite of the relative effect of these strategies to each underlying factor, these findings provide clear evidence that both the high and low-ability groups utilized these strategies, a finding that controverts the claims made by Rabinowitz and Chi (1987), who argued that students invoke strategies only at the beginning stages of language learning when they are consciously trying to learn, and that the strategies cease to be strategic at the later stages when language use has become automatized. Conversely, the data show that strategies contribute to each stage of the language learning and testing process as suggested by O'Malley and Chamot (1990). What does occur, however, is that the strategies variables for the low-ability group generally loaded more heavily on the strategy use factors than with the high-ability group. This finding might be explained by the psycholinguistic processes of automatization and restructuring put forth by McLaughlin (1987, 1990) in which automatized language is said to be accessed more quickly and with little effort. Given this notion, it may be that the high-ability test-takers felt less inclined to report

6. Multiple-group analyses

these strategies.

Turning now to the relationships between the metacognitive and cognitive strategy use when the models were analyzed simultaneously, we see that metacognitive strategy use produced a very strong, statistically significant, *direct* effect on COMP-MEM and RET with both groups. These results reconfirm the executive role of metacognitive strategy use over cognitive strategy use. A comparison of the direct effects, presented in Figures 6.3 and 6.4, showed that MSU had a greater impact on the COMP-MEM factor for the high-ability group (0.861) than for the low-ability group (0.631), whereas it had a stronger influence on the RET factor for the low-ability group (0.948) than for the high-ability group (0.709).

A closer examination of the effects of metacognitive strategy use on cognitive strategy use showed that for the low-ability group, MSU had on average a relatively strong, statistically significant, total effect on all the COMP-MEM and RET variables except for transferring from L1 to L2. For the low-ability group, values ranged from 0.286 for clarifying to 0.596 for repeating/rehearsing. For the high-ability group, MSU had a strong, significant total effect on analyzing inductively, associating, repeating, summarizing, applying rules and practicing naturalistically, with values from 0.258 for repeating to 0.530 for applying rules. For the high-ability group, MSU had a strong, significant total effect on analyzing inductively, associating, repeating, summarizing, applying rules and practicing naturalistically, with values from 0.285 for repeating to 0.530 for applying rules. However, the total effect of MSU was non-significant for clarifying/verifying, inferencing and transferring from L1 to L2. These results showed that although MSU played a strong role in how both groups used the cognitive strategies, it had, on average, a stronger total effect on the low ability-group model than it did on the high ability-group model, as seen in Table 6.6. This again suggests that information processing at the lower levels of proficiency appear to require more effort.

Table 6.6

Simultaneous Group Analysis: Total Effects of MSU on CSU for the High and Low-Ability Groups

The Effect of MSU on Observed CSU Variables

High Ability Group		Low Ability Group	
AI (V2)	0.383*	AI (V2)	0.564*
CLAR (V3)	0.158	CLAR (V3)	0.286*
INF (V4)	0.147	INF (V4)	0.437*
ASSOC (V6)	0.345*	ASSOC (V6)	0.264*
LPK (V7)	0.516*	LPK (V7)	0.502*
REP (V8)	0.285*	REP (V8)	0.596*
SUMM (V9)	0.412*	SUMM (V9)	0.349*
APR (V10)	0.530*	APR (V10)	0.523*
PN (V11)	0.352*	PN (V11)	0.551*
TRF (V12)	0.135	TRF (V12)	0.005

* = significant at the 0.05 level

CSU = Cognitive Strategy Use		MSU = Metacognitive Strategy Use	
AI = Analyzing Inductively		TRF = Transferring	
CLAR = Clarifying or Verifying		INF = Inferencing	
ASSOC = Associating		LPK = Linking with Prior Knowledge	
REP = Repeating or Rehearsing		APR = Applying Rules	
SUMM = Summarizing		PN = Practicing Naturalistically	

Finally, with regard to SLTP, the high and low-ability measurement models again produced an identical underlying factorial structure. As seen in Figures 6.3 and 6.4, SLTP was represented by a lexico-grammatical and reading ability factor, with L-G ability being measured by the grammar, vocabulary, word formation and sentence formation subtests, and RDG ability by passage comprehension and cloze.

A comparison of SLTP for both groups, presented in Table 6.7, showed that among the L-G ability variables, grammar loaded more heavily (0.566) on L-G ability with the high-ability group, whereas the loadings for vocabulary (0.609), word formation (0.558) and sentence formation (0.442) were stronger measures of L-G ability with the low-ability group. These results suggest that the grammar subtest is perhaps a better measure of L-G ability for the high-ability group, and the vocabulary subtest a better indicator of L-G ability for the low-ability group.

Table 6.7

Simultaneous Group Analysis: SLTP for the High and Low-Ability Groups

High-Ability Group	Low-Ability Group
GR = V17 = .181 SE +.566 L-G +.821 E17	GR = V17 = .185 L-G +.983 E17
VOC = V18 = .205 L-G +.979 E18	VOC = V18 = .609 L-G +.793 E18
PC = V22 = .345 RDG +.938 E22	PC = V22 = .470 RDG +.883 E22
WF = V23 = .374 L-G +.927 E23	WF = V23 = .558 L-G +.830 E23
CLZ = V26 = .196 SE +.843 RDG+.536 E26	CLZ = V26 = .320 RDG +.947 E26
SF = V27 = .154 SE +.233 L-G +.965 E27	SF = V27 = .442 L-G +.897 E27
RDG = F4 = .812 L-G +.584 D4	RDG = F4 = .694 L-G +.720 D4
L-G = F5 = -.883 C-M+.659 RET +.705 D5	L-G = F5 = -.701 C-M+.666 RET +.790 D5

SLTP = Second Language Test Performance

GR = Grammar
VOC = Vocabulary
PC = Passage Comprehension
CLZ = Cloze
WF = Word Formation
SF = Sentence Formation

C-M = Comprehending & Memory Processes
RET = Retrieval Processes
MSU = Metacognitive Strategy Use
RDG = Reading Ability
L-G = Lexico-Grammatical Ability
SE = Self-Evaluating

Then, among the RDG variables, the cloze subtest loaded more heavily (0.843) on RDG ability for the high-ability group, whereas the passage comprehension subtest showed a stronger loading (0.470) on RDG for the low-ability group, suggesting here that the cloze might be a better indicator of RDG ability for the high-ability group and the multiple-choice passage comprehension test a better indicator of reading for the low-ability group. These findings come as no surprise since it is generally believed that one of the challenges in doing cloze tests is the need to integrate top-down and bottom-up processing of the text in a productive mode, whereas in multiple-choice tests of reading, fewer items typically require top-down processing, which is the case in the *FCE Anchor Test*. Also, the task requires selection of answers rather than production, which could be a less confounding way of assessing reading ability for learners who have limited English production skills.

It is also interesting to note that when the models were analyzed simultaneously, the self-evaluating variable in the MSU measurement model again yielded a significant, direct effect on the grammar (0.181), sentence formation (0.154) and cloze (0.196) subtests for the high-ability group, but not for the low-ability group. Again, these findings suggest that the high-ability group appears to be more aware of the importance of checking their "grammar" before handing in their tests with the grammar-related sections of

6. Multiple-group analyses

the test and checking their answers on the cloze, which is perceived by most students to be a grammar, rather than a reading task. These results seem to reflect the high performers' preoccupation with grammatical accuracy, a common characteristic of learners in EFL situations. Nonetheless, this preoccupation, especially in the context of a language test, made a small, albeit significant, contribution to performance. These findings seem to support the notion that focused attention on grammar (i.e., grammatical awareness) contributes positively to the overall process of second language performance, thereby lending support to Schmidt's (cited in Loschky & Bley-Vroman, 1993) "consciousness hypothesis" which argues that attention to the features of input is a necessary condition for any learning to occur, and here, by extension for high performance on tests as well. These results again conflict with Krashen's (1985) claim that focused attention on the formal properties of the second language leads to unproductive monitoring.

With regard to the relationship between L-G ability and RDG ability, the L-G ability factor produced a strong, statistically significant effect on RDG ability with both groups, as seen in Table 6.7. The direct effect of L-G ability on RDG ability was 0.812 for the high-ability group and 0.694 for the low-ability group, suggesting that L-G ability might play a greater role in how test-takers performed on the RDG test for the high-ability group than for the low-ability group; however, given the size of the disturbances associated with the latent variables, these results must be viewed with some caution.

An examination of the total effects of L-G ability on the observed RDG variables, presented in Table 6.8, showed that for both groups, L-G ability produced a significant, total effect on both the passage comprehension and the cloze subtests. Interestingly, the effect of L-G ability on passage comprehension was 0.280 for the high-ability group and 0.326 for the low-ability group, while L-G ability had a total effect of 0.684 on the cloze test for the high-ability group and 0.223 for the low-ability group. In short, L-G ability seemed to play a large and different role in how test-takers performed on the RDG test.

Table 6.8

Simultaneous Group Analysis: Total Effects of L-G Ability on RDG Variables for the High and Low-Ability Groups

The Effect of L-G on Observed RDG Variables	
High-Ability Group	**Low-Ability Group**
PC (V22) 0.280*	PC (V22) 0.326*
CLZ (V26) 0.684*	CLZ (V26) 0.223*

* = significant at the 0.05 level

Simultaneous analyses: Strategy use and performance

With regard to the effects of strategy use on second language test performance in the simultaneously-analyzed models, the metacognitive strategy use factor again produced no significant, *direct* effect on L-G or RDG ability for either the high or low-ability groups, but when it came to its *total* effects, MSU had a differential effect on each group. A decomposition of the total effects of metacognitive strategy use and cognitive strategy use on SLTP is presented in Table 6.9.

Table 6.9

Simultaneous Group Analysis: Total Effects of MSU and CSU on SLTP for the High and Low-Ability Groups

The Effect of MSU on Observed and Latent SLTP Variables

High Ability Group		Low Ability Group	
GR (V17)	-.083	GR (V17)	0.035*
VOC (V18)	-.060	VOC (V18)	0.115*
PC (V22)	-.082	PC (V22)	0.061*
WF (V23)	-.110	WF (V23)	0.105*
CLZ (V26)	-.110	CLZ (V26)	0.042*
SF (V27)	-.002	SF (V27)	0.083*
RDG (F4)	-.238	RDG (F4)	0.131*
L-G (F5)	-.293	L-G (F5)	0.188*

The Effect of COMP-MEM on Observed SLTP Variables

High Ability Group		Low Ability Group	
GR (V17)	-.500*	GR (V17)	-.130*
VOC (V18)	-.181	VOC (V18)	-.427*
PC (V22)	-.248*	PC (V22)	-.229*
WF (V23)	-.330*	WF (V23)	-.391*
CLZ (V26)	-.604*	CLZ (V26)	-.156*
SF (V27)	-.206	SF (V27)	-.310*

The Effect of RET on Observed SLTP Variables

High Abiltiy Group		Low Ability Group	
GR (V17)	0.373	GR (V17)	0.123*
VOC (V18)	0.135	VOC (V18)	0.405*
PC (V22)	0.185	PC (V22)	0.217*
WF (V23)	0.247*	WF (V23)	0.372*
CLZ (V26)	0.451	CLZ (V26)	0.148*
SF (V27)	0.153*	SF (V27)	0.294*

The Effect of COMP-MEM and RET on RDG

High Ability Gropup		Low Ability Group	
COMP-MEM (F1)	-.717*	COMP-MEM (F1)	-.487*
RET (F2)	0.535*	RET (F2)	0.462*

* = significant at the 0.05 level

Table 6.9 (cont.)

SLTP = SL Test Performance
GR = Grammar
VOC = Vocabulary
PC = Passage Comprehension
CLZ = Cloze
WF = Word Formation
SF = Sentence Formation
COMP-MEM = Comprehending-Memory Processes
RET = Retrieval Processes
MSU = Metacognitive Strategy Use
RDG = Reading Ability
L-G = Lexico-Grammatical Ability
SE = Self-Evaluation

First, in addition to having no significant, *direct* effect on performance, metacognitive strategy use for the high-ability group showed no significant, *total* effect on L-G ability either. Nor did it have a significant impact on any of the L-G subtests. These results are surprising since they clearly suggest that MSU seems to have a diminished role in performance with the high-ability test-takers, or as mentioned previously, it may be that these strategies are more automatic for this group, resulting in less of a need for high-ability test-takers to report them.

However, even though MSU had no *direct* effect on performance with the low-ability group, it did show a small, but significant, *total* effect on L-G ability (0.188). It also had a very small, significant, *total* effect on each of the L-G variables (ranging from a negligible 0.035 for grammar to 0.115 for vocabulary). Similarly, metacognitive strategy use had a small, but significant, *total* effect on RDG ability (0.131) with a small, but significant effect on passage comprehension (0.061) and cloze (0.042). In sum, even though these differences do not appear great, the high and low-ability models do appear to be different with regard to the effect of MSU on SLTP.

Turning now to the effects of cognitive strategy use on SLTP, the COMP-MEM factor had a large, significant, direct, *negative* effect on L-G ability (-.883) with the high-ability group, as seen in Figures 6.2 and 6.3. It also showed a significant, total, *negative* influence on grammar (-.500), word formation (-.330) and sentence formation (-.206), but had no significant impact on the vocabulary subtest. Then, with the low-ability group, COMP-MEM also had a large, significant, direct, *negative* impact on L-G ability (-.701), as well as having a large, significant, negative total effect on all of the observed L-G variables (ranging from -.130 for grammar to -.427 for vocabulary). In short, these relationships again suggest that both high and low-ability test-takers who use test time to understand or remember input—strategies used in learning—are ultimately disadvantaged.

Then, COMP-MEM showed no significant, *direct* impact on RDG ability; however, it did produce a large, significant, negative, *total* effect on RDG ability (-.717) with the high-ability group and a significant, total negative effect on passage comprehension (-.248) and cloze (-.604). With the low-ability group, COMP-MEM also had a large, significant, *total* effect on RDG

6. Multiple-group analyses

ability (-.487), as well as a large, significant, negative impact on passage comprehension (-.229) and cloze (-.156). Surprisingly, for both ability-level groups, invoking the COMP-MEM strategies in the context of a reading test again seemed to detract from performance.

Unlike COMP-MEM, the RET factor had a large significant, direct, *positive* effect on L-G ability (0.659) with the high-ability group, as seen in Figure 6.3. Also, it had a significant, positive *total* effect on word formation (0.247) and sentence formation (0.153), but had no significant total effect on the grammar or vocabulary subtests with the high-ability group. With the low-ability group, RET again showed a large, significant, *direct* impact on L-G ability (0.666), as well as a large, significant, *total* impact on all of the observed L-G variables (ranging from 0.123 for grammar to 0.405 for vocabulary). Given the findings with the COMP-MEM strategies, these results are interesting since the RET strategies positively impacted L-G ability with both groups, but specifically, with the low-ability group, the RET strategies influenced all the subtests, while with the high-ability group, RET had a significant influence *only* on those subtests that required words to be transformed from one form to another (i.e., word formation) or a synonymous sentence to be completed based on minimal cues.

Finally, we see that RET again had no *direct* effect on RDG ability with either group. It also had no significant, *total* effect on RDG with the high-ability group. With the low-ability group, however, RET showed a fairly large, significant, *total* effect on RDG ability (0.462). Then, with regard to the RDG subtests, RET showed no significant *total* impact on passage comprehension or the cloze for the high-ability group, but it did have a significant, total impact on passage comprehension (0.217) and on the cloze (0.148) for the low-ability group.

Considering these reading models, the observed differences for the two groups with regard to the direct and especially the total effects of strategy use on reading ability seem to support the claims made by a number of researchers (e.g., Clapham, 1996; Coady, 1979; Cziko, 1980; McLeod & McLaughlin, 1986), who maintain that high and low-ability learners invoke different strategies to read. Clapham (1996) states:

> *I accept McLeod and McLaughlin's proposal (1986) that once an advanced learner is sufficiently familiar with the vocabulary and linguistic rules of a language to be able to decode written text automatically, the learner will be able to make full use of L1 reading processes. It is therefore reasonable to think that for L2 readers there is a continuum from the novice who is learning elementary decoding skills to the highly advanced learner who is capable of using the same reading processes in the first and the second languages (p. 195).*

6. Multiple-group analyses

The challenge still remains, however, to identify the specific nature of these differences.

To summarize, the high and low-ability models clearly showed that strategy use, operationalized by metacognitive strategy use, comprehending-memory and retrieval, had many similar ways of influencing lexico-grammatical and reading ability in the context of the *FCE Anchor Test*. Metacognitive strategy use for both groups produced no significant, *direct* effects on lexico-grammatical ability or reading ability, whereas the COMP-MEM processes for both groups produced a *negative* effect on L-G ability and the RET processes produced a *positive* effect. These models also showed that strategy use clearly affected L-G and RDG ability in a number of different ways, especially when the total effects of these strategies were considered. For example, metacognitive strategy use showed no significant total effect on L-G ability for the high-ability group, but showed a small, but significant total effect on L-G ability for the low-ability group. Similarly, the strategy use variables had total effects on the L-G and RDG subtests that were often very different for the two groups. These findings highlight the role of strategy choice in SLTP, demonstrating that the "effective" use of strategies in second language testing contexts is of primal importance, and they support findings by Chamot *et al.* (1988), who in the context of learning distinguished "effective" from "ineffective" learners based in part on their ability to choose strategies that were appropriate for the task.

Cross-group tests of invariance

While these cross-group comparisons are interesting, they do not indicate whether the parameters in these models are equivalent across groups from a statistical perspective. As a result, a series of cross-group equality constraints were imposed, and the invariance of these parameters was tested. An examination of the multivariate tests of equivalence for each parameter revealed that only seven of the original twenty equality constraints produced probability values associated with the LM Chi-Square statistics of greater than 0.05, indicating that the hypothesized equality for only seven parameters held across the two groups. These results suggest that the measures for metacognitive strategy use, cognitive strategy use and SLTP were not operating in completely the same way for both groups—nor were the relationships between some of the latent variables. The results of these tests of invariance are presented in Table 6.13.

6. *Multiple-group analyses*

Table 6.10

Multivariate Tests of Cross-Group Invariance

EQUALITY CONSTRAINTS	CHI-SQ.	PROB.
(ASSOC <— COMP-MEM)	3.531	.060 (SIG.)
(SF <— L-G)	2.471	.116 (SIG.)
(ASSIT <— MSU)	1.808	.179 (SIG.)
(AI <— RET)	1.521	.218 (SIG.)
(L-G <— COMP-MEM)	1.197	.274 (SIG.)
(SUMM <— COMP-MEM)	3.507	.061 (SIG.)
(RDG <— L-G)	.180	.671 (SIG.)

COMP-MEM = Comprehending-Memory   L-G = Lexico-Grammatical Ability
RET = Retrieval Processes   RDG = Reading Ability
MSU = Metacognitive Strategy Use   SF = Sentence Formation
ASSOC = Association   VOC = Vocabulary
ASSIT = Assessing the Situation
AI = Analyzing Inductively
SUMM = Summarizing

In the metacognitive strategy use model, only one parameter, assessing the situation (thought of as "planning"), held across the two groups; all the other variables were variant across ability level. These results provide clear evidence that the MSU variables load on MSU differently across ability groups. Given the previous analyses, it is not surprising that the high and low-ability groups may be utilizing monitoring, self-evaluating and self-testing differently. However, what is interesting is that the factor loadings of three of the four variables were variant across ability levels in spite of their seemingly equivalent factorial structures.

In the cognitive strategy use model, only three parameters were found to be equivalent across the two groups. These included the loadings between associating and COMP-MEM, summarizing and COMP-MEM, and analyzing inductively and RET. More interestingly, all other parameters were variant across ability levels, demonstrating again that many measures of cognitive strategy use appear to be operating in different ways across the two levels.

Finally, in the SLTP measurement model, only one cross-group equality constraint showed cross-group invariance; the loading between sentence formation and L-G ability operated invariantly across the groups, a curious finding given the nature of the task and the differences in the means for each group. All other parameters of L-G ability and RDG ability were variant across the two groups. Given the nature of these two groups, the fact that the measurement models might operate differently across the two groups comes as no surprise.

In the structural model, two equality constraints held across the two groups. The first involved the path from COMP-MEM to L-G ability. This result is interesting since it showed that in spite of the different path coefficients, the effect of the COMP-MEM strategies on L-G ability was

6. Multiple-group analyses

equivalent across the two groups, thereby suggesting that the use of the COMP-MEM strategies in the context of a test disadvantaged both groups in the same way. These findings further suggest that the differences in L-G ability between the high and low groups might be attributed to the different ways in which each group invoked the RET processes or the different ways in which MSU affected SLTP indirectly.

The second equality constraint in the structural model that held across the two groups involved the path from lexico-grammatical ability to reading ability. This result suggests that again despite the different path coefficients, the impact of L-G ability on RDG ability was equivalent across ability levels. In other words, based on the path coefficients between these variables, it appears clear that both groups rely heavily on their L-G ability to process the text and their reading scores seem to depend on this ability. These results strongly support Carrell's (1988) claim that most ESL students depend a great deal on bottom-up processing. They also clearly provide evidence against Barnett's (1989) assertion that bottom-up processing more typically describes beginning learners since both groups depend on their L-G ability to read. More interesting, however, is that given the cross-group equality of the influence of L-G ability on RDG ability, differences in reading ability might then be attributed to differences in how test-takers invoke both the metacognitive and retrieval strategies. This hypothesis certainly warrants further investigation.

Summary

The purpose of Chapter 6 was to investigate the multi-group relationships between strategy use and SLTP when separate and high and low-ability group models were estimated both individually and simultaneously. The aim was to show that in concurrence with the previous studies on successful and unsuccessful learners, differences exist in the ways that high and low-ability test-takers use strategies and that these different patterns of behavior have a significant impact on second language test performance. To examine these differences, separate baseline models of strategy use and performance were first established for the high and low-ability groups, and these group-sensitive models were estimated simultaneously with a number of cross-group equality constraints imposed. The observed similarities and differences in this simultaneously-analyzed, multi-group model provided the means for assessing the viability of the parameter estimates across ability levels.

Substantively, this chapter showed that the metacognitive strategy use and second language test performance models produced almost the exact same underlying factorial structure for each group, whereas cognitive strategy use produced somewhat different models for each group. These differences related to the observed cross-loadings in the low-ability group and to the different ways in which some strategy-type variables loaded on the underlying factors. Also, this study showed that in spite of these similar structures, metacognitive strategy use, cognitive strategy use and second language test performance appear to be operating, on the whole, in different ways across the two levels, since hypotheses relating to cross-group equivalence on the underlying variables could only be supported with factorial relationships involving assessing the situation, associating, summarizing, analyzing inductively and sentence formation.

Turning to the structural model, the data provided some evidence of cross-group equivalence. The impact of comprehending and storage/memory processes on lexico-grammatical ability and the impact of lexico-grammatical ability on reading ability appeared to be invariant across the two groups. This latter finding provides evidence that lexico-grammatical ability has an equally strong impact on reading ability with both groups. However, the tests of invariance across groups could not be uniformly supported in the data. First, the effect of metacognitive strategy use on cognitive strategy use was found to be variant across the two groups. In other words, with the low-ability group, the metacognitive strategies seemed to have, on average, a stronger total effect on the cognitive strategy and the SLTP variables than with the high-ability test-takers, a result which might be attributed to the fact that the high-ability test-takers have achieved a higher degree of automatization, and, therefore, less of a need to report using these strategies. Second, the effect of the retrieval processes on lexico-grammatical ability was also variant across the groups, implying that the variation in lexico-grammatical ability and reading ability stem from the test-takers' use of the retrieval processes in concert with the metacognitive use strategies.

Methodologically, multi-sample SEM has served as a powerful analytic tool for advancing theory of the relationships between strategy use and second language test performance. Rather than accepting a one-size-fits-all theory, multi-group SEM provides a direct method for simultaneous testing and evaluating cross-group hypotheses about group effects. It can also be used to estimate group-specific parameters of interest such as the factor loadings of the measurement model, the path coefficients of the structural models or other parameters (Scott-Lennox & Lennox, 1995).

Endnotes

1. An earlier and an abbreviated version of this chapter was presented at the 1997 Language Testing Research Colloquium held in Orlando, Florida. Also, an earlier version of this chapter appears in 1998 in *Language Testing, Vol. 15*, No. 3, 333–379, published by Arnold.
2. In this chapter, I performed several single-group analyses on the different components of the measurement models. I will, however, limit the discussion in this chapter to the full latent variable model of strategy use and performance used.
3. Bentler (1990) refers to the impact of one observed variable on another (as well as a host of other non F->V or F->F relationships) as a "special effect."

7 Conclusions

Introduction

This study investigated the relationships between test-takers' reported use of cognitive and metacognitive strategies on the one hand and their performance on second or foreign language tests on the other. This research was motivated by the notion proposed by Bachman (1990) that a portion of the variability in language test performance can be attributed to test-taker background characteristics such as their reported cognitive and metacognitive strategy use. This study also examined the differential performance of high and low-ability test-takers with relation to their cognitive and metacognitive strategy use. In this concluding chapter I will summarize the results of this research as it relates to the questions posed in Chapter 1. I will then briefly discuss the theoretical and methodological implications of the study. Finally, I will conclude by relating the findings in this study to broader issues of second or foreign language pedagogy and assessment.

The research questions: The entire-group analyses

Research question 1: The nature of cognitive strategy use

What is the trait structure of cognitive strategy use as measured by the Cognitive Strategies Questionnaire? In other words, what is the relationship (1) between the cognitive strategy item types (e.g., the "cla-rifying" strategy type) and the cognitive processes (e.g., comprehending, memory and retrieval). Also, what is the relationship (2) among these processes?

In response to this question, I performed a series of confirmatory factor analyses (CFAs) in which hypotheses related to the nature of cognitive strategy use were posited and tested. In the end, I found that a model with three intercorrelated factors, ten measured variables and three correlated errors provided a reasonable explanation of the correlations among the observed variables. These results supported the hypothesis that cognitive strategy use was a multidimensional construct consisting of three underlying processes, which included a comprehending processing factor, memory/storing processing factor and a retrieval processing factor. Each of these processes related to a host of individual strategy types. Also, these processes produced high interfactor correlations, as well as some cross-loadings and correlated errors. In sum, cognitive strategy use was seen as a set of complex, inter-related, cognitive behaviors, contributing differentially to performance.

Research question 2: The nature of metacognitive strategy use

What is the trait structure of metacognitive strategy use as measured by the Metacognitive Strategies Questionnaire? In other words, what is the relationship (1) between the metacognitive strategy item types (e.g., the "monitoring" strategy type) and the metacognitive processes (e.g., goal-setting, planning and assessment). Also, what is the relationship (2) among these processes?

In response to research question 2, I again performed a series of CFAs to examine the nature of metacognitive strategy use. The initially-hypothesized multidimensional construct of metacognitive strategy use consisting of "on-line assessment" and "post-assessment" strategies proposed by Wenden (1991) was rejected. Instead, the data supported a 1-factor model of metacognitive strategy use as an explanation of the correlations among the observed variables. In other words, metacognitive strategy use was not interpreted, as Wenden stated, according to when the behavior occurred—before, during or after the act. Rather, metacognitive strategy use was seen primarily as a single assessment process relating more to the behavior than to the time of the behavior. In this study metacognitive strategy use was measured by strategies for assessing the situation (i.e., planning), monitoring, self-evaluating and self-testing.

Research question 3: The nature of second language test performance

What is the trait structure of second or foreign language test performance as measured by the FCE Anchor Test*?*

Again, CFAs were performed on the SLTP variables and a 2-factor model of second language test performance was found as a reasonable explanation of the correlations among the observed variables. Similar to how the *FCE Anchor Test* had been designed (i.e., reading comprehension and use of English), the 2-factor model of second language test performance consisted of

7. Conclusions

an underlying "reading ability" and "lexico-grammatical ability" factor. The variance in "reading ability" was explained by the test items in the passage comprehension and the cloze tasks, while the variance in "lexico-grammatical ability" was explained by the items in the grammar, vocabulary, word formation and sentence formation tasks. This 2-factor solution produced a high interfactor correlation, suggesting that lexico-grammatical ability and reading ability, as measured by the *FCE Anchor Test*, were not purely independent measures of these abilities, but were highly inter-related. In other words, the ability to read in English was highly influenced by the test-takers' ability to use English grammar and vocabulary.

A closer examination of the subtests suggested that this inter-dependence might be attributed to both the underlying factorial structure of the tasks and the item types used to measure reading ability. In other words, both reading tasks required test-takers to decode input at the lexical and syntactic levels, seemingly triggering bottom-up processing of reading. These tasks also required test-takers to process input at the semantic and discourse levels and to relate information to prior knowledge schemata, invoking top-down processing of reading. However, given the degree of bottom-up processing required in each of these tasks, it follows that lexico-grammatical ability had such a close relationship with reading ability in the *FCE Anchor test*—if not in all standardized tests of reading ability of this type.

Research question 4: The effects of strategy use on SLTP

What is the relationship between the test-takers' reported use of cognitive and metacognitive strategies and their performance on second or foreign language tests?

The relationship between metacognitive strategy use and cognitive strategy use

Prior to looking at the effects of strategy use on second language test performance, the relationship between metacognitive and cognitive strategy use was examined. Metacognitive strategy use had a direct, *positive* impact on all three of the cognitive strategy use variables. More specifically, it had a moderate, *direct* influence on the comprehending processes and a strong, *direct* impact on both the memory and retrieval processes. All three links were statistically significant. These results provided empirical evidence in support of the notion put forth by several researchers (Bachman & Palmer, 1996; Brown *et al.*, 1983; Faerch & Kasper, 1983; O'Malley & Chamot, 1990; Wenden, 1991) that the metacognitive strategy use exert an executive function in the higher order thinking processes, which is used to oversee and manage the cognitive behaviors in language acquisition, use and testing.

7. Conclusions

The relationship between strategy use and SLTP

Then, in exploring the effects of cognitive and metacognitive strategy use on SLTP, I originally hypothesized that both cognitive and metacognitive strategy use would have a *direct*, positive impact on SLTP; however, this relationship was not borne out in the data. Metacognitive strategy use showed no *direct* impact on SLTP although it did have a significant, *indirect* impact on it. These results suggest that the use of metacognitive strategies *alone* does not appear to improve performance in testing contexts. Rather, these results show that "thinking" needs to work in concert with "actions" in order for learners to do well on language tests. More generally, metacognitive ability appears to be a co-requisite for learners to effectively regulate the cognitive strategies they will need in language acquisition, use and testing.

With regard to the effect of cognitive strategy use on SLTP, I had originally postulated that the comprehending, memory and retrieval processes would each have a direct impact on both reading and lexico-grammatical ability; however, again such a relationship was not seen in the data. The comprehending, memory and retrieval processes had a direct impact on lexico-grammatical ability, but unexpectedly, had no direct influence on reading ability.

A closer examination of these relationships showed that the comprehending processes had a very low and non-significant, direct effect on lexico-grammatical ability, suggesting that in the context of a language test, the use of the comprehending strategies had no noticeable effect on performance. This finding was again surprising since I had originally thought that test-takers would have at least needed to use the comprehending strategies to decode the reading. This, however, was not observed in the data.

Conversely, the memory processes produced a very large, direct, *negative* effect on lexico-grammatical ability, which was highly significant. This finding can be attributed to the fact that the strategies that explain the memory processes seemed to be more related to learning behaviors rather than language use or testing behaviors. Thus, it was not surprising to see that the more the test-takers reported the use of the memory processes in a language use or language testing context, the worse they would perform—a situation which might be compounded if the test-taker perceived the test to be speeded. On the other hand, the less a student used the memory strategies, the better they might perform. These findings suggest that "good" test-taking strategies might be empirically defined as the ability to retrieve information from long-term memory without spending time trying to "learn" or "remember" during a test.

Finally, the retrieval processes represented the only factor that had a statistically significant, direct, *positive* impact on lexico-grammatical ability. In other words, behaviors such as analyzing inductively, inferencing, linking

7. Conclusions

with prior knowledge, applying rules and practicing naturalistically seemed to have a *direct*, positive effect on lexico-grammatical ability, as well as an indirect effect on reading ability through the lexico-grammatical factor.

The research questions: The multi-group analyses

Multi-group analyses were used to examine the separate models of strategy use and SLTP for the high and low-ability groups. After examining the models separately, the high and low-ability group models were estimated simultaneously with a number of cross-group equality constraints imposed. The results showed that the high and low-group models of strategy use and performance produced very similar underlying factorial structures. Nonetheless, they also provided clear evidence that cross-group invariance was not uniformly observed in the data. Rather, only seven of the twenty parameters were found to be invariant across groups. In sum, the high and low-ability test-takers do indeed use strategies differently on language tests. In this section, I will briefly summarize these multi-group results.

Research question 5: The nature of SLTP across the high and low-ability groups

> *Is the factorial structure of SLTP as measured by the* FCE Anchor Test *equivalent across high and low ability-level groups? If not, what is the nature of these differences?*

In response to research question 5, the high and low-ability groups produced almost the exact same underlying factorial structure for second language test performance. In both cases, lexico-grammatical ability was represented by grammar, vocabulary, word formation and sentence formation, and reading ability by passage comprehension and cloze. When estimated simultaneously, the cloze task provided a better measure of reading ability for the high-ability group, an expected result given the inferential nature of this task, whereas for the low-ability group, the passage comprehension task was a better measure of reading ability, again a logical result given the limited number of gist and inferencing items and the high number of detail questions in the subtest.

Similarly, the grammar subtest appeared to be a stronger indicator of lexico-grammatical ability for the high-ability group, while the vocabulary and word formation subtests were stronger for the low-ability group. Surprisingly, the sentence formation subtest was found to be invariant across groups.

Finally, similar to the entire-group model, lexico-grammatical ability had a

7. Conclusions

strong, positive effect on reading ability for both groups. The only difference was that lexico-grammatical ability had a slightly greater effect on reading ability for the high group than for the low group. In spite of these differences, the relationship between lexico-grammatical ability and reading ability was found to be invariant across the two groups. In other words, lexico-grammatical ability seemed to play a uniformly large role in how the high and low-ability test-takers performed on the reading subtest.

Research question 6: The nature of cognitive strategy use and metacognitive strategy use across high and low-ability groups

Is the factorial structure of cognitive strategy use and metacognitive strategy use, as measured by the two questionnaires, equivalent across high and low ability-level groups? If not, what is the nature of these differences?

In response to this question, metacognitive strategy use for the high and low-ability groups also produced identical underlying factorial structures, and just as in the entire-group model, it was well-represented by self-testing, assessing the situation, self-evaluating and monitoring. The only difference between these models involved the factor loadings, which in the low-group model were higher than in the high-group model with regard to assessing the situation, self-evaluating and monitoring. Self-testing was the only loading larger in the high-ability group. In this model, in spite of the similar factorial structures, only one parameter, assessing the situation (thought of as planning), was found to be equivalent across the two groups; all other parameters were variant. In other words, metacognitive ability was used differently by the two ability-level groups.

With regard to cognitive strategy use, the high and low-ability groups produced models that differed significantly from the whole-group model. Unlike the whole-group model that supported a three-factor solution of cognitive strategy use, the high and low-group models supported a two-factor solution of cognitive strategy use. Additionally, the high and low-ability group models contained slightly different factorial structures. Each model consisted of underlying comprehending-memory (COMP-MEM) and retrieval factors. COMP-MEM for both groups was represented by clarifying/verifying, association, repeating/rehearsing, summarizing, and transferring from L1 to L2, but analyzing inductively loaded on COMP-MEM for the low-ability group and applying rules loaded on COMP-MEM for the high-ability group. In all cases, the strategies loaded more heavily on COMP-MEM for the low-ability group. A further difference between the high and

7. Conclusions

low-ability groups involved three cross-loadings, which occurred in the low-ability group only. Finally, in comparing the groups, only three parameters (i.e., associating, summarizing and analyzing inductively) were found to be equivalent; all others were variant. These findings provide clear evidence that the cognitive strategies are also utilized differently by different ability-level groups. Furthermore, these results show that cognitive strategy use *alone* is not a sufficient condition for high performance; rather, test-takers need to use strategies "effectively."

Turning to the relationships between metacognitive strategy use and cognitive strategy use, when the models were analyzed simultaneously, both the high and low-ability models were again identical with metacognitive strategy use yielding a strong, direct influence on both the COMP-MEM and RET processes. However, with the high group, MSU produced a stronger effect on COMP-MEM, while with the low group, it yielded a stronger effect on RET. In other words, the low performers exhibited an extremely high degree of metacognitive processing in retrieving information from long-term memory, an indication of lack of automaticity, whereas with the high performers, metacognitive strategy use contributed more to their understanding and remembering. In both instances, however, metacognitive strategy use proved to have a significant, strong effect on cognitive strategy use, just as it did with the entire-group model. In spite of this identical structure, all parameters between metacognitive and cognitive strategy use were found to be variant across the two groups, and metacognitive strategy use had, on average, a stronger total effect on cognitive strategy use with the low-ability group than it did with the high-ability group. These results provide further support for the regulatory role that metacognitive strategy use has over cognitive strategy use, as well as supporting the notion that information processing at the lower levels of second language proficiency appears to require more effort than at the higher levels, when linguistic recall is more automatized.

Research question 7: The effects of cognitive strategy use and metacognitive strategy use on second language test performance across high and low ability-level groups

Is the factorial structure of the relationships between the test takers' cognitive and metacognitive strategy use and their performance on the language test equivalent across high and low ability-level groups? If not, what is the nature of these differences?

In response to research question 7, metacognitive strategy use produced no significant, direct effect on lexico-grammatical ability for either group, but metacognitive strategy use did influence SLTP indirectly through the cognitive strategies. Again these results showed that for the high and low-ability groups, "thinking" and "action" need to work together to produce the best effects.

With regard to the effects of cognitive strategy use on SLTP, the high and low-ability groups produced similar patterns of behavior across the groups. For both groups, the COMP-MEM and RET factors showed no direct impact on reading ability, whereas the COMP-MEM processes had a significant, direct, negative effect on lexico-grammatical ability—a path that was found to be equivalent across groups. This invariance is interesting, since it suggests that the differences in lexico-grammatical ability between the high and low-ability groups might be attributed to the different ways in which the respective groups invoke the retrieval processes, or to the different ways in which metacognitive strategies use might affect SLTP indirectly. Finally, for both groups, the retrieval processes had a significant, direct, *positive* effect on lexico-grammatical ability, suggesting again that test-takers should direct their efforts toward retrieval during language tests, and not toward the more learning-oriented COMP-MEM strategies. More interesting, however, is that given (1) the cross-group equivalence of the effect of the COMP-MEM strategies on lexico-grammatical ability and (2) the cross-group equivalence of the effect of lexico-grammatical ability on reading ability, the differences in reading ability might be attributed to differences in how test-takers use both the metacognitive and retrieval strategies, a finding that certainly warrants deeper examination.

Theoretical implications

As this study drew on second language learner strategy research, second language assessment research and educational psychology to investigate the relationships between the reported cognitive and metacognitive characteristics of test-takers and their performance on language tests, the results presented in this study obviously have a number of implications relating to second language acquisition and second language assessment theory. In this section I will enumerate these.

The nature of strategy use and SLTP

It is clear from this study that prior to making cognitive claims about second language strategy use and performance, one must first define strategy use theoretically within a cognitive framework. The strategy use constructs must then be operationalized with reference to that framework and the instruments used to measure strategy use must be validated before further analyses are carried out. Without strong evidence of construct validation, inferences

7. Conclusions

relating to the nature of strategy use would certainly be suspect.

With this caveat in mind, I designed the questionnaires in the current study within an information-processing framework. The components of the information-processing model were operationalized by means of cognitive and metacognitive strategies. Items were then developed to elicit the test-takers' use of these strategies in the context of language learning, use and testing. Finally, the psychometric characteristics of the instruments were investigated before further analyses were performed.

In examining the construct validity of the questionnaires and the language test instrument, this study has provided several insights on the nature of cognitive strategy use, metacognitive strategy use and second language test performance as measured by the *FCE Anchor Test*.

1. This study first showed that cognitive strategy use, as measured by the Cognitive Strategies Questionnaire, was, in fact, a multi-dimensional construct consisting of a set of comprehending, memory and retrieval processes, and that different strategy types measured different underlying factors. Although some earlier studies have looked at the relationship between individual strategies and performance, the findings in this study clearly showed that cognitive strategy use constitutes a complex set of behaviors that work in concert with one another to affect performance in positive, negative and neutral ways.
2. This study also showed that metacognitive strategy use, as measured by the Metacognitive Strategies Questionnaire, represented a unidimensional construct consisting of a single set of assessment processes. In other words, strategies such as goal-setting, planning, monitoring, self-evaluating and self-testing, often thought of as separate metacognitive strategies, all form part of one underlying construct involving assessment. For example, when a learner sets goals, she *assesses* what she want to achieve; when she plans what do to next, she *assesses* the situation and *assesses* which actions to pursue; when she monitors her work, she *assesses* how she is carrying out the task at hand; when she evaluates her work, she *assesses* the quality of her actions; and when she tests her knowledge or understanding of something, she *assesses* what she thinks she knows or understands.
3. Next, this study showed that the *FCE Anchor Test* measured reading comprehension as UCLES had intended it to do; however, the tasks originally designated by UCLES as measures of reading ability were slightly different from the ones found in the analyses. In other words, reading ability was measured by the passage comprehension, but not by the grammar and vocabulary task as designed. Rather, reading was also measured by the cloze subtest. Also, the use of English section of the *FCE*

Anchor Test was, in fact, a test of lexico-grammatical ability measured by grammar, vocabulary, word formation and sentence formation tasks. More importantly, the results in the current study showed that the test-takers' lexico-grammatical ability was closely related to their reading ability. A closer examination of the reading subtests show that this finding might be expected given that the majority of the reading items were designed to invoke the bottom-up rather than top-down processing of reading. Nonetheless, given this finding, one wonders whether this result is not simply an artifact of the test design or whether this behavioral pattern can be observed with other similar tests of reading ability. One thing for sure, however, is that this pattern is repeatedly observed in all the analyses. Even in the multi-group analyses, a strong relationship between lexico-grammatical ability and reading ability was also observed; it was also found to be invariant across groups.

4. Finally, this study showed that in comparing high and low-ability groups, the parameters in the models of cognitive strategy use, metacognitive strategy use and second language test performance were, on average, variant across the two groups. Even though the models of these constructs produced similar underlying factorial structures, the two groups were approaching the language test from a strategic perspective in different ways.

The relationship between cognitive and metacognitive strategy use

In the 1970s and 1980s, several second language practitioners and researchers treated metacognitive strategies as a separate set of behaviors that could influence how students might perform on a variety of tasks, and more generally, how students would learn a second language. More recently, researchers have argued that the metacognitive processes have a regulatory function over the cognitive processes (which are then assumed to have a positive impact on performance). In other words, "metacognitive knowledge functions in the self-regulation of learning" (Wenden, 1998, p. 528)—and by extension, in the self-regulation of language use and language testing. This relationship is clearly depicted in Gagné, Yekovich and Yekovich's (1993) model of human information-processing.

The current study provides strong evidence that metacognitive processes do indeed exert an executive function over the cognitive processes, a finding that is observed in both single-group and multi-sample models. In other words, students who are capable of using the metacognitive strategies seem to have the wherewithal to use the cognitive strategies. For example, when a student is writing an essay on a test, he may very well *think about* checking

7. Conclusions

his work, but unless self-evaluation translates into specific cognitive behaviors, like applying rules or linking with prior knowledge, the final writing product will not be affected. The assumption is, then, that metacognitive ability influences cognitive ability, which, in turn, has a positive impact on performance.

The effects of strategy use on second language test performance

Probably the most important findings in this study relate to the effects of second language strategy use on SLTP. In this regard, the current study showed that simple linear associations between metacognitive strategy use and second language test performance or between cognitive strategy use and second language test performance are simplistic and inaccurate depictions of the complex nature of the interrelationships. In short, this study revealed that the strategies or the clusters of strategies test-takers report they use in language learning, use and testing do, indeed, appear to have a significant effect on second language test performance. And, in fact, as many strategy researchers have observed, many strategies or strategy clusters have a positive effect. However, what is rarely mentioned in the strategy research is that the use of some strategies or strategy clusters in certain contexts (i.e., testing) may have a negative effect on performance, a result which provides evidence against the commonly-held belief that the more strategies a learner can invoke the better. Rather, these findings clearly support the idea that learners need to know how to use both metacognitive and cognitive strategies effectively. Similarly, this study showed that the greater degree to which a strategy was used did not necessarily correspond to the better performance, another commonly-held belief in the strategy research. Rather, we see, especially in comparing the high and low-ability group behaviors, that the amount of effort expended in using these strategies seemed to depend on the degree to which the linguistic abilities needed to complete the task were automatized—a case in point is the role of metacognitive strategy use in the low-ability model. Finally, some strategies in some contexts have a negligible or no effect at all on performance, again a rarely mentioned observation.

In examining the model of the effects of strategy use on SLTP, this study has provided several insights on how cognitive and metacognitive strategies impact performance.

1. Surprisingly, this study showed that the cognitive and metacognitive processes had no direct effect on reading ability, as measured by the *FCE Anchor Test*. Rather, strategy use affected reading ability *indirectly* through lexico-grammatical ability. Similarly, the use of the comprehending processes produced no significant effect on lexico-grammatical ability.

2. This study also showed that the use of memory processes had a *negative* effect on lexico-grammatical ability, while the use of the retrieval processes had a *positive* effect. These relationships might help explain why some "good" students appear to be poor test-takers or why some "average" or "poor" students appear to be good test-takers. In other words, these relationships might be used to characterize test-taking style, which could be defined along a continuum ranging from product-oriented to process-oriented, where product-oriented test-takers are able to answer questions quickly and efficiently by retrieving information from long-term memory, while process-oriented test-takers might be more prone to spending time trying to comprehend or remember test input, rather than simply answering the question being asked. In timed testing situations, process-oriented test-takers would surely be disadvantaged. This finding is compelling and merits further empirical investigation, as it has serious implications for test validity.

Strategy use and SLTP with high and low-ability groups

One of the more compelling questions in this study relates to the notion that successful and unsuccessful learners invoke strategies differently, and that these strategies might help to explain why successful and unsuccessful learners perform as they do. In fact, questions relating to the differential performance of successful and unsuccessful learners have been central to the research on strategy use.

The current study was unique in that it not only modeled strategy use and SLTP with an entire group of test-takers, but it also modeled these relationships with high and low-ability groups in separate and simultaneous-group analyses. The goal of these multi-group analyses was twofold. First, I wanted to determine if the factorial structures of the effects of strategy use and SLTP were similar across groups. Second, I wished to see what parameters in the model would prove to be invariant across groups if the models were estimated simultaneously, since cross-group invariance could lead to insights about differential behaviors leading to performance. This study provided the following findings.

1. It showed that although the factorial structure of second language test performance was almost identical for both the high and low-ability groups, all of the parameters except one (sentence formation) were invariant across the two groups. In this case, the grammar subtest was a stronger measure of lexico-grammatical ability for the high-ability group than for the low-ability group. More interestingly, however, the relationship between lexico-grammatical ability and reading ability was

7. Conclusions

found to be invariant across the two groups. In other word lexico-grammatical ability influenced reading ability in the same way across the two groups. This finding suggests that differential performance in second language reading ability might not be due only to differences in top-down and bottom-up processing, as evidenced by the role that lexico-grammatical ability played in the reading test. Rather, performance on the reading subtests might also be due to other factors as well, such as the strategies students use.

2. This study also showed that although the underlying factorial structure of metacognitive strategy use was almost identical across the high and low-ability groups, all but one of the parameters (assessing the situation) were actually variant across the two groups. In other words, monitoring, self-evaluating and self-testing provided significantly stronger indicators of metacognitive strategy use for the low-ability group than they did for the high-ability group.

3 Also, this study showed that the underlying factorial structure of cognitive strategy use varied from model to model. Cognitive strategy use for the entire group produced a three-trait model, while a two-trait model was observed for both the high and low-ability groups. Generally speaking the low-ability group model was more complex and on average had higher loadings, a finding that might be explained by the low performers' lack of automaticity in their use of the English language. Then, when estimated simultaneously, the high and low-ability group models produced only four invariant cross-group parameters in the cognitive strategy use measurement model, again highlighting the cross-group differences in cognitive strategy use.

4. This study again showed that metacognitive strategy use had a strong influence over cognitive strategy use for both groups; however, this influence was found to be variant across the two groups in the simultaneous analyses.

5. With regard to the effects of strategy use on performance, this study clearly demonstrated that high and low-ability test-takers used some strategies in the same way. For example, the comprehending-memory strategies had a significant, negative effect on lexico-grammatical ability for both groups, as seen in the equivalence of this parameter across the two groups. However, it also showed the high and low-ability test-takers also used the majority of the strategies differently, differences which were related to test score variation. To illustrate, the retrieval strategies had a

significant, positive effect on lexico-grammatical ability for both groups; however, this parameter was found to be variant across the two ability-level groups. These findings further reinforce the notion that the effective use of strategies is associated with better performance and suggest perhaps that high-ability test-takers are more effective than are low-ability test-takers in their use of strategies.

Methodological implications

This study demonstrated the usefulness of multivariate, analytic procedures for investigating relationships between test-taker background characteristics and performance on second language tests. Exploratory factor analysis was useful for identifying the clustering of items in the strategy use questionnaires and for providing empirical information from which composite variables could be created. Then, confirmatory factor analysis and structural equation modeling provided insights concerning the inter-relationships between observed and latent variables and among latent variables based on substantive theory. Finally, this study was one of the first in second language acquisition and assessment research to demonstrate the usefulness of multi-sample structural equation modeling for estimating models simultaneously and for providing information on cross-group relationships.

Implications for practice

This study was primarily concerned with understanding selected factors internal to the test-taker that are important in the process of test-taking. This was not a study about second language pedagogy. Nonetheless, many of the research findings could certainly inform teachers about how second language strategy use can be interpreted within a system of human information-processing and how these strategies might contribute to "good" performance in a number of contexts. Although the specific findings in this study further our understanding of test-takers' cognitive and metacognitive processes, teachers should also understand that factors other than those examined, factors external to the test-taker such as the test task itself or other facets of the test, can potentially contribute to test score variation. Finally, the current research asked students to report on their general language learning strategy use. The responses were then associated with their scores on a second language proficiency test. Given the nature of the study, a direct application of the results to language acquisition (learning over a period of time) or language pedagogy must be viewed with a note of caution—even though, in reality, many similarities probably exist. Bearing these caveats in mind, I will discuss how the research findings in this study might be applied to classroom practice.

7. Conclusions

Learner awareness and strategy training

Most second language educators accept the premise that second language acquisition is a complex, cognitive and linguistic process. Most would also agree that one of the first steps toward language learning in most contexts is an awareness of what is to be learned. Without launching into an in-depth discussion of the research on attention, awareness or consciousness-raising (for more information, see Gass, 1997; Schmidt 1990; Sharwood Smith, 1988; Tomlin & Villa, 1994), awareness in second language acquisition contexts could be accomplished in a number of ways: through selective attention, comprehensible input, metalinguistic analysis, input enhancement via instruction, explicit correction or other forms of negative evidence, or even through a trigger to the learner's innate universal grammar. In short, it is generally held that a degree of linguistic awareness or "noticing" on some level is a necessary condition for many aspects of language learning to take place.

Second language strategy researchers have made similar claims about the cognitive component of language learning, arguing that an increased awareness of how to process a second language contributes to acquisition and performance. In other words, an explicit knowledge of learning strategies can be effective in enhancing learning and performance. To demonstrate this, O'Malley (1987) examined the effectiveness of explicit strategy training with ESL students learning vocabulary, listening comprehension and speaking. In addition to being trained in the three language skill areas, a "metacognitive" group was instructed in metacognitive, cognitive and social-affective strategy use; a "cognitive" group was provided training in cognitive and social-affective strategy use; and a control group was given no explicit strategy instruction. Results of the post-tests generally provided evidence that explicit strategy training was effective in improving performance, especially with the listening and speaking components of the course. Given these results and the results from other strategy training studies, the implication for teachers is that we should be teaching strategies explicitly and incorporating them into our lessons whenever appropriate. By extension, this implication would extend to strategy awareness training for students in the context of test-taking.

As we have learned from the current study, however, we must be cautious not to assume that all strategies are appropriate for all contexts. Some strategies appear to benefit second language test performance (or by extension learning in certain contexts), and others do not. For example, in the context of test-taking, the use of metacognitive and retrieval strategies seem to benefit performance, whereas the use of the memory strategies inhibit it. Therefore, from a practical perspective, it is important for students to be aware of how they process tests, also known as their test-taking style. Are they product-oriented test-takers (i.e., do they principally rely on retrieval strategies)? Are they more process-oriented (i.e., do they rely on memory or comprehending strategies)? If students discover they lean toward a process-oriented approach to test-taking, they might take the appropriate steps to change their orientation with certain kinds of tests. Finally, are they locking in critical thinking (i.e., do they not use metacognitive strategies or are they unable to implement 'thinking' into 'action'?). In short, the results of this study can help teachers provide their students with this kind of formative information.

The current study also showed us that it may be inaccurate to assume that the more strategies we use, the better we will perform on language tests. The truth of the matter is that as students learn more language, they process input more quickly. Linguistic recall becomes much more proceduralized, and so do the strategies students use to process input. In fact, the results of this study suggest that at the high-ability level, students on average seem to report strategy use to a lesser degree. What is more important than the amount of strategies we use is the way we use strategies, or the degree to which we use them appropriately and efficiently, given the specific learning goal. Therefore, classroom teachers should concentrate on making students aware of the strategies they use, and they should help them consider if these strategies are the most appropriate for the task at hand and if they are the most efficient to invoke in language learning or test-taking contexts.

In the current study, strategy use was not conceptualized as an atheoretical list of "good" behaviors. Rather, it linked strategy use to human information processing. In other words, strategy use was contextualized with a larger, more complex system of inter-related behaviors. Similarly, in thinking about what strategies to teach and how to do so, teachers could refer to the taxonomies presented in this study as they relate to a model of human learning. Then, in planning for strategy training, they need to organize their classroom tasks and activities so that strategies are not used in isolation, but rather, with the goal of developing both metacognitive strategies along with cognitive strategies. For example, in a pronunciation lesson, students might be introduced to a topic—consonant assimilation. They can then be presented with a part of a written dialogue and asked to "apply the rules." After that, they can work with a partner and compare their answers, discussing how the rules were applied. Finally, teachers can present them with an audiotape of the dialogue so they can "evaluate" their work or "test their knowledge." These, multi-tasked activities, in the context of language learning or language assessment, will promote the use of strategies. Finally, teachers (and students) need to understand that these strategies are not only relevant to language learning contexts, but to other content learning contexts as well.

To a certain extent depending on the students' level of proficiency, I

7. Conclusions

believe students should be made aware that strategy use relates to human information-processing. An effective way of introducing intermediate and advanced students to this topic is by means of a theme-based unit on "learning" or "learning and the brain." [1] One or more reading passages can be selected for students to examine the topic. The passages could include information on the strategies used to comprehend language, remember it, and use it in different contexts, as well as the strategies used to regulate these processes. Once students understand how individual strategies constitute the different stages of the learning process, they will be more ready to examine their own strategy use explicitly. Finally, a unit on human learning also provides teachers with a natural opportunity for administering strategy use questionnaires to students.

Lastly, in preparing to incorporate strategy instruction into classroom practice, teachers should be sure to organize strategy training around language learning or test-taking tasks and activities. Assuming students are trying to learn a language, strategy use should be presented in such a way that students understand the role that strategies play in helping them achieve their goals. In other words, students should learn that strategies facilitate information processing whether it be in the context of language learning, use or assessment. More specifically, they should know that efficient and appropriate strategy use can contribute to the process of achieving a linguistic (or other subject matter) product. In incorporating strategies in the classroom, students and teachers alike should maintain a clear focus on the final learning goal, and not pursue strategy training in and of itself. Strategy use is a means to the broader goal of acquisition or performance just as language learning is a means to the broader goal of communication. Certainly most second language educators would question a decontextualized approach to strategy training in which strategies were not closely related to other curricular exigencies, just as we have questioned decontextualized language learning.

Strategy assessment and strategy instruction

Just as most teachers would formulate a coherent and systematic plan for presenting linguistic or skill-based learning points to students, they should also approach strategy training with the same care and thoughtfulness. Therefore, in implementing strategy training into the classroom, teachers should introduce students to the notion of strategies and to the importance of strategy use in achieving their goals. A second step teachers need to follow to implement strategy training into the classroom is to gather information on the strategies their students are currently using (or currently think they use). Strategy assessment can be accomplished through a number of strategy elicitation methods. Some common ways to gather strategy use information include, but are not limited to: structured interviews, surveys, questionnaires,

7. Conclusions

think-aloud protocols, learning logs and dialogue journals. Each method has its strengths and weaknesses and many researchers have written extensively on this (for an excellent review, see Nunan, 1992).

One of the more controlled and systematic ways of gathering information on self-reported strategy use is the questionnaire. In this respect, the current study can serve as a valuable resource for students and teachers alike. The present study provides two validated language learning questionnaires: one for students to report their cognitive strategy use (see Appendix D) and one for their metacognitive strategy use (see Appendix F).

In order to gain information on the patterns of strategy use reported by students, teachers should have the students fill out the questionnaires on a separate answer sheet (since the questionnaire may be administered several times during a semester). Then, students should be directed to record their responses to each strategy item on the tally sheet provided in Figure 7.1.

7. Conclusions

Table 7.1
Second Language Learning and Test-Taking Strategy Inventory: Tally Sheet

1. Record your responses to the strategy questionnaire on the lines.
2. Total each column.
3. Calculate the average for each strategy type.

Cognitive Strategy Use

Part 1 Analyze Inductive	Part 2 Clarify/ Verify	Part 3 Inference	Part 4 Associate	Part 5 Linking w/ Prior Kn.	Part 6 Repeat/ Rehearse	Part 7 Summarize	Part 8 Applying Rules	Part 9 Practice Natural	Part 10 Transfer L1-L2
36. ___	20. ___	34. ___	10. ___	1. ___	4. ___	7. ___	8. ___	21. ___	15. ___
39. ___	38. ___	37. ___	11. ___	2. ___	27. ___	33. ___	18. ___	23. ___	16. ___
40. ___			12. ___	6. ___	28. ___		32. ___	25. ___	19. ___
			13. ___	22. ___	29. ___			26. ___	24. ___
					30. ___			35. ___	
SUM ___ ÷ 3 = ___ (Average)	SUM ___ ÷ 2 = ___ (Average)	SUM ___ ÷ 2 = ___ (Average)	SUM ___ ÷ 4 = ___ (Average)	SUM ___ ÷ 4 = ___ (Average)	SUM ___ ÷ 5 = ___ (Average)	SUM ___ ÷ 2 = ___ (Average)	SUM ___ ÷ 3 = ___ (Average)	SUM ___ ÷ 5 = ___ (Average)	SUM ___ ÷ 4 = ___ (Average)

Part A Comprehend	Part B Memory	Part C Retrieve	Part D Metacog.
Average from Parts	Average from Parts	Average from Parts	Average from Parts
1. ___	4. ___	2. ___	11. ___
2. ___	6. ___	3. ___	12. ___
	7. ___	5. ___	13. ___
	8. ___	8. ___	14. ___
	10. ___	9. ___	
SUM ___ ÷ 2 = ___ (Average)	SUM ___ ÷ 5 = ___ (Average)	SUM ___ (From this subtract the average from Part 10.) ___ ___ (SUM) ___ (Pt. 10) ÷ 5 = ___ (Average)	SUM ___ ÷ 4 = ___ (Average)

Metacognitive Strategy Use

Part 11 Assess the Situation	Part 12 Monitor	Part 13 Self- Evaluate	Part 14 Self- Testing
41. ___	52. ___	47. ___	45. ___
42. ___	57. ___	49. ___	46. ___
58. ___	60. ___	59. ___	50. ___
63. ___	68. ___	62. ___	51. ___
65. ___		64. ___	61. ___
66. ___		69. ___	70. ___
67. ___		71. ___	74. ___
72. ___		73. ___	76. ___
		78. ___	
		79. ___	
SUM ___ ÷ 8 = ___ (Average)	SUM ___ ÷ 4 = ___ (Average)	SUM ___ ÷ 10 = ___ (Average)	SUM ___ ÷ 3 = ___ (Average)

7. Conclusions

Once the item responses have been recorded, the students are ready to create a profile of their strategy use. They should first be instructed to add the item responses for each strategy type. For example, in Part 1, students would add their responses to items 36, 39 and 40, and record the total next to the word "SUM." Then, they should divide the total by the number of items (indicated on the form), and record the average amount of strategy use on the line above the word "Average." The score in Part 1 would be the mean score for "analyzing inductively." Students should repeat this calculation for all ten parts of the Cognitive Strategy Use questionnaire and all four parts of the Metacognitive Strategy Use questionnaire.

Once the students have calculated an average for each strategy they say they use, they can learn the general strategic patterns of behavior in language learning, use and testing. More specifically, they can learn how these patterns of behavior relate to Gagné, Yekovich and Yekovich's (1993) model of human information-processing. In other words, students can calculate the degree to which they report using the comprehending, memory, retrieval processes related to cognitive strategy use, and the assessment processes related to metacognitive strategy use. This information can be used to make students aware of how they use strategies and how they process information. To calculate this, students should record the strategy averages in the four boxes labeled Part A, B, C and D in the lower right hand corner. They should then add the parts, record the sum on the appropriate line, divide by the number of parts, and record the average for each underlying process on the line. For example, a student who receives an average score of 2.5 in Part A under the comprehending strategies reports that he or she uses this cluster of strategies to understand input. In part C, after students total the average of each of the five strategy types, they must account for the negative effect of transferring on retrieval. As a result, they should subtract the average for transferring (the SUM for Part 10) from the sum of the five strategies in Part C. After recording this product, it should be divided by 5 to produce the mean score for retrieval.

Once students have calculated these four averages, they should transfer this information from the tally sheet (Figure 7.1) to the strategy use profile sheet in Figure 7.2, where they can get a profile of their general strategic processes relating the language learning, use and testing.

7. Conclusions

Table 7.2
Strategy Use Profile: What Second Language Learning and Test-Taking Processes You Use

Part	Average
A. Strategies For Understanding a SL: This refers to the degree to which... • you analyze your SL by using clues to understand and make sense of it; • you ask yourself questions to help with your own understanding of what you have read or heard; • you ask yourself (or others) questions to check that what you have understood is correct.	A. _____
B. Strategies For Remembering a SL: This refers to the degree to which... • you group or make associations about SL to learn or remember it; • you repeat words or phrases or you rehearse your SL to remember it; • you make mental (or written) summaries to remember your SL; • you are able to remember information about the SL by applying the rules you have learned to different contexts; • compare your first language to your SL or to some other language you already know so that you can remember it better.	B. _____
C. Strategies for Using a SL: This refers to the degree to which you ... • ask yourself (or others) questions to help with your own understanding of what you have read or heard in a SL; • ask yourself (or others) questions to see if what you have understood is correct; • use cues to guess the meaning of what you have heard or read in a SL; • link what you already know to what you are hearing, reading or learning; • apply the rules about your SL to different contexts; • actively read in your SL or have conversations with speakers of that language; • compare items in your first language with those in your SL or with those in some other language you already know.	C. _____
D. Strategies for Managing Your Second Language Learning, Testing or Use: This refers to the degree to which you manage how well you learn a SL, take a SL test or use the SL by... • taking stock of what you need to do with the SL so that you can set goals and make plans; • monitoring how well you understand what you hear or read in the SL, how well you remember items in the SL and how well you can use the SL; • evaluating how well you have understood what you have heard or read, how well you have remembered items in the SL and how well you have used the SL; • testing yourself to see how well you can understand aspects of the SL, how well you can remember them and how well you can use them when you need them.	D. _____
Add the scores for parts A, B, C, and D.	Total _____
Divide the SUM by 4, and record the overall strategy use average	Overall Average _____

7. Conclusions

When the students have recorded the averages for each underlying process, they should total them and divide by four to obtain the overall strategy use average.

This information can be plotted onto the graph in Figure 7.3, and students can keep track of their general strategy use during the course of a semester.[2] Each time students complete the questionnaire and calculate their general strategy use behaviors, these response patterns can be plotted on the same graph in a different color pen in order to facilitate comparison of strategy use over time. Teachers should remember that the degree of strategy use may have a differential effect on performance. As seen in the current study, for example, high ability test-takers typically used "self-evaluating" more than the low-ability test-takers, and this strategy seemed to improve test scores, especially in the context of checking their answers on the test. However, the high-ability test-takers used "transferring from L1 to L2" much less and this also seemed to benefit test performance. In short, the issue of degree of strategy use is complex and not fully understood in second language acquisition and assessment research. For now, teachers need to help students contextualize these strategic patterns of behavior. What is important for most classrooms is that students become sensitized to the range of strategies they could use when they are learning a language, using it in conversation or taking language tests.

7. Conclusions

Figure 7.3

Plot of the Strategy Use Profile

A: **Understanding Your Strategy Use Averages**

Very High	4.1 – 5.0	I always or almost always use the strategies.
High	3.1 – 4.0	I often use the strategies.
Medium	2.1 – 3.0	I sometimes use the strategies.
Low	1.1 – 2.0	I rarely use the strategies.
Very Low	0.0 – 1.0	I never or almost never use the strategies.

B: **Graph of the Strategy Use Averages**

Plot the average score from your strategy use profile.

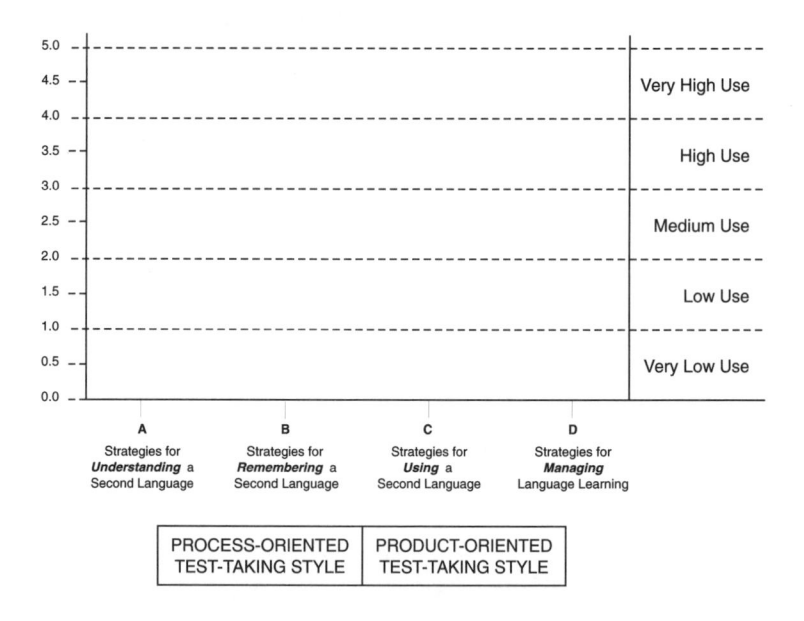

```
5.0  ─────────────────────────────────────────
4.5                                              Very High Use
4.0  ─────────────────────────────────────────
3.5                                              High Use
3.0  ─────────────────────────────────────────
2.5                                              Medium Use
2.0  ─────────────────────────────────────────
1.5                                              Low Use
1.0  ─────────────────────────────────────────
0.5                                              Very Low Use
0.0
        A           B           C           D
   Strategies for  Strategies for  Strategies for  Strategies for
   Understanding a Remembering a   Using a         Managing
   Second Language Second Language Second Language Language Learning
```

PROCESS-ORIENTED TEST-TAKING STYLE	PRODUCT-ORIENTED TEST-TAKING STYLE

For teachers, these strategy profiles can provide information on how an individual learner reports his or her approach to learning or test-taking. Teachers can use the results from these questionnaires (or any other elicitation procedure described above) to plan for individualized training if they estimate that performance has suffered from the ways in which students are approaching learning or test-taking.

These individual profiles can also be used to create a strategy use profile for the entire class. Again, this information could be used to make pedagogical decisions about learning or test-taking. For example, a teacher might see that his students, as a group, are not using the assessment strategies in test-taking. In this case, instructional intervention can be planned and monitored.

The current study asked students to report the types of strategies they thought they used in language acquisition, use and testing. The aim was to elicit information on a wide range of strategies. Additionally, the strategies were not associated with any particular learning event or test-taking task. (The questionnaires were always given before the language test.) The strategy questionnaires did, however, ask students to report the strategies they used while reading, writing and so forth. Although the goal of the current study was not to look at these specific areas, teachers might want to understand the strategies their students use while they read or write, for example. In this case, the strategy questionnaire in this study can be adapted to allow students to report the strategies they use with relation to more specific language learning or test-taking activities. Figure 7.4 presents an example of a checklist that has been adapted to elicit cognitive and metacognitive strategy use information relating to a reading task.

Figure 7.4

Strategies Checklist for Reading

Name _____ Date _____			
After reading the story, read the strategies and indicate how often you used these following strategies. Put a check in the appropriate box.			
Strategies	**Often**	**Sometimes**	**Almost Never**
1. I tried to understand by asking myself questions about the story.			
2. I made associations between different parts of the story while I read.			
3. I read some sentences more than once.			
4. I took time to summarize in my mind what I had just read.			
5. I thought about grammar rules while reading.			
6. I tried to read in English like I read in my own language.			
7. I tried to figure out new grammar items in the reading.			
8. I tried to use the story to figure out new vocabulary words.			
9. I tried to relate the story to something in my own life.			
10. While reading, I thought about what was going to happen next in the story.			
11. While I was reading, I wondered if I understood the story correctly.			
12. After I read stories like this, I think about how I can read better.			

This type of strategy checklist can be used both as a means of checking the strategies students report using in a learning or test-taking task, and it can also be presented to students as a list of behaviors they might want to consider in the future.

Similar to the reading strategies checklist, teachers can provide students with self-evaluation tasks designed to target specific areas of writing. Figure 7.5 provides another example of a focused self-evaluation task that promotes cognitive and metacognitive strategy use.

Figure 7.5

Focused Self-Evaluation of Writing

Author's Name _____ Date _____
Title of Paper _____

	yes	no
Purpose and Organization		
1. I oriented the reader to my topic.	❏	❏
2. I stated the purpose clearly.	❏	❏
3. I provided the proper support for my ideas.	❏	❏
4. My paper has a conclusion.	❏	❏
Coherence		
5. The sentences in my paragraphs are logically related to each other.	❏	❏
6. I used transition words to link the ideas between paragraphs.	❏	❏
7. I used logical connectors within paragraphs to help link ideas.	❏	❏
Language		
8. I used correct subject–verb agreement.	❏	❏
9. I used the correct verb tenses.	❏	❏
10. I used complete sentences.	❏	❏

What aspect of your writing will you work on improving the next time? How will you go about it?

Finally, the results in the current study showed that self-evaluating, aside from its role as an indicator of metacognitive strategy use, had a significant, special effect with the high-ability group on performance. This strategy seemed to reflect how high-ability students were responsive to being asked to check their work before handing in their test. More generally, this reflects how students were asked to focus their attention on the quality of their responses. Based on these findings, self-evaluating could be proactively applied to classroom learning in the form of self-assessment. This conceptualization of self-assessment departs from the traditional notion of self-assessment, where students are asked to evaluate their language performance in a certain content domain—for example, a job applicant who is asked to rate her ability to speak or understand French. Rather, self-assessment in this context refers to a concerted effort to "notice" whether an answer on a test is correct or not. From this research, self-assessment in the form of self-evaluating certainly seems important to test-taking. I would hypothesize it has an equal importance in all learning contexts, and perhaps should be developed more systematically in classroom practices.

To summarize, an awareness of the strategies students use in language learning, use and testing actively involves them in these activities and encourages them to take more responsibility for their learning. This knowledge will hopefully motivate students to question how they learn and take tests, to experiment with new learning and test-taking strategies, and ultimately provide them with a greater sense of autonomy.

Suggestions for further research

Although this study used sophisticated, statistical tools that allowed for a confirmatory approach to model analysis, it was exploratory in nature. In this regard, it demonstrated the usefulness of exploratory factor analysis, confirmatory factor analysis and structural equation modeling to investigate the relationships between strategy use and second language test performance. However, this type of strategy research is still in its initial stages and could profit from further in-depth investigation.

One area of future research relates to the operationalization of the variables in this study. It is obvious that the use of the *FCE Anchor Test* as the sole measure of second language test performance provides only a limited view of this construct. Reading and lexico-grammatical ability are but two of a host of areas of communicative language ability that could be related to strategy use. In addition to reading and lexico-grammatical ability, future studies should include a variety of tasks that measure other areas of language ability, such as pragmatic knowledge, and other language skill areas such as listening, speaking and writing.

Also, the types of strategies used to measure cognitive and metacognitive processing provide only a partial list of the possible strategies a test-taker could invoke during an exam. As this study makes no claim at providing a comprehensive list of strategies, future research might be conducted with a greater variety of strategy-type variables.

A second important area of future research suggested by this study relates to other test-taker characteristics that might have an influence on test scores, but were not modeled in this study. For example, several strategy researchers have hypothesized the effect of social and affective strategies on second language test performance, but these variables were not included in the current study; nor were variables relating to the test-takers' attitudes, motivation, effort or other socio-psychological or sociocultural variables—in spite of the fact that research has shown many of these variables have a significant effect on performance. Future research on test-taker characteristics might include a greater number of test-taker background characteristics in the models of second language test performance, so that the differential effect of all these variables on second language test performance can be assessed.

A third area of future research suggested by this study relates to the robustness of the proposed models of strategy use and performance across

7. Conclusions

different types of groups. The current study looked at high and low-ability groups, but never looked to see if the models held across gender or some other variables. As this study included participants that could be grouped in a number of ways, further research could look at group-specific models of the relationships between strategy use and second language test performance. A few questions to be addressed in these studies might include the following:

1. To what extent do the models of strategy use and second language test performance hold across nationality? Are the Spanish/Catalan, Czech and Turkish models of strategy use and performance equivalent when modeled simultaneously? How are these models similar and different?
2. To what extent do the models of strategy use and second language test performance hold across age? Are the models of strategy use and second language test performance similar when the younger participants (e.g., 15 through 17 years old) and the older participants (e.g., 23 and older) models are estimated simultaneously? How are these models similar and different?
3. To what extent do the models of strategy use and second language test performance hold across gender? How are these models similar and different?

A fourth area of future research relates to the cognitive characteristics of test tasks. The results of this study have demonstrated that test-takers' strategy use has an effect on performance. In other words, the strategies a test-taker uses accounts for some of the variability in test scores. The stimulus for strategic processing, however, is the task—whether it be in the context of learning or testing. It would follow, then, that test tasks—or items within a task—possess prototypical characteristics that place certain cognitive demands on test-takers. However, to what degree do test developers take in account these cognitive demands when they develop tasks for tests? Traditionally, language test developers have focused their energy on devising tasks that elicit the types of linguistic behaviors they wish to measure. In other words, the focus is on the content domain. Test developers have also focused on issues of test method in an effort to maximize test reliability. Perhaps, it is now time for test developers to consider test tasks in light of the types of strategies they might invoke. In other words, language assessment researchers need to begin looking anew at the cognitive demands of test tasks related to the strategies and processes they elicit within a system of human information processing.

Finally, a vital area of future research emerging from this study relates to the validity of self-report methods for eliciting information on test-takers' mental processes. Given the scope of the current study, multiple data elicitation methods were not used. However, in future studies, the potential threats to external validity would be minimized if multiple data collection procedures were used, even on a small scale, and the results from the various methods cross-validated.

Conclusion

This study designed strategy use questionnaires according to a model of human information-processing so that test-takers' reported cognitive and metacognitive strategy use could be measured and compared to their performance on second or foreign language tests. Without restating the specific findings in the study, the results showed that the relationships between strategy use and performance on second language tests are complex and subtle, given the nature of the constructs involved and the number of possible interactions that could occur. In spite of this complexity, the issues raised in this study are of vital importance if we wish to gain insights into how we understand, remember, retrieve information for use in carrying out academic tasks or in how we manage these processes. This is especially of import if language educators wish to utilize this information to help students develop learning processes as well as products.

This study also investigated models of strategy use and second language test performance with high and low-ability test-takers and provided clear evidence that these groups use strategies differently, incurring a significant impact on performance. In other words, the tests of invariance across groups could not be uniformly supported in the data, suggesting then that second language test-takers generally approach the cognitive task of test-taking in very different ways.

From a methodological perspective, this study has demonstrated the value of using a number of statistical procedures, but especially, structural equation modeling as a research tool for investigating multiple variables simultaneously and for providing insights into the inter-relationships among these variables.

From a pedagogical perspective, this study has a number of implications for strategy use awareness through strategy use assessment. Following an understanding of the students' strategy use, learners can be provided with information on how they report using strategies and how they might learn to use them more efficiently and appropriately in different contexts. Strategy assessment will also provide teachers with strategy use profiles of their students individually and as a group. This information can be the point of departure for incorporating strategy training in their classroom practices.

In closing, it is my hope that the present study has made a contribution to the formulation of a more comprehensive theory of second or foreign

7. Conclusions

language performance in which cognitive and metacognitive strategy use have an articulated role.

Endnotes

1. For an example of a theme-based lesson on learning, see Unit 1 in Purpura, J. E. & Pinkley, D. (1999). *On Target (2nd Edition)*. White Plains, NY: Pierson Education.

2. Teachers should be the judge of what information would be helpful for students in their classes. They could also devise plots for the individual strategies and students could keep track of these over time.

References

Abraham, R. G., Vann, R. J. (1987). Strategies of two language learners: A case study. In Wenden, A., Rubin, J. (Eds.) *Learner strategies in language learning* (pp.85–102). London: Prentice Hall International.

Anderson, J. R. (1980). *Cognitive psychology and its implications*. San Francisco: Freeman.

Anderson, J. R. (1981). *Cognitive skills and their acquisition*. Hillsdale, NJ: Lawrence Erlbaum.

Anderson, J. R. (1982). Acquisition of cognitive skills. *Psychological Review, 89*: 369–406.

Anderson, J. R. (1983). A spreading activation theory of memory. *Journal of Verbal Learning and Verbal Behavior, 22*: 261–95.

Anderson, J. R. (1985). *Cognitive psychology and its implications* (2nd ed.). New York: Freeman.

Anderson, N. J. (1989). *Reading comprehension tests versus academic reading: What are second language readers doing?* Doctoral dissertation. Austin: The University of Texas, Austin, TX.

Asher, J. (1977). *Learning another language through actions: The complete teachers' guidebook*. Los Gatos, CA: Sky Oaks Publications.

Atkinson, R. C., Shiffrin, R. M. (1968). Human memory: A proposed system and its control processes. In Spence K. W. & Spence, J. T. (Eds.) *The Psychology of learning and motivation: Advances in research and theory* (Vol. 2). New York: Academic Press.

Bachman, L. F. (1990). *Fundamental considerations in language testing*. Oxford: Oxford University Press.

Bachman, L. F., Cushing, S. T., Purpura, J. E. (1993). *Development of a questionnaire item bank to explore test-taker characteristics*. Interim Report submitted to University of Cambridge Local Examination Syndicate.

Bachman, L. F., Davidson, F., Milanovic, M. (1993). *The use of test method characteristics in the content analysis and design of EFL proficiency tests*. Paper presented at the 13th Annual Language Testing Colloquium, Princeton, NJ.

References

Bachman, L. F., Davidson, F., Ryan, K., Choi, I.-C. (1993). *An investigation into the comparability of two tests of English as a foreign language: The Cambridge-TOEFL comparability study.* Cambridge: Cambridge University Press.

Bachman, L. F., Kunnan, A., Vanniarajan, S., Lynch, B. (1988). Task and ability analysis as a basis for examining content and construct comparability in two EFL proficiency test batteries. *Language Testing, 5*(2): 128–159.

Bachman, L. F., Palmer, A. S. (1981). The construct validation of the FSI oral interview. *Language Learning, 31*: 67–86.

Bachman, L. F., Palmer, A. S. (1982). The construct validation of some components of communicative proficiency. *TESOL Quarterly, 16*(4): 449–65.

Bachman, L. F., Palmer, A. S. (1983). Oral Interview Test of Communication Proficiency in English. Urbane, IL: Photo-Offset.

Bachman, L. F., Palmer, A. S. (1996). *Language testing in practice.* Oxford: Oxford University Press.

Barnett, M. A. (1989). *More than meets the eye.* Englewood Cliffs, NJ: Prentice Hall Regents.

Bentler, P. M. (1990). Comparative fit indexes in structural models. *Psychological Bulletin, 107*: 238–246.

Bentler, P. M. (1992). EQS structural equations program manual. Los Angeles, CA: BMDP Statistical Software, Inc.

Bentler, P. M. (1995). EQS structural equations program manual. Los Angeles: BMDP Statistical Software, Inc.

Bentler, P. M., Dijkstra, T. (1985). Efficient estimation via linearization in structural models. In Krishnaiah, P. R. (Ed.) *Multivariate analysis VI,* (pp.9–42). Amsterdam: North-Holland.

Bentler, P. M., Weeks, D. G. (1979). Intercorrelation of models for the analysis of moment structures. *Multivariate Behavioral Research, 14*: 169–185.

Bentler, P. M., Weeks, D. G. (1980). Linear structural equations with latent variables. *Psychometrica, 45*: 289–308.

Bentler, P. M., Wu, E. C. (1995). *EQS for Macintosh user's guide.* Encino, CA: Multivariate Software, Inc.

Bialystok, E. (1978). A theoretical model of second language learning. *Language Learning, 28*: 69–83.

Bialystok, E. (1981). The role of conscious strategies in second language proficiency. *Modern Language Journal, 65*: 24–35.

Bialystok, E. (1983). Some factors in the selection and implementation of communication strategies. In Faerch, C., Kasper, G. (Eds.) *Strategies in interlanguage communication* (pp.100–18). London: Longman.

References

Bialystok, E. (1990). *Communication strategies: A psychological analysis of second-language use.* Cambridge, MA: Basil Blackwell.

Bollen, K. A. (1989). *Structural equations with latent variables.* New York: Wiley.

Bollen, K. A., Long, J. S. (1993). *Testing structural equation models.* Newbury Park, CA: Sage Publications.

Borkowski, J. G. (1985). Signs of intelligence: Strategy generalization and metacognition. In Yussen, S. R. (Ed.) *The growth of reflection in children* (pp.105–144). Orlando, FL: Academic Press.

Brown, A. L., Bransford, J. D., Ferrara, R., Campione, J. C. (1983). Learning, remembering and understanding. In Flavell, J. H., Markman, E. M. (Eds.) *Carmichael's Manual of child psychology,* Vol. 1. New York: Wiley.

Brown, A. L., Palinscar, A. S. (1982). Inducing strategic learning from texts by means of informed self-control training. *Topics in Learning and Learning Disabilities, 2*: 1–17.

Brown, T., Perry, F. (1991). A comparison of three learning strategies for ESL vocabulary acquisition. *TESOL Quarterly, 25*: 655–670.

Byrne, B. M. (1989). *A primer of LISREL: Basic applications and programming for confirmatory factor analytic models.* New York: Springer Verlag.

Byrne, B. M. (1994). *Structural equation modeling with EQS and EQS/Windows.* Thousand Oaks, CA: Sage Publications.

Byrne, B. M., Shavelson, R. J., Muthén, B. (1989). Testing for the equivalence of factor covariance and mean structures: The issue of partial measurement invariance. *Psychological Bulletin, 105*: 456–466.

Campione, J. C., Brown, A. L. (1978). Toward a theory of intelligence: Contributions from research with retarded children. *Intelligence, 2*: 279–304.

Canale, M. (1983). On some dimensions of language proficiency. In Oller, J. (Ed.) *Issues in language testing research* (pp.333–342). Rowley, MA: Newbury House.

Canale, M., Swain, M. (1980). From communicative competence to communicative language pedagogy. In Richards, J. C., Schmidt, R. (Eds.) *Language and communication.* London: Longman.

Carrell, P. L. (1988). Some causes of text boundedness and schema interference in ESL reading. In Carrell, P. L., Devine, J., Eskey, D. E. (Eds.) *Interactive approaches to second language reading* (pp.101–113). Cambridge: Cambridge University Press.

Carroll, J. B. (1961). Fundamental considerations in testing for English language proficiency of foreign students. Center for Applied Linguistics, *Testing the English proficiency of foreign students* (pp.313–320). Washington, DC. Reprinted in Allen & Campbell (1972).

References

Carroll, J. B. (1968). The psychology of language testing. In Davies, A. (Ed.) *Language testing symposium: A psycholinguistic approach* (pp.46–69). London: Oxford University Press.

Carroll, J. B. (1981). Twenty-five years of research on foreign language aptitude. In Diller, K. C. (Ed.) *Individual differences and universals in language learning aptitude* (pp.83–118). Rowley, MA: Newbury House.

Carroll, J. B. (1983). Psychometric theory and language testing. In Oller, J. W. (Ed.) *Issues in language testing research* (pp.137–155). Rowley, MA: Newbury House.

Carroll, J. B. (1985). Second language abilities. In Sternberg, R. J. (Ed.) *An information processing approach* (pp.83–101). New York: W. H. Freeman and Company.

Carroll, J. B. (1993). *Human cognitive abilities: A survey of factor-analytic studies*. Cambridge: Cambridge University Press.

Chamot, A. U. (1987). The learning strategies of ESL students. In Wenden, A., Rubin, J. (Eds.) *Learner strategies in language learning* (pp.71–82). New York: Prentice Hall.

Chamot, A. U., Küpper, L. (1989). Learning strategies in foreign language instruction. *Foreign Language Annals, 22*: 13–24.

Chamot, A. U., Küpper, L., Impink-Hernandez, M. (1988). *A study of learning strategies in foreign language instruction: Findings of the longitudinal study*. McLean, VA: Interstate Research Associates.

Chapelle, C. A., Abraham, R. G. (1990). Authenticity in language testing: Cloze method: What difference does it make? *Language Testing, 7*(2): 121–146.

Chesterfield, R., Chesterfield, K. (1985). Natural order in children's use of second language learning strategies. *Applied Linguistics, 6*: 45–59.

Chou, C. P., Bentler, P. M. (1995). Estimates and tests in structural equation modeling. In Hoyle, R. H. (Ed.) *Structural equation modeling: concepts, issues and applications*. Thousand Oaks, CA: Sage Publications.

Clapham, C. (1996). *The development of IELTS: A study of the effect of background knowledge on reading comprehension*. Cambridge: Cambridge University Press.

Clarke, M. A. (1980). The short circuit hypothesis of ESL reading – or when language competence interferes with reading performance. *Modern Language Journal, 64*: 203–09.

Clahsen, H. (1987). Connecting theories of language processing and (second) language acquisition. In Pfaff, C. (Ed.) *First and second language acquisition* (pp.137–155). Cambridge, MA: Newbury House.

References

Clement, R., Kruidenier, B. (1985). Aptitude, attitude, and motivation in second language proficiency: A test of Clément's model. *Journal of Language and Social Psychology, 4*: 21–37.

Coady, J. (1979). A psycholinguistic model of the ESL reader. In Mackay, R., Barkman, B., Jordan, R. R. (Eds.) *Reading in a second language: Hypotheses, organization and practice* (pp.5–12). Rowley, MA: Newbury House.

Cohen, A. (1984). On taking language tests: What the students report. *Language Testing, 1*: 70–81.

Cohen, A. (1987). The use of verbal and imagery mnemonics in second-language vocabulary learning. *Studies in Second Language Acquisition, 9*: 43–62.

Cohen, A., Aphek, E. (1981). Easifying second language learning. *Studies in Second Language Acquisition, 3*: 221–236.

Cohen, A. Hosenfeld, C. (1981). Some uses of mentalistic data in second language research. *Language Learning, 31*: 285–313.

Corder, P. (1983). A role of the mother tongue. In Gass, S., Selinker, L. (Eds.) *Language transfer in language learning* (pp.85–97). Rowley, MA: Newbury House.

Craik, F. I., Lockhart, R. S. (1972). Levels of processing: A framework for memory research. *Journal of Verbal Learning and Verbal Behavior, 11*: 671–684.

Cziko, G. A. (1980). Language competence and reading strategies: A comparison of first and second-language oral reading errors. *Language Learning, 30*: 101–116.

Dansereau, D. F., McDonald, B. A., Collins, K. W., Garland, J. C., Holley, C. D., Diekhoff, G. M., Evans, S. H. (1979). Evaluation of a learning strategy system. In O'Neil Jr., H. F., Spielberger, C. D. (Eds.) *Cognitive and affective learning strategies*. New York: Academic Press.

DeKeyser, R. (1995). Learning second language grammar rules: An experiment with a miniature linguistic system. *Studies in Second Language Acquisition, 17* (3): 379–410.

DeKeyser, R. (1998). Beyond focus form: Cognitive perspectives on learning and practicing second language grammar. In Doughty, C. and Williams, J. (Eds.) *Focus on form in classroom second language acquisition* (pp.42–63). Cambridge: Cambridge University Press.

Dulay, H. C., Burt, M. K., Krashen, S. D. (1982). *Language two.* New York: Oxford University Press.

EFL Division of UCLES (1994). *First Certificate in English Handbook.* Cambridge: University of Cambridge Local Examinations Syndicate.

Ellis, N. (1993). Rules and instances in foreign language learning: Interactions of implicit and explicit knowledge. *European Journal of Cognitive Psychology, 5*(3): 289–319.

Ellis, R. (1985). *Understanding second language acquisition*. Oxford: Oxford University Press.
Ellis, R. (1994). *The study of second language acquisition*. Oxford: Oxford University Press.
Faerch, C., Kasper, G. (1983). *Strategies in interlanguage communication*. London: Longman.
Faerch, C., Kasper, G. (1984). Two ways of defining communication strategies. *Language Learning, 34*: 46–63.
Fillmore, L. W., Swain, M. (1984). Child second language development: View from the field on theory and research. Paper presented at TESOL Houston, TX.
Flavell, J. (1979). Metacognition and cognitive monitoring: A new area of cognitive developmental inquiry. *American Psychologist, 34*: 906–911.
Fouly, K. (1985). *A confirmatory multivariate study of the nature of second language proficiency and its relationships to learner variables*. Unpublished doctoral dissertation. University of Illinois, Urbana, IL.
Gagné, E. D., Yekovich, C. W., Yekovich, F. R. (1993). *The cognitive psychology of school learning*. New York, NY: HarperCollins College Publishers.
Gardner, R. C. (1983). Learning another language: A true social psychological experiment. *Journal of Language and Social Psychology, 2*: 219–239.
Gardner, R. C. (1985). *Social psychology and second language learning: The role of attitude and motivation*. London: Edward Arnold.
Gardner, R. C., Lalonde, R., Moorcroft, R., Evers, F. T. (1987). Second language attrition: The role of motivation and use. *Journal of Language and Social Psychology, 6*: 1–47.
Gardner, R. C., Lalonde, R. N., Pierson, R. (1983). The socio-educational model of second language acquisition: An investigation using LISREL causal modeling. *Journal of Language and Social Psychology, 2*, 1, 1–15.
Gass, S. M. (1997). *Input, interaction and the second language learner*. Mahwah NJ: Lawrence Erlbaum Associates, Publishers.
Gillette, B. (1987). Two successful language learners: An introspective report. In Faerch, C., Kasper, G. (Eds.) *Introspection in second language research* (pp.267–279). Clavedon, Avon: Multilingual Matters.
Grabe, W. (1997). Developments in reading research and their implications for computer-adaptive reading assessment. Paper presented at 19th Annual Language Testing Research Colloquium, Orlando, FL.
Grotjahn, R., Stemmer, B. (1985). On the development and evaluation of a C-Test for French. *Fremdsprachen und Hochschule 13*(14): 101–120.
Hansen, J., Stansfield, C. (1981). The relationship of field dependent–independent cognitive styles to foreign language achievement, *Language Learning, 31*: 349–367.

References

Hatch, E. (1978). Discourse analysis, speech acts and second language acquisition. In Ritchie, W. (Ed.) *Second Language Acquisition Research* (pp.137–155). New York: Academic Press.

Hosenfeld, C. (1976). Learning about learning: discovering our students' strategies. *Foreign Language Annals, 9*: 117–129.

Hosenfeld, C. (1977a). *A learning-teaching view of second-language instruction: The learning strategies of second-language learners with reading-grammar tasks*, Unpublished doctoral dissertation. Ohio State University, Columbus, OH.

Hosenfeld, C. (1977b). A preliminary investigation of the reading strategies of successful and non-successful language learners. *System, 5*: 110–123.

Hosenfeld, C. (1984). Case studies of ninth grade readers. In Alderson C. J., Urquhart, A. H. (Eds.) *Reading in a foreign language* (pp.231–244). London: Longman.

Huang, X.-H., Van Naerssen, M. (1985). Learning strategies for oral communication. *Applied Linguistics, 6*: 287–307.

Hunt, M. (1982). *The universe within: A new science explores the human mind*. New York: Simon & Schuster.

Hymes, P. H. (1982). *Towards linguistic competence*. Philadelphia, PA. Graduate School of Education, University of Pennsylvania.

Jamieson, J., Chapelle, C. (1987). Working styles on computers as evidence of second language learning strategies. *Language Learning, 37*(4): 523–544.

Jöreskog, K. G. (1993). Testing structural equation models. In Bollen, K., Long, J. S. (Ed.) *Testing structural equation models*: 294–316. Newbury Park: Sage Publications.

Jöreskog, K. G., Sörbom, D. (1989). *LISREL 7: A Guide to the program and applications* (2nd ed.). Chicago: Jöreskog & Sörbom/SPSS Inc.

Jöreskog, K. G., Sörbom, D. (1993). *PRELIS 2: User's Reference Guide*. Chicago: SSI Scientific Software, Inc.

Kaiser, H. F. (1958). The varimax criterion for analytic rotation in factor analysis. *Psychometrica, 23*: 187–200.

Kim, J. O., Mueller, C. W. (1978a). *Introduction to factor analysis: What it is and how to do it*. Newbury Park, CA: Sage University Press.

Kim, J. O., Mueller, C. W. (1978b). *Factor analysis: statistical methods and practical issues*. Newbury Park, CA: Sage University Press.

Klatsky, R. L. (1980). *Human memory: structures and processes*. San Francisco: Freeman.

Krashen, S. (1985). *The input hypothesis: Issues and implications*. London: Longman.

Kunnan, A. J. (1995). *Test-taker characteristics and performance: A structural equation modeling approach*. Cambridge: Cambridge

University Press.
Lado, R. (1961). *Language Testing*. New York: McGraw-Hill.
Lefebvre-Pinard, M. (1983). Understanding and auto-control of cognitive functions: Implications for the relationship between cognition and behavior. *International Journal of Behavioral Development, 39*: 375–395.
Lennon, P. (1989). Introspection and intentionality in advanced second-language acquisition. *Language Learning, 6*: 15–35.
Long, M. H. (1988). Instructed interlanguage development. In Beebe, L. M. (Ed.) *Issues in second language acquisition* (pp.115–141). New York, NY: Newbury House.
Loschky, L., Bley-Vroman, R. (1993). Grammar and task-based methodology. In Crookes, G., Gass, S. M. (Eds.) *Tasks and language learning: Integrating theory and practice* (pp.123–167). Clevedon: Multilingual Matters LTD.
Lyons, J. (1968). *Introduction to theoretical linguistics*. Cambridge: Cambridge University Press.
MacCallum, R. C. (1995). Model specification: Strategies, procedures and related issues. In Hoyle, R. H. (Ed.) Structural Equation Modeling: Concepts, Issues and Applications (pp.16–36). Thousand Oaks: Sage Publications.
MacCallum, R. C., Roznowski, M., Newcowitz, L. B. (1992). Model modifications in covariance structure analysis: The problem of capitalization on chance. *Psychological Bulletin, 111*: 490–504.
Mangubhai, F. (1991). The processing behaviours of adult second language learners and their relationship to second language proficiency. *Applied Linguistics, 12*: 268–298.
McCombs, B. (1991). The definition and measurement of primary motivational processes. In Wittrock, M. C., Baker, E. L. (Eds.) *Testing and Cognition* (pp.62–81). Englewood Cliffs, NJ: Prentice Hall.
McLaughlin, B. (1987). *Theories in second-language learning*. London: Edward Arnold.
McLaughlin, B. (1990). Restructuring. *Applied Linguistics, 11*: 113–128.
McLaughlin, B., Rossman, T., McLeod, B. (1983). Second language learning: An information-processing perspective. *Language Learning, 33*: 135–158.
McLeod, B., McLaughlin, B. (1986). Restructuring or authenticity? Reading in a second language. *Language Learning, 36*: 108–123.
Microsoft EXCEL Version 5.0. (1993). Microsoft Corporation.
Naiman, N., Fröhlich, M., Stern, H. H., Todesco, A. (1978). The good language learner. *Research in Education Series* 7. Ontario Institute for Studies in Education.
Neisser, U. (1967). *Cognitive psychology*. New York, NY: Appleton, Century, Crofts.

References

Nevo, N. (1988). Test-taking strategies on a multiple-choice test. Unpublished paper.

Nunan, D. (1992). *Research methods in language learning*. Cambridge: Cambridge University Press.

O'Malley, M. (1987). The effects of training in the use of learning strategies. In Wenden, A. and Rubin, J. (Eds.) *Learner strategies in language learning* (pp.133–144). New York: Prentice Hall.

O'Malley, M. J., Chamot, A. U. (1990). *Learning strategies in second language acquisition*. Cambridge: Cambridge University Press.

O'Malley, M. J., Chamot, A. U., Küpper, L. (1989). Listening comprehension strategies in second language acquisition. *Applied Linguistics, 10*(4): 418–437.

O'Malley, M. J., Chamot, A. U., Stewner-Manzanares, G., Küpper, L., Russo, R. (1985). Learning strategies used by beginning and intermediate ESL students. *Language Learning, 35*: 21–46.

O'Malley, M. J., Chamot, A. U., Walker, C. (1987). Some applications of cognitive theory to second language acquisition. *Studies in second language acquisition, 9*: 287–306.

Oller Jr., J. W. (1979). *Language tests at school*. London: Longman.

Oller Jr., J. W. (1981). Language as intelligence? *Language Learning, 31*: 465–492.

Oller Jr., J. W. (1983). A consensus for the eighties? In Oller Jr., J. W. (Ed.) *Issues in language testing research*. Rowley, MA: Newbury House.

Oxford, R. (1986). *Development of the strategy inventory for language learning. Manuscript*. Washington, DC: Center for Applied Linguistics.

Oxford, R. (1989). Use of language learning strategies: A synthesis of studies with implications for teacher training. *System, 17*: 235–247.

Oxford, R. (1990). *Language learning strategies: What every teacher should know*. New York: Newbury House Publisher.

Oxford, R. (1996). Language Learning Strategies Around The World: Cross-Culture Perspectives. Honolulu, HI: Second Language teaching & Curiculum Center, University of Hawaii.

Oxford, R., Nyikos, M., Crookall, D. (1987). Learning strategies of university foreign language students: A large-scale, factor analytic study. Paper presented at the annual convention of Teachers of English to Speakers of Other Languages. Miami, FL.

Pienemann, M. (1985). Psycholinguistic principles of second language teaching, Unpublished manuscript. Department of German, University of Sydney.

Pintrich, P. R. (1988). A process-oriented view of student motivation and cognition. In Stark, J. S., Mets, L. A. (Eds.) *Improving teaching and learning through research* (pp.65–79). New Dimensions for Institutional Research, San Francisco: Jossey-Bass.

References

Politzer, R. L., McGroarty, M. (1985). An exploratory study of learning behaviors and their relationship to gains in linguistic and communicative competence. *TESOL Quarterly, 19*: 103–123.

Poulisse, N., Bongaerts, T., Kellerman, E. (1987). The use of retrospective verbal report in the analysis of compensatory strategies. In Faerch, C. Kasper, G. (Eds.) *Introspection in second language research* (pp.213–229). Philadelphia: Multilingual Matters.

Purcell, E. T. (1983). Models of pronunciation accuracy. In Oller, J. (Ed.) *Issues in language testing research* (pp.133–153). Rowley, MA: Newbury House.

Purpura, J. E. (1994). Using EFA to validate a metacognitive strategy questionnaire. Unpublished paper.

Purpura, J. E. (1996). *Modeling the relationships between test takers' reported cognitive and metacognitive strategy use and performance on language tests*. Unpublished doctoral dissertation. Department of TESL/Applied Linguistics. University of California, Los Angeles.

Purpura, J. E. (1998). The development and construct validation of an instrument designed to investigate selected cognitive background characteristics of test takers. In Kunnan, A. J. (Ed.) *Validation in language assessment* (pp.111–139). Hillsdale, NJ: Lawrence Erlbaum Associates.

Rabinowitz, M., Chi, M. T. (1987). An interactive model of strategic processing. In Ceci, S. J. (Ed.) *Handbook of cognitive, social and neuropsychological aspects of learning disabilities* (pp.83–102). Hillsdale, NJ: Erlbaum.

Reiss, M. (1983). Helping the unsuccessful language learner. *The Canadian Review, 39*: 257–266.

Reiss, M. (1985). The good language learner: Another look. *Canadian Modern Language Review, 41*: 511–523.

Rindskopf, D., Rose, T. (1988). Some theory and applications of confirmatory second-order factor analysis. *Multivariate Behavioral Research, 23*: 51–67.

Rubin, J. (1975). What the "good language learner" can teach us. *TESOL Quarterly, 9*: 41–51.

Rubin, J. (1981). The study of cognitive processes in second language learning. *Applied Linguistics, 2*: 117–131.

Rubin, J. (1987). Learner Strategies: Theoretical assumptions, research history and typology, pp.15–30. In Wenden, A., Rubin, J. (Eds.) *Learner strategies in language learning* (pp.145–58). London: Prentice Hall International.

Rubin, J. (1989) The language learning disc. In Soreth, W. F. (Ed.) *Modern technology in foreign language education* (pp 267–275). Lincolnwood, IL: National Textbook Company.

Rubin, J., Thompson, I. (1982). *How to be a more successful language learner*. Boston, MA: Heinle & Heinle Publishers, Inc.

References

Sasaki, M. (1991). *Relationships among second language proficiency, foreign language aptitude, and intelligence: A structural equation modeling approach*. Unpublished doctoral dissertation, University of California, Los Angeles.

Satorra, A., Bentler, P. M. (1988a). *Scaling corrections for statistics in covariance structure analysis*. (UCLA Statistics Series 2). Los Angeles: University of California at Los Angeles, Department of Psychology.

Satorra, A., Bentler, P. M. (1988b). Scaling corrections for chi-square statistics in covariance structure analysis. *Proceedings of the American Statistics Association*: 308–313.

Satorra, A., Bentler, P. M. (1994). Corrections to statistics and standard errors in covariance structure analysis. In von Eye, A., Clogg, C. C. (Eds.) *Latent variables analysis: Applications for developmental research* (pp.309–419). Thousand Oaks, CA: Sage.

Schachter, J. (1983). A new account of language transfer. In Gass, S., Selinker, L. (Eds.) *Language transfer in language learning* (pp.98–111). Rowley, MA: Newbury House.

Schmidt, R, (1990). The role of consciousness in second language learning. *Applied Linguistics, 11*: 129–158.

Scott-Lennox, J. A., Lennox, R. D. (1995). Sex-race differences in social support and depression in older low-income adults. In Hoyle, R. H. (Ed.) *Structural equation modeling: Concepts, issues and applications* (pp.199–216). Thousand Oaks, CA: Sage Publications.

Seliger, H. W. (1983). The language learner as linguist: of metaphors and realities. *Applied Linguistics, 4*: 179–191.

Seliger, H. W. (1984). Processing universals in second language acquisition. In Eckman, F. R., Bell, L. H., Nelson, D. (Eds.) *Universals of second language Acquisition*. Rowley, MA: Newbury House.

Sharwood Smith, M. (1988). Consciousness-raising and the second language learner. In Rutherford, W. amd Sharwood Smith (Eds.) *Grammar and second language teaching* (pp.51–60). Boston, MA: Heinle and Hurle Publishers.

Skehan, P. (1989). *Individual differences in second-language learning*. London: Edward Arnold.

Spolsky, B. (1973). What does it mean to know a language: Or how do you get someone to perform his competence? In Oller, J. W., Richards, J. C. (Eds.) *Focus on the learner: pragmatic perspectives for the language teacher* (pp.164–176). Rowley, MA: Newbury House.

Spolsky, B. (1985). The limits of authenticity in language testing. *Language Testing* 3(2): 164–176.

SPSS Version 4.0.4. (1990) SPSS Inc.

SPSS incorporated. (1988). *SPSS-X User's Guide* (3rd ed.). Chicago, IL: SPSS Inc.
Stansfield, C., Hansen, J. (1983). Field-dependence-independence as a variable in second language cloze test performance. *TESOL Quarterly, 17*: 29–38.
Stemmer, B. (1991). What's on a C-test taker's mind? Mental processes in C-test taking. *Manuskripte zur Sprachlehrforshung Band 36*. Bochum: Universitatsverlag Dr. N. Brockmeyer.
Stern, H. H. (1983). *Fundamental concepts in language teaching*. Oxford: Oxford University Press.
Sternberg, R. J. (1980). Sketch of a componential subtheory of human intelligence. *Behavioural and Brain Science, 3*, 573–654.
Sternberg, R. J., Powell J. S. (1983). Comprehending verbal comprehension. *American Psychologist, 38*: 878–893.
Swanson, H. L. (1985). Assessing learning disabled children's intellectual performance: An information processing perspective. In Gadow, K. D. (Ed.) *Advances in learning and behavioral disabilities* (Vol. 4, pp.225–272). Greenwich, CT: JAI Press.
Tarone, E. (1981). Some thoughts on the notion of communication strategy. *TESOL Quarterly, 24*(2): 177–198.
Tomlin, R. S., Villa, V. (1994). Attention in cognitive science and second language acquisition. *Studies in second language acquisition, 16*: 183–203.
Van Dijk, T. A., Kintsch, W. (1983). *Strategies of discourse comprehension*. New York: Academic Press.
Vann, R. J., Abraham, R. G. (1990). Strategies of unsuccessful language learners. *TESOL Quarterly, 24*(2): 177–198.
VanPatten, B. (1996). *Input processing and grammar instruction: theory and practice. Norwood, NJ: Ablex Publishing Corporation.*
Victori, R. M. (1992). *Investigating the metacognitive knowledge of students of English as a second language.* Unpublished M. A. thesis in TESL, UCLA.
Volmer, H. J., Sang, F. (1983). Competing hypotheses about second language ability: A plea for caution. In Oller, J. W. (Ed.) *Issues in language testing research* (pp. 29–79). Rowley, MA: Newbury House.
Wald, A. (1943). Tests of statistical hypotheses concerning several parameters when the number of observations is large. *Transactions of the American Mathematical Society, 54*: 426–482.
Wang, L.-S. (1988). *A causal analysis of achievement models for language minority students in the U.S.: A linear structural relations (LISREL) Approach.* Unpublished Ph.D. dissertation, Urbana: University of Illinois.

References

Weinstein, C. E. (1987). *LASSI user's manual*. Clearwater, FL: H & H Publishing Company, Inc.

Weinstein, C. E., Mayer, D. (1986). The teaching of learning strategies. In Wittrock, M. (Ed.) *Handbook of research on teaching*. New York: MacMillan.

Weinstein, C. E., Schulte, A. C., Cascallar, E. C. (1983). The learning and study strategies inventory (LASSI): Initial design and development. Manuscript. Austin: University of Texas.

Wenden, A. (1987a). How to be a successful language learner: Insights and prescriptions from L2 learners. In Wenden, A., Rubin, J. (Eds.) *Learner strategies in language learning* (pp.103–118). London: Prentice Hall International.

Wenden, A. (1987b). Incorporating learner training in the classroom. In Wenden, A., Rubin, J. (Eds.) *Learner strategies in language learning* (pp.159–168). London: Prentice Hall International.

Wenden, A. (1991). *Learner strategies for learner autonomy*. Englewood Cliffs, NJ: Prentice-Hall.

Wenden, A. (1998). Metacognitive knowledge and language learning. *Applied Linguistics, 19* (4): 515–537.

Wenden, A., Rubin, J. (1987). Conceptual background and utility. In Wenden, A., Rubin, J. (Eds.) *Learner strategies in language learning* (pp.3–13). Englewood Cliffs, NJ: Prentice-Hall.

Wesche, M. (1987). SL performance testing: the Ontario Test of ESL as an example. *Language Testing, 4*(1): 28–47

Westney, P. (1994). Rules and pedagogical grammar. In Odlin, T. (Ed.) *Perspectives on pedagogical grammar* (pp.72–96). Cambridge: Cambridge University Press.

Widdowson, H. G. (1978) *Teaching language communication*. Oxford: Oxford University Press.

Wittrock, M. C. (1978). The cognitive movement in instruction. *Educational psychologist, 13*: 87–95.

Wong-Fillmore, L. (1976). *The second time around: Cognitive and social strategies in second language acquisition*. Unpublished doctoral dissertation, Stanford University.

Wong-Fillmore, L. (1979). Individual differences in second language acquisition. In Fillmore, C. J., Wang, W.-S. Y., Kempler, D. (Eds.) *Individual differences in language ability and language behavior*. New York: Academic Press.

Zimmerman, B. J., Pons, M. M. (1986). Development of a structured interview for assessing student use of self-regulated learning strategies. *American Educational Research Journal, 23*: 614–628.

Appendices

Appendix A Participants by Country and Test Center
Appendix B Participants by Course Level
Appendix C Participants by Native Language
Appendix D Learning Strategies Questionnaire: part 1
Appendix E Cognitive Strategy Questionnaire by item type
Appendix F Learning Strategies Questionnaire: part 2
Appendix G Metacognitive Strategy Questionnaire by item type
Appendix H The *FCE Anchor Test*
Appendix I The *FCE Anchor Test* Answer Sheet
Appendix J UCLES Scoring Rubric
Appendix K Model 1.2 CSU: Correlation Matrix
Appendix L Model 2.2 MSU: Correlation Matrix
Appendix M Model 3.1 SLTP: Correlation Matrix
Appendix N Model 4.2 Full Latent Variable Model: Correlation Matrix
Appendix O Covariance Matrix for the High-Ability Group
Appendix P Covariance Matrix for the Low-Ability Group

Appendix A
Participants by Country and Test Center

Participants by Country

Country	Frequency	Percent
Czech Republic	132	9.5
Spain	225	16.3
Turkey	1025	74.2
Total	1382	100.0

Participants by Test Center

		Cum %
Sehremini HS, Istanbul, Turkey	150	10.9
Dokuz Eylul U, Izmir, Turkey	56	4.1
Dokuz Eylul U, Izmir, Turkey	19	1.4
Hacettepe U, Ankara, Turkey	23	1.7
Erciyes U, Kayseri, Turkey	7	0.5
Tuglacilar HS, Tekirdat, Turkey	43	3.1
Orhan Cemal Fersoy HS, Istanbul, Turkey	179	13.0
Hasan Polatkan HS, Istanbul, Turkey	119	8.6
Dvorakovo HS, Kralupy, Czech Republic	95	6.9
Liberac U, Liberac, Czech Republic	37	2.7
Barcelona U, Barcelona, Spain	224	16.2
Turkish-American Assoc., Ankara, Turkey	126	9.1
Berna Unsal HS, Istanbul, Turkey	55	4.0
Oya Aksoy HS, Istanbul, Turkey	96	6.9
Serpil Akkan HS, Istanbul, Turkey	11	8.5
ITBA Language School, Istanbul, Turkey	29	2.1
Berin, Istanbul, Turkey	6	0.4
Total	1275	100.0%

Legend: **HS** = High School   **U** = University

Appendix B
Participants by Course Level

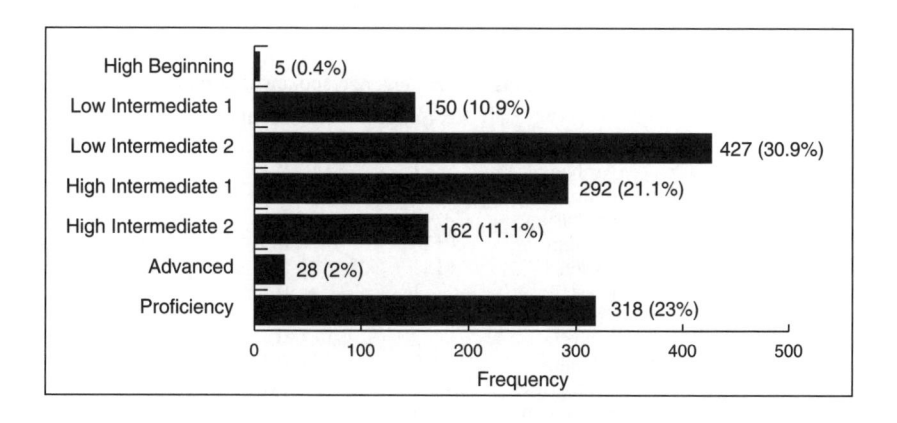

Course Level	Frequency
High Beginning	5 (0.4%)
Low Intermediate 1	150 (10.9%)
Low Intermediate 2	427 (30.9%)
High Intermediate 1	292 (21.1%)
High Intermediate 2	162 (11.1%)
Advanced	28 (2%)
Proficiency	318 (23%)

Appendix C
Participants by Native Language

Native Language (The language spoken at home)

	Frequency	Percent
Albanian	1	0.1
Amharic	1	0.1
Arabic	4	0.3
Bulgarian	2	0.1
Catalan	118	8.5
Czech	131	9.5
Farsi	1	0.1
French	1	0.1
Hebrew	2	0.1
Korean	2	0.1
Portuguese	1	0.1
Romanian	1	0.1
Spanish	106	7.7
Turkish	1008	72.9
Ukrainian	2	0.1
Urdu	1	0.1
Total	1382	100.0

Appendix D
Learning Strategies
Questionnaire: Part 1

```
Never                              Always
<-------------------------------------->
0      1      2      3      4      5
```

(0) Never   (2) Sometimes   (4) Usually
(1) rarely   (3) Often   (5) Always

When I am learning new material in English...

1. I try to connect what I am learning with what I already know.
2. I try to somehow organize the material in my mind.
3. I ask for examples of how to use a word or expression.
4. I repeat words to make sure that I have understood them correctly.
5. I look for similarities and differences between English and my own language.
6. I use what I know from my past experiences to help me learn more.
7. I make written summaries of information that I hear or read in English.
8. I learn best when I am taught the rules.
9. I translate it into my native language.

I learn new words in English by...

10. relating the sound of the new word to the sound of a familiar word.
11. remembering where the new word was located on the page, or where I first saw it or heard it.
12. associating them with how they look, feel, smell, sound or taste.
13. thinking of words I know that sound like the new word.
14. translating them into my own language.

I learn grammar in English by...

15. using the grammar of my own language to help me learn the rules.
16. comparing grammar rules in my own language with grammar rules in English.
17. looking for similarities in different sentences.
18. memorizing the rules and applying them to new situations.

Appendix D

I try to improve my English by...
19. looking for words in my own language that are similar to words in English.
20. asking other people to tell me if I have understood or said something correctly.
21. spending time with English speaking people.

I try to improve my English by...
22. applying what I have learned to new situations.
23. looking for opportunities to speak English as much as possible.
24. identifying and using words that are similar to words in my own language.

I try to improve my listening by...
25. watching TV programs in English.
26. listening to programs in English on the radio.

I try to improve my speaking in English by...
27. repeating what I've learned out loud.
28. pronouncing new sounds until I can say them like a native speaker.
29. repeating sentences in English until I can say them easily.
30. repeating what I hear native speakers say.
31. using familiar words in different combinations to make new sentences.
32. using my knowledge of grammar rules to help me form new sentences.

I try to improve my reading in English by...
33. summarizing new information to remember it.
34. trying to understand without looking up every new word.
35. reading English books and magazines.
36. looking for the ways that writers show relationships between ideas.
37. guessing the meaning of new words from context.

I try to improve my writing in English by...
38. showing my writing to another person.
39. analyzing how other writers organize their paragraphs.
40. analyzing the ways that other writers show relationships between ideas.

Appendix E
Cognitive Strategy Questionnaire by item type

Comprehending Processes

Process	Strategy	Item
COMP	AC5	When I am learning new material in English, I look for similarities and differences between English and my own language.
COMP	AC16	I learn grammar in English by comparing grammar rules in my own language with grammar rules in English.
COMP	AC17	I learn grammar in English by looking for similarities in different sentences.
COMP	AI36	I try to improve my reading in English by looking for the ways that writers show relationships between ideas.
COMP	AI39	I try to improve my writing in English by analyzing how other writers organize their paragraphs.
COMP	AI40	I try to improve my writing in English by analyzing the ways that other writers show relationships between ideas.
COMP	CLAR3	When I am learning new material in English, I ask for examples of how to use a word or expression.
COMP	CLAR4	When I am learning new material in English, I repeat words to make sure that I have understood them correctly.
COMP	CLAR20	I try to improve my English by asking other people to tell me if I have understood or said something correctly.
COMP	CLAR38	I try to improve my writing in English by showing my writing to another person.
COMP	INF34	I try to improve my reading in English by trying to understand without looking up every word.
COMP	INF37	I try to improve my reading in English by guessing the meaning of new words from context.
COMP	TRL9	When I am learning new material in English, I translate it into my native language.
COMP	TRL14	I learn new words in English by translating them into my own language.

Appendix E

Storing or Memory Processes

Process	Strategy	Item
MEM	ASSOC10	I learn new words in English by relating the sound of the new word to the sound of a familiar word.
MEM	ASSOC11	I learn new words in English by remembering where the new word was located on the page, or where I first saw it or heard it.
MEM	ASSOC12	I learn new words in English by associating them with how they look, feel, smell, sound or taste.
MEM	ASSOC13	I learn new words in English by thinking of words I know that sound like the new word.
MEM	LPK1	When I am learning new material in English, I try to connect what I am learning with what I already know.
MEM	LPK2	When I am learning new material in English, I try to somehow organize the material in my mind.
MEM	LPK6	When I am learning new material in English, I use what I know from my past experiences to help me learn more.
MEM	REP27	I try to improve my speaking in English by repeating what I have learned out loud.
MEM	REP28	I try to improve my speaking in English by pronouncing new sounds until I can say them like a native speaker.
MEM	REP29	I try to improve my speaking in English by repeating sentences in English until I can say them easily.
MEM	REP30	I try to improve my speaking in English by repeating what I hear native speakers say.
MEM	SUM7	When I am learning new material in English, I make written summaries of information that I hear or read in English.
MEM	SUM33	I try to improve my reading in English by summarizing new information to remember it.

Appendix E

Using or Retrieval Processes

Process	Strategy	Item
RET	APR8	When I am learning new material in English, I learn best when I am taught the rules.
RET	APR18	I learn grammar in English by memorizing the rules and applying them to new situations.
RET	APR22	I try to improve my English by applying what I have learned to new situations.
RET	APR31	I try to improve my speaking in English by using familiar words in different combinations to make new sentences.
RET	APR32	I try to improve my speaking in English by using my knowledge of grammar rules to help me form new sentences.
RET	PN21	I try to improve my English by spending time with English speaking people.
RET	PN23	I try to improve my English by looking for opportunities to speak English as much as possible.
RET	PN25	I try to improve my listening in English by watching TV programs in English.
RET	PN26	I try to improve my listening in English by listening to programs in English on the radio.
RET	PN35	I try to improve my reading in English by reading English books and magazines.
RET	TRF15	I learn grammar in English by using the grammar of my own language to help me learn the rules.
RET	TRF19	I try to improve my English by looking for words in my own language that are similar to words in English.
RET	TRF24	I try to improve my English by identifying and using words that are similar to words in my own language.

Appendix F
Learning Strategies Questionnaire: Part 2

Never   Always
<--->
0   1   2   3   4   5

(0) Never   (2) Sometimes   (4) Usually
(1) rarely   (3) Often   (5) Always

41. Before I use English, I think about whether my grammar is good enough to express my ideas.
42. Before I begin an English test, I try to see which parts will be easy and what parts will be difficult.
43. When I begin studying English, I plan what I am going to do so I can use my time well.
44. When I speak English, I know what I need to change so that people will understand me.
45. I think about how I learn languages best.
46. When I have learned a new word or phrase in English, I test myself to make sure I have memorized it.
47. Before I hand in my English test, I check my work.
48. I try to understand the purpose of activities in my English classes.
49. When I listen to English, I realize when I have not understood something.
50. I test my knowledge of English grammar rules by applying them to new situations.
51. I test my knowledge of new English words by using them in new situations.
52. When I am speaking English, I know when I have not pronounced something properly.
53. I set goals for myself in language learning.
54. I think about whether I am making progress in learning English.
55. When I am taking an English test, I know how much time has gone by.
56. When I begin learning a new language, I think about how well I want to learn it.

Appendix F

57. When I speak English, I recognize when I have said something that sounds like a native speaker.
58. Before I begin an English test, I think about how the test will be scored.
59. When someone is speaking English, I try to concentrate on what the person is saying.
60. When I speak English, I know when I make grammar mistakes.
61. After I have taken a test in English, I think about how I can do better next time.
62. I try to learn from the mistakes I make in English.
63. Before I begin an English test, I think about which parts of the test are the most important.
64. When I am taking an English test, I try to concentrate on what I am doing.
65. Before I begin an English assignment, I think about whether I know enough of English to do it.
66. Before I begin an English test, I decide how important it is for me to get a good grade on the test.
67. Before I use my English, I think about how I can ask for help if I cannot express myself clearly or if I do not know a word.
68. When I listen in English, I recognize other people's grammar mistakes.
69. After I finish a conversation in English, I think about how I could say things better.
70. I try to find out all I can about language learning by reading books or articles.
71. After I say something in English, I check whether the person I am talking to has really understood what I meant.
72. Before I talk to someone in English, I think about how much the person knows about what I'm going to say.
73. When someone does not understand my English, I try to understand what I said wrong.
74. When I have learned a new English grammar rule, I test myself to make sure I know how to use it.
75. When I speak English, I know when someone does not understand something I said.
76. After I learn something in English, I test myself to make sure I have really learned it.
77. I know what helps me to remember new words in English.
78. Before I begin an English assignment, I make sure I have a dictionary or other resources.
79. Before I write a composition in English, I plan my work.
80. When I am taking an English class, I think about my final goals.

Appendix G
Metacognitive Strategy Questionnaire by item type

Goal-Setting Processes

Process	Strategy	Item
GS	GS43	When I begin studying my English, I plan what I am going to do so I can use my time well.
GS	GS53	I set goals for myself in language learning.
GS	GS54	I think about whether I am making progress in learning English.
GS	GS56	When I begin learning a new language, I think about how well I want to learn it.
GS	GS80	When I am taking an English class, I think about my final goals.

Planning Processes

Process	Strategy	Item
PLAN	FPL48	I try to understand the purpose of activities in my English class.
PLAN	FPL59	When someone is speaking English, I try to concentrate on what the person is saying.
PLAN	FPL64	When I am taking an English test, I try to concentrate on what I am doing.
PLAN	FPL78	Before I begin an English assignment, I make sure I have a dictionary or other resources.
PLAN	FPL79	Before I write a composition in English, I plan my work.
LLRN	LLRN45	I think about how I learn languages best.
LLRN	LLRN70	I try to find out all I can about language learning by reading books or articles.
LLRN	LLRN77	I know what helps me to remember new words in English.

Appendix G

Assessment Processes

Process	Strategy	Item
ASSESS	ASIT41	Before I use my English, I think about whether my grammar is good enough to express my ideas.
ASSESS	ASIT42	Before I begin an English test, I try to see which parts will be easy and what parts will be difficult.
ASSESS	ASIT58	Before I begin an English test, i think about how the test will be scored.
ASSESS	ASIT63	Before I begin an English test, I think about which parts of the test are the most important.
ASSESS	ASIT65	Before I begin an English assignment, I think about whether I know enough English to do it.
ASSESS	ASIT66	Before I begin an English test, I decide how important it is for me to get a good grade on the test.
ASSESS	ASIT67	Before I use my English, I think about how I can ask for help if I cannot express myself clearly or if I do not know a word.
ASSESS	ASIT72	Before I talk to someone in English, I think about how much the person knows about what I'm going to say.
ASSESS	MON44	When I speak English, I know what I need to change so that people will understand me.
ASSESS	MON47	Before I hand in my English test, I check my work.
ASSESS	MON49	When I listen to English, I realize when I havae not understood something.
ASSESS	MON52	When I am speaking English, I know when I have not pronounced something correctly.
ASSESS	MON55	When I am taking an English test, I know how much time has gone by.
ASSESS	MON57	When I speak English, I recognize when I have said something that sounds like a native speaker.
ASSESS	MON60	When I speak English, I know when I make grammar mistakes.
ASSESS	MON68	When I listen to English, I recognize other people's grammar mistakes.
ASSESS	MON75	When I speak English, I know when someone does not understand something I said.

Appendix G

Assessment Processes – cont.

Process	Strategy	Item
ASSESS	EVAL46	When I have learned a new word or phrase in English, I test myself to make sure I have memorized it.
ASSESS	EVAL51	I test my knowledge of new English words by using them in new situations.
ASSESS	EVAL61	I test my knowledge of English grammar rules by applying them to new situations.
ASSESS	EVAL62	After I have taken a test in English, I think about how I can do better the next time.
ASSESS	EVAL69	I try to learn from the mistakes I make in English.
ASSESS	EVAL71	After I finish a conversation in English, I think about how I could say things better.
ASSESS	EVAL73	After I say something in English, I check whether the person I am talking to has really understood what Imeant.
ASSESS	MON74	When someone does not understand my English, I try to understand what I said wrong.
ASSESS	MON74	When I have learned a new English grammar rule, I test myself to make sure I know how to use it.
ASSESS	EVAL76	After I learn something in English, I test myself to make sure I have really learned it.

Appendix H
The *FCE Anchor Test*

Candidate name: _____

Centre Number: [ ] Candidate Number: [ ]

University of Cambridge Local Examinations Syndicate [A1]

ENGLISH LANGUAGE TEST

Time allowed: 1 hour 30 minutes

Instructions to candidates:

DO NOT OPEN THE TEST PAPER UNTIL YOU ARE TOLD TO DO SO.

There are **two** sections in this test:
Section A: Reading Comprehension   Questions 1 to 30
Section B: Use of English   Questions 31 to 66

Answer **all** the questions

Put your answers in pencil **on the separate sheet** provided.

Read and follow carefully the instructions given on the separate sheet.

You may write on the test paper, but you must **transfer your answers to the separate answer sheet** within the time limit.

Appendix H

SECTION A
READING COMPREHENSION

Part One

Questions 1 to 20
*For each question, you must choose the word or phrase which best completes the sentence. Mark the appropriate box on the **answer sheet**.*

EXAMPLE
00   Is there _____ of food for everybody?
A   adequate   B   enough   C   sufficient   D   plenty

00   A ⬚   B ⬚   C ⬚   D ■

1. Price control seems to be the only _____ to the problem of the rising cost of living.

   A way   B explanation   C possibility   D solution

2. Most people prefer _____ vegetables to frozen or tinned ones.

   A fresh   B new   C refreshing   D ripe

3. When you stay in a country for some time, you get used to the people's _____ of life.

   A habit   B custom   C way   D system

4. What do you mean, he's watching television? He's _____ to be in bed.

   A supposed   B hoped   C should   D thought

5. I'm sorry I'm late. I never _____ the taxi to take so long to get here.

   A waited for   B depended on   C expected   D planned

6. When you are riding a bicycle you should _____ the handlebars firmly.

   A handle   B hold   C hand   D control

7. After the death of her parents the girl was _____ by her grandparents.

   A brought up   B grown up   C taken up   D given up

Appendix H

8. Although I spoke to him many times, he never took any _____ of what I said.

   A notice **B** remark **C** warning **D** attention

9. I've had this cold for ages. I just can't get _____ of it.

   A rid **B** better **C** over **D** out

10. By the time you receive this letter, I _____ for Japan.

    A will leave **B** have left **C** would have left **D** will have left

11. Mr. Smith only _____ that shop, he doesn't own it.

    A rules **B** orders **C** leads **D** runs

12. How much do you _____ for cleaning a suit?

    A cost **B** account **C** demand **D** charge

13. He asked an artist to _____ some drawings to illustrate what he had written.

    A show **B** do **C** paint **D** describe

14. I am absolutely _____ to go ahead with my plan, whatever you say.

    A ensured **B** intended **C** determined **D** designed

15. I can't advise you what to do: you must use your own _____ .

    A opinion **B** guesswork **C** justice **D** judgement

16. Copies of this book are _____ direct from the publisher.

    A attainable **B** acceptable **C** available **D** capable

17. I have no _____ in recommending Ms. Smith for the head teacher's post.

    A opposition **B** caution **C** care **D** hesitation

18. When he was a student, his parents gave him a monthly _____ towards his expenses.

    A salary **B** allowance **C** wage **D** money

19. She was _____ with murder.

    A accused **B** arrested **C** charged **D** convicted

20. I had no _____ in my lawyer's decision.

    A confidence **B** defence **C** doubt **D** fault

Appendix H

Part Two

Questions 21 to 30
*You will find after each passage a number of questions or unfinished statements about the passage, each with four suggested answers or ways of finishing. You must choose the one which you think fits best. On your **answer sheet**, indicate the letter **A, B, C** or **D** against the number of each question from **21 to 30**, for the answer you choose. Read each passage right through before choosing your answers.*

Passage One

> Koko is the first gorilla* to learn a human language. Now nearly eleven he was born in a children's zoo in America. Here he was 'adopted' by a young research psychologist who tried to teach the gorilla human sign language.
>
> Each morning before the zoo opened the psychologist would carry Koko for walks through the children's zoo. She felt it was important to get Koko outside his cage so that he would develop confidence. He soon began to regard the psychologist as his mother.
>
> Koko was terrified of the large animals, particularly a baby elephant, and refused to leave his 'mother's' side.
>
> When Koko was one year old his 'mother' developed games to show him the usefulness of his hands. She breathed on the glass of the large windows in his house and then drew stars and simple faces on the misted surface. Koko loved these games and would try to draw as well. By the second year of the project the researcher found that she had become fond of Koko and that he was as affectionate as any human infant. When Koko sensed that his 'mother' was about to leave he would hang on so fiercely that he sometimes left black and blue finger marks on her arms. Like a parent, the psychologist was fascinated by Koko's development. The gorilla helped to clean the house, imitated movements, played games and finally even laughed.
>
> One of the first signs his 'mother' tried to teach Koko was BIRD, a sign made by placing the forefinger and thumb together in front of the mouth in imitation of a bird's beak. Koko watched the researcher's hands carefully and then he made a sign like a bird but with his fingers away from his mouth.
>
> One of Koko's pastimes was drawing and he was able to make reasonably good copies of things, especially birds. He also spent a good deal of time talking to and playing games with his toys. But this was a private pastime and he did not like being watched while doing it.
>
> As Koko grew larger some of his favourites games – such as riding around on shoulders – were out of the question. With most visitors Koko was extremely gentle. He used to put out his hand, lead them round the room, sit down with them and put his face close to theirs. One of Koko's favourites activities was a car ride when he sat up in the front seat and was able to stare at various things on the journey. Out in the country he enjoyed sitting in the trees, clapping with excitement and sliding down the trunks. Sometimes he would hang from a branch by his arms and move cautiously out towards the end until the branch broke off and he would fall down in a shower of leaves.
>
> The sight of Koko playing freely in the countryside gave the researcher the idea of finding a place which could be like that every day. So now Koko lives with the psychologist on an old farm. The farm is small but it is quiet and private, surrounded by trees and rough land.
>
> * A gorilla is a large kind of monkey.

Appendix H

21. The psychologist took Koko for walks so that he would

    A get exercise out of doors.
    B meet large animals.
    C be in human company.
    D overcome his nervousness.

22. Koko learned to use his hands by

    A touching the psychologist's face.
    B making simple drawings.
    C cleaning the windows.
    D copying basic words.

23. When Koko was learning sign language he

    A tried to copy the psychologist's movements.
    B tried to draw the signs on the ground.
    C put his finger and thumb in his mouth.
    D watched the psychologist's mouth movements.

24. As Koko grew up he

    A became fierce with strangers.
    B lost interest in his games.
    C began to like journeys by car.
    D developed round shoulders.

25. When playing in trees Koko most enjoyed

    A breaking up branches.
    B jumping from branches.
    C swinging carefully along branches.
    D throwing leaves from branches.

Appendix H

Passage Two

Polly and Ted got back to their first-floor flat one night to find everything upside down and £300 missing. They had a life-time's habit of putting to one side money for regular expenses, like groceries, electricity and insurance, and placing the cash in envelopes in a desk with a weak lock. The thieves had seen the flat in darkness, taken tools from a neighbour's shed, piled some handy wooden boxes against the building and calmly pushed their way in through an upstairs lavatory window. As Polly said months afterwards, it wasn't so much the money as the shock.

The sudden experience of being robbed produces an enormous range of feelings in anybody. All the people in this position to whom I have spoken remember feeling first of all a sense of loss and injustice. Psychologists describe the effect on people as similar to that of the death of someone close to them and say it happens even when the amount of actual damage or loss is relatively slight.

Human beings have many ways of dealing with such problems. A few people will have little difficulty, once they have recovered from the first shock, in putting their lives back together. But most people's psychological resources are to some extent inadequate. It may be that they already have some problem that they have to live with, such as illness, or loneliness brought about by divorce or widowhood, which will make it more difficult for them.

It is at this point that support and understanding are badly needed. Very often, people cannot recover from the experience of crime on their own. Yet, strangely, most of the people interviewed said they were unwilling to involve their families and friends. This was particularly noticeable where the person lived alone and it may suggest that people feel they need to protect their right to independence; that talking to anyone they know well about their problems would be admitting failure. In the long term, this unwillingness may prevent recovery, with the person losing all confidence in himself or herself and the world outside his or her own four walls.

Appendix H

26. When Polly and Ted got back to their flat one night they found that
    - A most of their possessions had been stolen.
    - B they had lost some of their savings.
    - C the front door had been broken down.
    - D their property was not insured against theft.

27. The burglars had entered the flat by
    - A stealing some boxes from a neighbour's shed.
    - B breaking in from the flat downstairs.
    - C gaining entry when everyone was asleep.
    - D climbing in through one of the windows.

28. Some people have difficulty in getting over the experience of being robbed because they
    - A have lived alone all their lives.
    - B are already upset or depressed.
    - C are having difficulties in their marriages.
    - D feel lonely without their possessions.

29. Although people often need the help of others to recover from being robbed they often
    - A hesitate to discuss it with people they know.
    - B feel they must confide in their relatives again.
    - C immediately discuss it with their neighbours.
    - D never mention the crime again.

30. The writer of the passage has found that people who lived alone seemed to feel that if they talked about their worries they would
    - A delay their long-term recovery.
    - B be taken into their relatives' protection.
    - C show that they could not manage on their own.
    - D embarrass their family and friends.

Appendix H

SECTION B
USE OF ENGLISH

Part One

Questions 31 to 40
*The word in capitals beside each of the following sentences can be used to form a word that fits suitably in the blank space. Fill each blank in this way. Write your answer in the space provided on the **separate answer sheet**.*

EXAMPLE
00 He said 'Good morning' in a _____ way.   **FRIEND**

00 .... *friendly* ....

31. Although we tried hard, all our efforts ended in _____ . **FAIL**

32. "Could you lend me five pounds?" he asked _____ . **HOPE**

33. He gave me a _____ of nuts and raisins. **HAND**

34. There is a _____ that life exists on other planets. **BELIEVE**

35. Everybody in this _____ works at the local factory. **NEIGHBOUR**

36. Thanks to their neighbours' _____ they managed to collect enough money for their child's operation. **GENEROUS**

37. Although he arrived _____ , we were able to provide him with a meal. **EXPECT**

38. To guarantee _____ to the course you should apply very early. **ADMIT**

39. He refused to follow any rules and had to be punished for _____ . **OBEY**

40. The cat examined the new kind of food _____ . **SUSPECT**

Appendix H

Part Two

Questions 41 to 60
*Find a suitable word to fill each of the numbered blanks in the passage. Use only **one** word for each space. Write your answers in the space provided on your **separate answer sheet**.*

EXAMPLE

00 ....*in*........................

The use of audio-description – a technique designed to enable blind people to enjoy the theatre – was pioneered in America .....(**00**)..... 1981. While continuing to listen in the .....(**41**)..... way to stage dialogue and sound, visually-impaired .....(**42**)..... of the audience also receive a commentary on what is .....(**43**)..... seen.

For .....(**44**)..... who reluctantly give up the theatre when they begin to lose their .....(**45**)..... , audio-description can revive a valued interest. For those, however, who have always enjoyed the theatre .....(**46**)..... total blindness, audio-description presents a whole new dimension.

It is not .....(**47**)..... to see the lights go down to be caught up in .....(**48**)..... sense of antcipation which gradually silences and unites the audience. .....(**49**) the curtain has gone up, it is simply a case of total concentration .....(**50**)..... as not to miss one word, tone, nuance or stage sound that .....(**51**)..... provide a clue .....(**52**)..... some visual happening.

Even .....(**53**)..... sight, theatre can be a delight, but there are innumerable gaps to be filled. Audio-description is the .....(**54**)..... solution. It .....(**55**)..... you in the picture by providing explanatory comments before the curtain goes up, and then audio commentary is relayed .....(**56**)..... an earphone by a person .....(**57**)..... is standing at the side or back of the stage .....(**58**)..... the performance.

Obviously .....(**59**)..... can replace lost sight but to a wonderful and perhaps surprising .....(**60**)..... audio-description makes it possible to *see* a play without sight. It is an exciting glimpse of things to come.

Appendix H

Part Two

Questions 61 to 66
Finish each of the following sentences in such a way that is as similar as possible in meaning to the sentence printed before it. Write your answer in the space provided on your **separate answer sheet**.

EXAMPLE

00   I expect that he will get there by lunchtime.
     I expect him ....

---

00   *to get there by lunchtime*

---

61. You might feel cold on the boat, so take a warm jacket.
    Take a warm jacket ....

62. Edward regretted telling his friend the secret.
    Edward wished ....

63. It was so foggy the plane couldn't take off.
    Thick fog prevented ....

64. I don't intend to apologise to either of them.
    I have ....

65. No one can buy more than four tickets for the dance.
    Four tickets ....

66. They are installing the finance department's new computer system tomorrow.
    The finance department is ....

Appendix I
The *FCE Anchor Test* Answer Sheet

Candidate Name: _____ _____ _____
                              (Last Name)   (First Name)   (Middle Initial)

Center Number: _____ **Candidate Number:** _____

English Language Test - Answer Sheet
Section A   Reading Comprehension

Part One (Circle one)

1. A B C D	6. A B C D	11. A B C D	16. A B C D
2. A B C D	7. A B C D	12. A B C D	17. A B C D
3. A B C D	8. A B C D	13. A B C D	18. A B C D
4. A B C D	9. A B C D	14. A B C D	19. A B C D
5. A B C D	10. A B C D	15. A B C D	20. A B C D

Part Two (Circle one)

21. A B C D	24. A B C D	26. A B C D	29. A B C D
22. A B C D	25. A B C D	27. A B C D	30. A B C D
23. A B C D		28. A B C D	

Appendix I

Section B Use of English
Part One

31. _____ 36. _____
32. _____ 37. _____
33. _____ 38. _____
34. _____ 39. _____
35. _____ 40. _____

Part Two

41. _____ 51. _____
42. _____ 52. _____
43. _____ 53. _____
44. _____ 54. _____
45. _____ 55. _____
46. _____ 56. _____
47. _____ 57. _____
48. _____ 58. _____
49. _____ 59. _____
50. _____ 60. _____

Part Three

61. _____

62. _____

63. _____

64. _____

65. _____

66. _____

Appendix J
UCLES Scoring Rubric

1. GRAMMAR AND VOCABULARY			
Item	UCLES Key	NS Errors*	Rubric Modifications**
8	A	1 NS put "C"	no change to rubric
13	B	2 NSs put "C"	"paint" vs. "do drawings" Considered correct in the dialect of 2 NS. No change to rubric.
18	B	1 NS did not answer	no change
20	A	1 NS put "C"	"no doubt" vs. "confidence"; multiple answers are possible; item deleted from analyses

* Based on the version of the UCLES rubric I was given, these answer choices were considered wrong.
** The "Rubric Modifications" column contains information on whether the "different" answer options were judged correct or not.

2. PASSAGE COMPREHENSION			
Item	UCLES Key	NS Errors	Rubric Modifications
21	D	C	no change to rubric
25	C	1 NS put "A" & 1 put "B"	multiple answers are possible; item deleted from analyses

3 WORD FORMATION			
	UCLES Key	NS Errors	Rubric Modifications
32	hopefully	1 NS put "hoping"	"hoping" added to rubric as correct
38	admission	all 5 NSs put "admittance"	"admittance" added to rubric as correct
39	disobedience	4 NSs put "disobeying"	"disobeying" added to rubric as correct

Appendix J

4. CLOZE

Item	UCLES Key	NS Errors	Rubric Modifications***
41	usual, normal; conventional; ordinary; NOT same	1 NS put "traditional"---> 1 NS put "customary" -->	credit given credit given ADDITIONAL TT CHOICES**: standard; old
42	members		ADDITIONAL TT CHOICES: people
43	being		ADDITIONAL CHOICES: not; next; actually; can be; going to be
44	those; people; some	1 NS put "theater-goers"---------->	credit given ADDITIONAL TT CHOICES: audiences; most; some
45	sight; vision; eyesight;		ADDITIONAL TT CHOICES: senses; patience; attention; enthusiasm; concentration; capacities
46	despite	3 NSs put "in" -----------> 1 NS put "visually" ------>	credit given no credit given
47	necessary; essential	unusual -------------------> unexpected --------------->	no credit given no credit given ADDITIONAL TT CHOICE: important
48	that; the; a		ADDITIONAL TT CHOICE: some
49	after; once; when		ADDITIONAL TT CHOICE: as
51	can; could; will; would; may; might		ADDITIONAL TT CHOICE: helps
52	to	1 NS put "of"--> 1 NS put "that" ---------->	no credit given no credit given
53	without	1 NS put "with" ----------> 1 NS put "lacking" ------>	no credit given credit given

Appendix J

4. CLOZE			
Item	UCLES Key	NS Errors	Rubric Modifications***
54	ideal; perfect; best NOT only; latest; obvious; ultimate	2 NSs put "latest" ------>	no given credit
		1 NS put "optimal" ----->	credit given
		1 NS put "final" --------->	no credit given
		1 NS put "elegant" ----->	no credit given
		1 NS put "perfect" ------>	credit given
		1 NS put "happy" ------->	no credit given
			ADDITIONAL TT CHOICES: main, modern, right, real; one
55	puts; NOT keeps	1 NS put "places" ------>	credit given
		1 NS put "situates" ---->	credit given
		1 NS put "lets" --------->	no credit given
			ADDITIONAL TT CHOICES: involves, gets
56	through; via; NOT over	1 NS put "by" ---------->	not possible
			ADDITIONAL TT CHOICES: to; into
58	during; throughout; describing		ADDITIONAL TT CHOICE: watching
59	nothing		ADDITIONAL TT CHOICES no one; audio-description; sound; audio
60	extent degree	1 NS put "technique"--->	no credit given
		1 NS put "result" ------->	no credit given
			ADDITIONAL TT CHOICE: measure

*** The ADDITIONAL TT CHOICE section refers to answers that one or more test-takers supplied, where the answer was considered to be correct.

5. SENTENCE FORMATION			
Item	UCLES Key	NS Errors	Rubric Modifications
61	(just) in case; because	1 NS put "so that" ------->	credit given
		1 NS put "to avoid" ----->	credit given
62	it's/it might be/you feel/ you might feel cold on the boat.	1 NS put "(with 'so that') you won't" ----------------->	credit given
		1 NS put "(with 'to avoid') feeling cold" ---->	credit given
65	the plane (from) taking off; the take-off of the plane	1 NS put "the plane's takeoff" ------------------>	credit given
		1 NS put "the plane's departure" ---------------->	credit given

241

Appendix K
Model 1.2 CSU: Correlation Matrix

Model Correlation Matrix for Measured and Latent Variables

		AI V2	CLAR V3	INF V4	ASSOC V6	LKP V7
AI	V2	1.000				
CLAR	V3	0.325	1.000			
INF	V4	0.225	0.100	1.000		
ASSOC	V6	0.247	0.185	0.114	1.000	
LPK	V7	0.327	0.145	0.231	0.166	1.000
REP	V8	0.345	0.259	0.160	0.294	0.232
SUMM	V9	0.286	0.214	0.132	0.243	0.192
APR	V10	0.295	0.180	0.169	0.206	0.246
PN	V11	0.342	0.151	0.241	0.174	0.350
TRF	V12	0.059	0.179	-0.026	0.296	-0.037
F1	F1	0.586	0.555	0.179	0.334	0.261
F2	F2	0.539	0.404	0.249	0.459	0.363
F3	F3	0.565	0.250	0.398	0.287	0.579

		REP V8	SUMM V9	APR V10	PN V11	TRF V12
REP	V8	1.000				
SUMM	V9	0.340	1.000			
APR	V10	0.287	0.238	1.000		
PN	V11	0.414	0.201	0.257	1.000	
TRF	V12	0.174	0.144	0.066	-0.039	1.000
F1	F1	0.466	0.386	0.325	0.273	0.200
F2	F2	0.641	0.530	0.448	0.379	0.272
F3	F3	0.401	0.332	0.424	0.605	-0.065

		F1 F1	F2 F2	F3 F3
F1	F1	1.000		
F2	F2	0.728	1.000	
F3	F3	0.451	0.626	1.000

Appendix L
Model 2.2 MSU: Correlation Matrix

Model Correlation Matrix for Measured and Latent Variables

		ST V13	ASSIT V14	SE V15	MON V16	F1 F1
ST	V13	1.000				
ASSIT	V14	0.346	1.000			
SE	V15	0.529	0.391	1.000		
MON	V16	0.397	0.294	0.450	1.000	
F1	F1	0.684	0.506	0.774	0.581	1.000

Appendix M
Model 3.1 SLTP: Correlation Matrix

Model Correlation Matrix for Measured and Latent Variables

		GR V17	VOC V18	PC V22	WF V23	CLZ V26
GRAM	V17	1.000				
VOC	V18	0.571	1.000			
PC	V22	0.602	0.481	1.000		
WFORM	V23	0.746	0.597	0.629	1.000	
CLZ	V26	0.691	0.552	0.608	0.722	1.000
SFORM	V27	0.713	0.570	0.601	0.746	0.690
F1	F1	0.827	0.661	0.728	0.864	0.835
F2	F2	0.845	0.676	0.712	0.883	0.817

		SFORM V27	F1 F1	F2 F2
SFORM	V27	1.000		
F1	F1	0.826	1.000	
F2	F2	0.844	0.979	1.000

Appendix N
Model 4.2 Full Latent Variable Model: Correlation Matrix

Model Correlation Matrix for Measured and Latent Variables

		AI V2	CLAR V3	INF V4	ASSOC V6	LKP V7
AI	V2	1.000				
CLAR	V3	0.328	1.000			
INF	V4	0.218	0.107	1.000		
ASSOC	V6	0.199	0.120	0.119	1.000	
LPK	V7	0.327	0.160	0.227	0.179	1.000
REP	V8	0.302	0.182	0.181	0.272	0.271
SUMM	V9	0.228	0.138	0.137	0.206	0.205
APR	V10	0.293	0.161	0.189	0.215	0.284
PN	V11	0.331	0.162	0.230	0.181	0.345
TRF	V12	0.009	0.150	-0.014	0.269	-0.020
STL	V13	0.471	0.284	0.282	0.317	0.423
ASSIT	V14	0.230	0.307	0.138	0.155	0.207
EPL	V15	0.329	0.199	0.197	0.221	0.296
MON	V16	0.263	0.159	0.158	0.177	0.236
GRAM	V17	-0.029	-0.044	0.140	-0.125	0.124
VOC	V18	-0.022	-0.033	0.106	-0.095	0.094
PC	V22	-0.024	-0.037	0.177	-0.105	0.104
WFORM	V23	-0.030	-0.045	0.143	-0.128	0.126
CLZ	V26	-0.028	-0.043	0.136	-0.122	0.120
SFORM	V27	-0.029	-0.044	0.139	-0.125	0.123
F1	F1	0.595	0.551	0.194	0.218	0.290
F2	F2	0.469	0.283	0.281	0.424	0.422
F3	F3	0.560	0.274	0.389	0.306	0.584
F4	F4	0.543	0.328	0.326	0.366	0.488
F5	F5	-0.034	-0.052	0.165	-0.148	0.146
F6	F6	-0.035	-0.052	0.167	-0.150	0.148

Appendix N

Model Correlation Matrix for Measured and Latent Variables (cont.)

		REP V8	SUMM V9	APR V10	PN V11	TRF V12
REP	V8	1.000				
SUMM	V9	0.313	1.000			
APR	V10	0.326	0.247	1.000		
PN	V11	0.438	0.208	0.287	1.000	
TRF	V12	0.119	0.090	0.052	-0.021	1.000
STL	V13	0.481	0.364	0.426	0.428	0.073
ASSIT	V14	0.235	0.178	0.208	0.209	0.190
EPL	V15	0.336	0.254	0.298	0.299	0.051
MON	V16	0.269	0.203	0.238	0.239	0.041
GRAM	V17	-0.190	-0.144	-0.093	0.007	-0.134
VOC	V18	-0.144	-0.109	-0.071	0.005	-0.102
PC	V22	-0.160	-0.121	-0.079	0.006	-0.113
WFORM	V23	-0.194	-0.147	-0.096	0.007	-0.138
CLZ	V26	-0.185	-0.140	-0.091	0.007	-0.131
SFORM	V27	-0.189	-0.143	-0.093	0.007	-0.134
F1	F1	0.330	0.250	0.292	0.294	0.050
F2	F2	0.643	0.486	0.508	0.427	0.185
F3	F3	0.465	0.351	0.486	0.591	-0.035
F4	F4	0.555	0.420	0.492	0.494	0.085
F5	F5	-0.224	-0.170	-0.110	0.009	-0.159
F6	F6	-0.228	-0.172	-0.112	0.009	-0.161

		STL V13	ASSIT V14	EPL V15	MON V16	GRAM V17
STL	V13	1.000				
ASSIT	V14	0.367	1.000			
EPL	V15	0.525	0.377	1.000		
MON	V16	0.419	0.205	0.426	1.000	
GRAM	V17	-0.098	-0.001	0.188	0.058	1.000
VOC	V18	-0.074	-0.001	0.142	0.044	0.527
PC	V22	-0.082	-0.001	0.158	0.049	0.585
WFORM	V23	-0.100	-0.100	0.193	0.059	0.712
CLZ	V26	-0.095	-0.001	0.183	0.056	0.677
SFORM	V27	-0.097	-0.001	0.188	0.058	0.693
F1	F1	0.516	0.252	0.360	0.288	-0.079
F2	F2	0.748	0.365	0.523	0.418	-0.295
F3	F3	0.725	0.354	0.506	0.405	0.012
F4	F4	0.867	0.423	0.605	0.484	-0.113
F5	F5	-0.115	-0.001	0.222	0.068	0.822
F6	F6	-0.117	-0.001	0.226	0.069	0.834

Appendix N

Model Correlation Matrix for Measured and Latent Variables (cont.)

		VOC V18	PC V22	WFORM V23	CLZ V26	SFORM V27
VOC	V18	1.000				
PC	V22	0.443	1.000			
WFORM	V23	0.619	0.598	1.000		
CLZ	V26	0.513	0.587	0.693	1.000	
SFORM	V27	0.525	0.583	0.710	0.675	1.000
F1	F1	-0.060	-0.067	-0.081	-0.077	-0.079
F2	F2	-0.224	-0.248	-0.302	-0.287	-0.294
F3	F3	0.009	0.010	0.013	0.012	0.012
F4	F4	-0.085	-0.095	-0.115	-0.110	-0.112
F5	F5	0.622	0.712	0.841	0.824	0.819
F6	F6	0.631	0.701	0.854	0.812	0.831

		F1	F2	F3	F4	F5
F1	F1	1.000				
F2	F2	0.514	1.000			
F3	F3	0.498	0.722	1.000		
F4	F4	0.595	0.863	0.837	1.000	
F5	F5	-0.094	-0.349	0.014	-0.133	1.000
F6	F6	-0.095	-0.354	0.015	-0.135	0.985

		F6
F6	F6	1.000

Appendix O
Covariance Matrix for the High-Ability Group (N=234)

		AI V2	CLAR V3	INF V4	ASSOC V6	LPK V7
AI	V2	1.320				
CLAR	V3	.181	1.255			
INF	V4	.232	.055	.917		
ASSOC	V6	.168	.149	.069	.648	
LPK	V7	.351	.078	.113	.212	.640
REP	V8	.224	.136	.001	.229	.225
SUMM	V9	.269	.133	-.010	.126	.163
APR	V10	.134	.141	.061	.100	.176
PN	V11	.270	.147	.113	.064	.255
TRF	V12	.029	.245	.078	.201	.049
ST	V13	.375	.111	.043	.146	.273
ASSIT	V14	.126	.174	.083	.092	.071
SE	V15	.162	.157	.003	.030	.118
MON	V16	.128	-.047	.073	.065	.114
GRAM	V17	.224	.031	.057	-.043	.209
VOC	V18	.043	-.078	-.074	-.022	.123
PC	V22	-.186	-.157	-.031	-.041	-.033
WF	V23	.032	.024	.010	-.043	.046
CLZ	V26	.111	.303	.002	-.014	.306
SF	V27	.249	.171	.042	-.053	.176

Appendix O

		REP V8	SUMM V9	APR V10	PN V11	TRF V12
REP	V8	1.082				
SUMM	V9	.268	1.495			
APR	V10	.205	.447	1.048		
PN	V11	.198	.105	.109	.746	
TRF	V12	.157	.120	.173	-.108	.951
ST	V13	.299	.379	.380	.218	.083
ASSIT	V14	.112	.014	.270	-.104	.218
SE	V15	.094	.105	.204	.020	.098
MON	V16	.168	-.010	.017	.123	-.016
GRAM	V17	-.076	-.134	-.326	.148	.100
VOC	V18	.024	-.035	.079	.099	-.031
PC	V22	-.120	-.194	-.162	-.063	.040
SF	V23	.034	.093	-.121	.091	.047
CLZ	V26	-.211	-.299	-.674	-.248	.384
SF	V27	.010	.054	.079	.053	.241

		ST V13	ASSIT V14	SE V15	MON V16	GRAM V17
ST	V13	.616				
ASSIT	V14	.195	.841			
SE	V15	.176	.184	.288		
MON	V16	.193	.109	.073	.557	
GRAM	V17	-.081	-.049	.124	-.064	2.911
VOC	V18	.045	-.058	.002	.036	.216
PC	V22	-.139	-.079	-.018	-.018	.259
WF	V23	-.002	-.052	.049	.088	.542
CLZ	V26	-.421	-.014	.197	-.071	1.609
SF	V27	.108	-.017	.125	-.025	.676

		VOC V18	PC V22	WF V23	CLZ V26	SF V27
VOC	V18	.828				
PC	V22	.206	1.813			
WF	V23	.175	.010	2.292		
CLZ	V26	.222	.918	1.097	6.720	
SF	V27	.201	.140	.505	1.134	3.019

Appendix P
Covariance Matrix for the Low-Ability Group (N=931)

		AI V2	CLAR V3	INF V4	ASSOC V6	LPK V7
AI	V2	1.035				
CLAR	V3	.468	1.442			
INF	V4	.256	.129	.984		
ASSOC	V6	.202	.248	.109	.767	
LPK	V7	.239	.145	.216	.190	.621
REP	V8	.387	.326	.222	.179	.236
SUMM	V9	.407	.276	.120	.251	.235
APR	V10	.265	.183	.216	.124	.219
PN	V11	.425	.231	.260	.137	.253
TRF	V12	.067	.230	-.050	.252	.069
ST	V13	.353	.208	.257	.128	.263
ASSIT	V14	.222	.311	.140	.159	.112
SE	V15	.222	.183	.200	.116	.190
MON	V16	.271	.154	.264	.087	.150
GRAM	V17	-.174	-.160	-.008	-.056	-.026
VOC	V18	.146	-.100	.130	-.061	.051
PC	V22	-.104	-.182	.051	-.136	.065
WF	V23	.005	-.119	.160	-.097	.009
CLZ	V26	-.030	-.111	.117	-.063	-.013
SF	V27	-.062	-.198	.159	-.097	.040

Appendix P

		REP V8	SUMM V9	APR V10	PN V11	TRF V12
REP	V8	.820				
SUMM	V9	.356	1.309			
APR	V10	.266	.174	.778		
PN	V11	.456	.235	.255	.974	
TRF	V12	.075	.236	.034	-.094	1.157
ST	V13	.357	.273	.292	.345	.001
ASSIT	V14	.185	.178	.171	.130	.188
SE	V15	.232	.150	.229	.209	.001
MON	V16	.240	.109	.229	.270	-.029
GRAM	V17	-.130	-.045	-.058	-.108	-.088
VOC	V18	.015	-.135	.162	.088	-.250
PC	V22	-.071	-.060	.001	-.037	-.098
WF	V23	-.030	-.164	.102	.083	-.205
CLZ	V26	-.004	-.069	0.000	.115	-.069
SF	V27	-.052	-.209	.064	.028	-.174

		ST V13	ASSIT V14	SE V15	MON V16	GRAM V17
ST	V13	.515				
ASSIT	V14	.206	.604			
SE	V15	.298	.226	.407		
MON	V16	.282	.224	.254	.647	
GRAM	V17	-.087	-.125	-.033	-.073	2.025
VOC	V18	.156	-.004	.134	.200	.289
PC	V22	.012	-.117	.050	.016	.223
WF	V23	.079	.025	.097	.160	.186
CLZ	V26	-.006	-.056	.054	.057	.064
SF	V27	.028	-.031	.091	.052	.138

		VOC V18	PC V22	WF V23	CLZ V26	SF V27
VOC	V18	2.037				
PC	V22	.461	2.552			
WF	V23	.725	.456	1.956		
CLZ	V26	.267	.328	.148	1.827	
SF	V27	.390	.299	.376	.267	1.485

Subject Index

A
ANOVA 3, 37
affective strategies 24, 184
assessment strategies 76, 124, 140, 1454, 147, 186

B
baseline model 41, 116, 120, 135–137
bottom-up processing 119, 120, 161

C
CLZ, cloze test 35, 79, 84, 106, 148, 150, 161, 164–65, 172, 178
cognitive factors 14, 17, 18, 21, 22, 180
cognitive processing 6, 8, 17, 33, 45, 179
cognitive processing variables 50
cognitive strategies 28, 35, 41, 46, 74, 87, 137, 185
Cognitive Strategy Questionnaire 4, 46, 68, 70, 88, 170, 178, 186, 187, 189
CSU, cognitive strategy use 4, 6, 7, 88, 90, 93, 96, 110, 125, 127, 137, 140, 142–146, 149–152, 154, 156–159, 163, 164, 166, 170, 172, 173, 175, 176, 177, 179, 182, 188
cognitive strategy-type variables 51
communicative language ability 15, 20
communication strategies 19, 39
composite variables 57, 70
COMP-MEM, comprehending and memory process 143, 145, 147–150, 156, 164
CFA, confirmatory factor analysis 4, 9, 58, 59, 61, 106, 118, 170, 171
cross-group invariance 136–137

D
declarative knowledge 34

E
EFA, exploratory factor analysis 2, 4, 8, 37, 41, 58, 81
EQS 143

F

factor analysis, see exploratory factor analysis
FCE, First Certificate of English 3, 49
FCE Anchor Test 78, 87, 110, 129, 151, 166, 171, 172, 178, 179, 180
foreign language aptitude 10, 39

G

goodness-of-fit index 92, 104, 108
group-specific model 135

H

high-ability group 41, 135–136, 138–144, 148–154, 156–161, 161–162, 164–166, 168–170, 174–176, 179–182
human information processing 7, 9, 24, 26, 30, 31, 43, 44

I

information processing model 33, 34, 35, 39, 45, 144
information retrieval process 32
item-level analysis 57, 60, 67, 69, 75, 87, 88

L

language knowledge 5, 17
language processing 34
latent (unobserved) variables 8, 9, 38, 50, 61, 93, 95, 107, 110, 125
latent variable model 114, 116
learning strategies 21, 22, 36, 39
lexico-grammatical ability 119, 120, 129-131, 140-144, 145, 148, 150, 151, 162, 166–169, 172–174, 175–177, 179–183
LTM, long-term memory 32, 96, 129, 130
low-ability learners 22, 39, 41, 136–137, 139, 147–150, 152–153, 156–162, 164–166, 168–169, 174–176, 179–182

M

metacognitive processes 4, 61, 99, 179–180
metacognitive processing variables 50
metacognitive process-type variables 54
metacognitive strategies 6, 24–26, 28, 35–36, 41, 87, 180, 185
Metacognitive Strategy Questionnaire 44, 47, 74, 100, 121, 171, 178, 186, 189

Subject Index

MSU, metacognitive strategy use 6, 28, 48, 61, 74, 76, 88, 102, 105, 121–123, 127, 137, 140, 142–145, 147, 149, 155, 156, 159, 163, 164, 166, 168, 170-73, 175–77, 182
metacognitive strategy-type variables 53
modeling 8, 83
monitoring 20, 76, 140, 144, 147, 167, 175, 182
multi-group analysis 41, 151, 153, 174, 179, 181
multi-group structural equation model 136
multiple regression analysis 3, 57
multi sample covariance structure analysis 10

N
normality 136, 138, 140

O
observable variables 3, 8, 9, 38, 61, 93, 96, 102, 109, 110, 112, 116, 131–132, 144

P
path analysis 3, 105
personal characteristics of test-takers 15
procedural knowledge 31, 34

R
random factors 15
RDG, reading ability 144, 145, 151, 156, 160, 162, 164, 165
reliability analysis 2, 46, 58
RET, retrieval processes 52, 70, 91, 96, 142–143, 145–149, 156–158, 165, 167, 168, 176, 177

S
second language proficiency 10
second language performance 24
second language test performance 2, 135
SLTP, second language test performance model 114, 118, 127, 129, 131, 133, 137, 139–146, 150, 152, 154, 163, 166–169, 171, 173, 174, 176, 177, 180, 181
second language test performance variables 54
selective perception processes 32
self-management strategies 6, 35, 36, 140, 144, 150, 151, 167, 179, 180
self-report method 11, 124, 126

Subject Index

self-testing strategy 76, 124, 182
separate group analysis 59, 140
simultaneous group analysis 59, 156
single group analysis 10, 41, 136, 137
social strategies 24
strategic processing 20
strategy scales 2, 29
SILL, Strategy Inventory for Language Learning 26
strategy use questionnaires 42, 43
strategy use profile 141
strategy use variables 50, 87
SEM, structural equation modeling 3, 8, 37, 38, 41, 56, 58, 59, 61, 136, 169
successful learners 27, 135

T

test method factors 15
test-performance variables 50
test-takers characteristics 5
think-aloud protocols 27, 35, 186

U

unsuccessful learners 27

V

variance 110
vocabulary knowledge 119

Author Index

A
Abraham, R. G. 10, 14, 28
Anderson, J. R. 6, 31, 34,
Anderson, N. J. 2, 9, 14, 28, 34, 43
Asher, J. 30
Atkinson, R. C. 30

B
Bachman, L. F. 2, 5, 6, 15, 16, 21, 38, 43, 44, 45, 46, 47, 48, 58, 127, 128, 144, 170, 172
Barnett, M. A. 120, 168
Bentler, P. M. 58, 59, 61, 63, 64, 65, 92, 113, 116, 131, 132, 134, 143
Bialystok, E. 7, 14, 22, 29, 30, 37
Bollen, K. A. 63, 64
Borkowski, J. G. 33, 43
Brown, A. L. 6, 14, 24, 34, 125, 172
Brown, T. 10
Byrne, B. M. 11, 59, 62, 63, 64, 136, 137

C
Campione, J. C. 33, 43
Canale, M. 18, 19, 20, 21
Carrell, P. L. 120, 168
Carroll, J. B. 2, 17, 60
Chamot, A. U. 14, 23, 24, 27, 28, 135, 166
Chapelle, C. A. 14
Chesterfield, R. 6, 37
Chou, C. P. 63
Clahsen, H. 14, 22
Clapham, C. 165
Clarke, M. A. 120
Clement, R. 16, 38
Coady, J. 120, 165
Cohen, A. 2, 14, 33, 37, 43

Corder, P. 122
Craik, F. I. 31
Cziko, G. A. 165

D
Dansereau, D. F. 14
DeKeyser, R. 97, 148
Dulay, H. C. 2

E
EFL Division of UCLES 66
Ellis, N. 97
Ellis, R. 2, 11, 12, 23, 26, 97

F
Faerch, C. 6, 19, 20, 22, 23, 24, 36, 44, 45, 48, 100, 105, 125, 172
Fillmore, L. W. 2, 20
Flavell, J. 23, 36
Fouly, K. 38

G
Gagné, E. D. 12, 31, 32, 38, 44, 46, 98, 121, 123, 125, 179
Gardner, R. C. 10, 16, 38
Gass, S. M. 184
Gillette, B. 2, 37
Grabe, W. 82, 88, 120
Grotjahn, R. 33, 43

H
Hansen, J. 130
Hatch, E. 2
Hosenfeld, C. 10, 14, 27, 33, 43
Huang, X.-H. 2, 10, 14, 27, 30,
Hunt, M. 7, 12, 31, 35, 44, 45, 46,
Hymes, P. H. 20

J
Jamieson, J. 14
Jöreskog, K. G. 8, 9, 58, 64, 95

Author Index

K
Kaiser, H. F. 60
Kim, J. O. 8, 37, 60
Klatsky, R. L. 31, 46
Krashen, S. 144, 162
Kunnan, A. J. 10, 16, 38, 39

L
Lado, R. 17
Lefebvre-Pinard, M. 23, 36
Lennon, P. 2, 37
Long, M. H. 97
Loschky, L. 162
Lyons, J. 119

M
MacCallum, R. C. 138
Mangubhai, F. 10, 12, 30
McCombs, B. 14
McLaughlin, B. 2, 22, 23, 34, 35, 158
McLeod, B. 165
Microsoft EXCEL Version 5.0 58

N
Naiman, N. 2, 10, 27, 34
Neisser, U. 18
Nevo, N. 9
Nunan, D. 187

O
O'Malley, M. J. 1, 6, 11, 12, 14, 21, 24, 25, 26, 28, 29, 33, 34, 35, 36, 37, 43, 44, 45, 47, 91, 100, 105, 125, 158, 172, 183
Oller, J. W. Jr. 2, 10, 17, 18, 19, 21, 38
Oxford, R. 1, 2, 11, 23, 24, 25, 29, 36, 37, 45, 46, 91, 100, 105, 125

P
Pienemann, M. 22
Pintrich, P. R. 33
Politzer, R. L. 1, 2, 9, 10, 14, 28, 29, 37
Poulisse, N. 33, 43
Purcell, E. T. 10, 38

Purpura, J. E. 43

R
Rabinowitz, M. 158
Reiss, M. 2, 10, 27
Rindskopf, D. 134
Rubin, J. 2, 11, 23, 24, 25, 27, 34, 37

S
Sasaki, M. 10, 38, 39, 63
Satorra, A. 63, 64
Schachter, J. 122
Schmidt, R. 184
Scott-Lennox, J. A. 169
Seliger, H. W. 7, 11
Sharwood-Smith, M. 184
Skehan, P. 2, 11
Spolsky, B. 17
SPSS incorporated 58
Stansfield, C. 130
Stemmer, B. 35
Stern, H. H. 7, 23
Sternberg, R. J. 7, 33, 43
Swanson, H. L. 32

T
Tarone, E. 20
Tomlin, R. S. 184

V
Van Dijk, T. A. 33, 43
Vann, R. J. 10, 27, 28
VanPatten, B. 97
Victori, R. M. 2, 37
Volmer, H. J. 18

W
Wald, A. 65
Wang, L.-S. 10, 38
Weinstein, C. E. 2, 23, 31, 37, 45, 46

Author Index

Wenden, A. 2, 6, 7, 11, 14, 21, 24, 35, 36, 37, 43, 44, 45, 48, 76, 91, 100, 104, 123, 125, 171, 172, 179
Wesche, M. 27, 28, 31, 99, 135
Westney, P. 97, 148
Widdowson, H. G. 20
Wittrock, M. C. 14
Wong-Fillmore, L. 25

Z
Zimmerman, B. J. 2, 9, 37